A B C D E F G

MORE PERFECT
ILLUSTRATIONS
FOR EVERY TOPIC AND OCCASION

P Q R S T U V W X Y Z

Compiled by the editors of

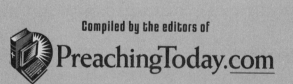
PreachingToday.com

Tyndale House Publishers, Inc.
WHEATON, ILLINOIS

Visit Tyndale's exciting Web site at www.tyndale.com

Visit PreachingToday's Web site at www.PreachingToday.com

Edited by David P. Barrett

Designed by Ron Kaufmann

Library of Congress Cataloging-in-Publication Data

More perfect illustrations for every topic and occasion / compiled by the editors of www.PreachingToday.com.
    p. cm.
Includes bibliographical references and indexes.
  ISBN 0-8423-6005-0 (pbk.)
  1. Homiletical illustrations. I. PreachingToday.com.
  BV 4225.3 .M67 2003
  251'.08—dc21   2002015641

Printed in the United States of America

08 07 06 05 04 03
 7   6   5   4   3   2   1

CONTENTS

Preaching experts sometimes advise, "Don't use 'canned' illustrations." *Canned* suggests that the illustration is not fresh. It is secondhand, processed. The preacher cannot escape two or more degrees of separation.

Although the intent of the advice is good, it is undiscriminating. Taken to its logical conclusion, it implies that any illustration that does not originate in personal experience is unfit. That rules out historical illustrations. That precludes illustrations from television programs, TV and radio newscasts, newsmagazines, newspapers, and literature. That bars all third-person illustrations. If the characteristic that makes a third-person illustration canned is that it did not come from one's own experience, that means we should not use even stories from the Bible!

Obviously no one advocates excluding all third-person illustrations. Even those who deride "canned" illustrations will illustrate in ways such as: "I saw an amazing story in the newspaper this morning. . . ." Or, "At a family gathering last month my brother told me something I will never forget. . . ." Or, "I read an interview in *Time* magazine recently in which Bono, lead singer of U2, said. . . ." Or, "Recent research published in the *New England Journal of Medicine* says that those who go through a divorce are. . . ." Or, "In a recent ad, Madonna said. . . . But Scripture says. . . ."

In all these examples, the only thing that makes the content personal is that the preacher saw or heard it himself, not that he personally experienced it. Is that really any different than if he read that identical story or statistic from *USA Today* in a sermon-illustration resource? Obviously not.

What, then, is intended when discerning homileticians scorn canned illustrations or when savvy preachers say, "I illustrate only from my own experience"? What problem have they rightly recognized? A discriminating view of third-person illustrations finds that the problem is not third-person illustrations, per se, nor their medium, but rather the *quality* of third-person illustrations and the *skill* with which they are used. The purpose of this book is to help you overcome the first hurdle (I hope you will come to PreachingToday.com to develop your skill!). We are confident you will find within the pages of this book first-rate illustrations.

Not all third-person illustrations are aluminum; some are like a tree cutting that we can graft into a bountiful olive tree. Chosen with care and used with skill, these illustrations can bud and flourish and bear fruit like a branch native to the tree. In fact, far from hurting a sermon, top-quality third-person illustrations add enormous benefits:

- *They broaden the message.* Listeners see examples of the truths of Scripture that transcend the small world of the preacher and spouse and kids and dog and yard and hobbies. Sermon illustration is not all about us.
- *They deepen our reservoir.* One person can have only so many illustrative experiences, and we can tell them only so many times.
- *They enable average communicators to use excellent illustrations.* The church has a limited number of Lucados and Swindolls. For the vast majority of preachers who are so-so storytellers and poets, third-person illustrations provide an invaluable resource they cannot develop in quantity on their own.
- *They bring other voices into the sermon.* Sometimes a third-person illustration brings in a contrasting voice, a foil, that brings energy—for example, the words of Carl Sagan on why he could not believe in God. At other times an illustration confirms what we say, as we bring authorities and respected cultural figures into the witness seat. For instance, when George Bush says he depends on prayer.

In this book are enough "olive shoots" to use one a week for six years, some 300 illustrations to graft and grow. May God use them for his glory.

Craig Brian Larson
Editor, PreachingToday.com and Preaching Today audio
The preaching resources of Christianity Today International

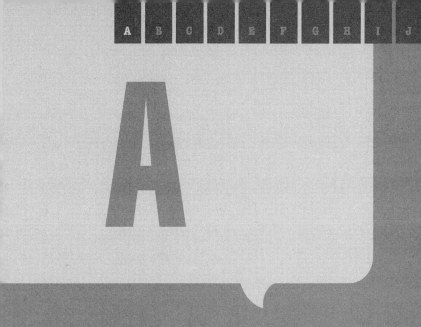

A B C D E F G H I J K L M

N O P Q R S T U V W X Y Z

A

ABORTION

KATHY TROCCOLI'S SONG BIRTHS CHILDREN

1 Samuel 1:1-11; Psalm 20:4; Psalm 21:2; Psalm 37:4; Psalm 139:13-16
Abortion; Desires; Dreams; Fulfillment; Goals; Hope; Ministry; Mission

Christian music star Kathy Troccoli shares how her ministry has filled an important place in her life:

> Being single at 42, I'm realizing I may never have a child. But God has repeatedly brought me stories from women who have chosen life over an abortion as a result of hearing a song I wrote.
>
> At a concert in Dallas, I had just finished singing when a 21-year-old woman's voice came over the loudspeaker. She talked about when she was pregnant with her second child and was being encouraged to abort the baby. During that time, she had come to one of my concerts. I'd sung, "A Baby's Prayer":
>
> "But if I should die before I wake, I pray her soul you'll keep. 'Forgive her, Lord; she doesn't know that you gave life to me.'"
>
> The Holy Spirit used that song to clinch her decision. She kept her baby.
>
> God has shown me that more children have been born through that song than I could ever bear.

Citation: Kathy Troccoli and Dee Brestin, Falling in Love with Jesus *(Word, 2001)*

ABSTINENCE

ABSTINENCE PLEDGES WORK

1 CORINTHIANS 6:12-20; GALATIANS 5:16-25; 1 THESSALONIANS 4:1-8
Abstinence; Commitment; Sex; Teenagers

Teens who take public pledges to remain virgins wait about 18 months longer to have sex than those who don't, says a new study published in the *American Journal of Sociology*. "Adolescents who pledge are much less likely to have intercourse than adolescents who do not pledge," wrote Peter S. Bearman of Columbia University and Hannah Bruckner of Yale University, the authors of the study. "The delay effect is substantial and robust. Pledging delays intercourse for a long time. In this sense, the pledge works."

It works, they say, because taking a public stand for virginity helps to give teens a sense of identity and community. Unfortunately, if a school's students accept the pledge as a fashionable stance (with more than 30 percent pledging), the effect diminishes dramatically. The results come from the *National Longitudinal Study of Adolescent Health*, which surveyed about 90,000 American teens and found that by 1995 about 10 percent of teen boys and 16 percent of teen girls had taken virginity pledges—that's about 2.5 million teens.

The University of North Carolina's J. Richard Udry, who helped design the survey, told Canada's *National Post*, "We were cynical about the likelihood that the pledge would produce [significant results]. But we were wrong."

Citation: Ted Olsen, ChristianityToday.com (1-04-01)

ACCEPTING CHRIST

DALE EARNHARDT: PREVENTABLE DEATH?

JOHN 1:12; ACTS 2:37-39; 1 THESSALONIANS 5:9; HEBREWS 2:3
Accepting Christ; Choices; Decisions; Neglect; Receiving Christ; Salvation and Lostness; Salvation, gift of

On Sunday, February 18, 2001, NASCAR lost one of its greatest drivers. Dale Earnhardt Sr., also known as "The Intimidator," was in third place on the last lap of the Daytona 500 when his car was tapped from behind and sent head-on into the wall at 180 mph.

In a matter of moments it was evident something was terribly wrong. Dale Earnhardt died in the crash. On the following Monday an autopsy report revealed he had died of blunt force trauma to the head.

Some have suggested that if Earnhardt had been wearing the HANS (Head and Neck Safety Device) he would have survived the crash. Although this device was available, Earnhardt, like many other drivers that day, neglected to use it. His neglect of this safety device may have cost him his life.

The Bible tells us that every individual is on a collision course with God's judgment. God, too, has provided a safety device—one designed to keep people from suffering eternal death and separation from God. But like Dale Earnhardt and the other drivers in the race that day, each of us must decide whether to accept or neglect this offer.

Citation: Michael Owenby; Carrollton, Georgia

■

ACCEPTING CHRIST

GOD'S CONSTANT INVITATION

JOHN 1:12; EPHESIANS 5:31-32; REVELATION 22:17

Accepting Christ; Bride; Conversion; Invitation; Marriage; Receiving Christ; Romance; Salvation and Lostness

Tedd Kidd was five years older than Janet, finished college before her, and started to work in a city hundreds of miles from her. They always seemed to be at different places in their lives. But they had been dating for seven years.

Every Valentine's Day, Tedd proposed to her. Every Valentine's Day, Janet would say, "No, not yet."

Finally, when they were both living in Dallas, Texas, Tedd reached the end of his patience. He bought a ring, took Janet to a romantic restaurant, and was prepared to reinforce his proposal with the diamond. Another no would mean he had to get on with his life without her.

After salad, entree, and dessert, it was time. Tedd summoned up his courage. Knowing that Janet had a gift for him, however, he decided to wait. "What did you bring me?" he asked. She handed him a box the size of a book. He opened the package and slowly peeled away the tissue paper. It was a cross-stitch Janet had made that simply said, "Yes."

Yes—it is the word that God, in his tireless pursuit of the sinner, longs to hear.

Citation: Rubel Shelly; Nashville, Tennessee; story told at Janet's funeral after 17 years of marriage to Tedd

■

ACHIEVEMENT
JOHN WOODEN'S INDIVIDUAL ACHIEVEMENT

PROVERBS 3:34; 1 CORINTHIANS 3:6-8; JAMES 4:6
Achievement; Humility; Modesty; Success; Work

Legendary basketball coach John Wooden turned 90 on October 14, 2000. The Wizard of Westwood led his UCLA men's basketball teams to ten national championships—seven of them in a row. Although his condominium is filled with photos, trophies, and plaques, there is one he treasures above the others.

"When I graduated from Purdue, I received the Big Ten medal as the senior athlete with the highest grade-point average," he told a reporter. "I did that. The other awards, my teams won."

Citation: The Tennessean (11-09-00), p. 3B; submitted by Rubel Shelly; Nashville, Tennessee

■

ADDICTION
ACTOR GARY BUSEY ON ADDICTION

PSALM 10:4; ROMANS 3:10-12; ROMANS 6:16; 2 PETER 2:19
Addiction; Conversion; Sin; Ungodliness

In July 1998, Oscar-winning actor Gary Busey discussed his faith on *The 700 Club*. Though he has starred in over 60 films, including such hits as *Lethal Weapon* and *The Firm*, Busey's off-screen party-boy reputation and arrest record took center stage. After attending a Promise Keepers conference, his life changed dramatically. When asked if he thought about God when he was sinking into debauchery, Busey states:

"Of course not. There's no way to think about God. There's no reason to . . . 'cause your number-one relationship is with the dark side of you. . . . I learned that addiction is a failed search for spirituality."

Citation: Melissa Park; Des Plaines, Illinois; source: The 700 Club, *CBN*

ADULTERY

HOW-TO BOOK ON ADULTERY

EXODUS 20:14; ROMANS 1:21-32; 1 THESSALONIANS 4:1-8; HEBREWS 13:4

Adultery; Deception; Marriage; Sex; Sin; Temptation

The publisher's review of a recent book describes it as "a thoughtful, detailed discussion of every aspect of considering, preparing for, beginning, and conducting a successful and emotionally fulfilling extramarital affair." The book is called *Affair! How to Manage Every Aspect of Your Extramarital Relationship with Passion, Discretion, and Dignity* (by Cameron Barnes, UPublish.com, 1999). For just $19.95, plus shipping and handling, you can get a practical summary of the lies the devil would have you believe concerning adultery.

Citation: Bill White, pastor of Emmanuel Church; Paramount, California

---

ADVENT

PRISON CELL: PICTURE OF ADVENT

LUKE 1:76-79

Advent; Christmas; Freedom; Grace; Hope; Waiting

Dietrich Bonhoeffer, imprisoned by Hitler during World War II, writes to his fiancée on one lesson learned from life in prison:

"A prison cell, in which one waits, hopes, does various unessential things, and is completely dependent on the fact that the door of freedom has to be opened *from the outside* is not a bad picture of Advent."

Citation: Dietrich Bonhoeffer, in Letters and Papers from Prison; *in a letter to his fiancée, Maria von Wedemeyer, from Tegel Prison in Germany, November 21, 1943; submitted by Bill White; Paramount, California*

ADVERSITY

ADVERSITY AND THE LESSON OF THE COFFEE BEAN

JOHN 16:33; ROMANS 5:3-5; ROMANS 8:31-39; ROMANS 12:21; JAMES 1:2-4; 1 PETER 4:1

Adversity; Attitude; Bitterness; Faith and Circumstances; Hardness of Heart; Obstacles; Overcoming; Perseverance; Suffering; Trust; Victorious Living; Victory

A daughter complained to her father about how hard things were for her. "As soon as I solve one problem," she said, "another one comes up. I'm tired of struggling."

Her father, a chef, took her to the kitchen where he filled three pots with water and placed each on a high fire. Soon the pots came to a boil. In one he placed carrots; in the second, eggs; and in the last, ground coffee beans. He let them sit and boil, without saying a word.

The daughter impatiently waited, wondering what he was doing. After a while, he went over and turned off the burners. He fished out the carrots and placed them in a bowl. He pulled the eggs out and placed them in a bowl. He poured the coffee into a bowl. Turning to her he asked, "Darling, what do you see?"

"Carrots, eggs, and coffee," she replied.

He brought her closer and asked her to feel the carrots. She did and noted that they were soft. He then asked her to take an egg and break it. After pulling off the shell, she observed the hard-boiled egg. Finally, he asked her to sip the coffee. She smiled, as she tasted its rich flavor.

She asked, "What does it mean, Father?" He explained that each of them had faced the same adversity—boiling water—but each reacted differently. The carrot went in strong, hard, and unrelenting, but after being subjected to the boiling water, it softened and became weak.

The egg was fragile. Its thin outer shell had protected its liquid interior, but after sitting through the boiling water, its inside hardened.

The ground coffee beans were unique, however. By being in the boiling water, they changed the water.

He asked his daughter, "When adversity knocks on your door, which are you?"

Citation: From the Internet; submitted by Eric Reed, managing editor, Leadership Journal

ADVERSITY

ITZHAK PERLMAN OVERCOMES ADVERSITY

2 Corinthians 4:8-9

Adversity; Difficulties; Endurance; Excellence; Hardship; Overcoming; Perseverance; Problems

World-renowned violinist Itzhak Perlman was stricken with polio as a child. As a result, he wears braces on both legs and walks with the aid of crutches. At concerts, getting on stage is no small achievement for him. He slowly crosses the stage until he reaches his chair. He lays his crutches on the floor, slowly undoes the clasps on his legs, tucks one foot back and extends the other foot forward. Then he bends down and picks up the violin, puts it under his chin, nods to the conductor, and proceeds to play.

One fall evening in 1995, while performing at Avery Fisher Hall at Lincoln Center in New York City, Perlman had to deal with one additional handicap. Jack Reimer, a columnist with the *Houston Chronicle,* described the scene. "Just as he finished the first few bars, one of the strings on his violin broke. You could hear it snap—it went off like gunfire across the room. There was no mistaking what that sound meant."

There was no mistaking what he had to do. People who were there said, "We figured he would have to get up . . . to either find another violin or find another string for this one."

But he didn't. Instead Perlman waited a moment, closed his eyes, and then signaled the conductor to begin again. The orchestra and he played from where he had left off. He played with passion and power.

Of course, it is impossible to play a symphonic work with just three strings. But that night Itzhak Perlman refused to know that. You could see him modulate, change, recompose the piece in his head. At one point, it sounded like he was detuning the strings to get new sounds they had never made before.

Citation: Submitted by Greg Asimakoupoulos; source: Houston Chronicle *(11-18-95)*

ADVOCATE

CONNECTIONS IN HIGH PLACES

Ephesians 3:20; Philippians 4:6; 2 Timothy 4:18; Hebrews 4:16; 1 Peter 5:7

Advocate; Christ, mediator; Dependence on God; Help from God; Intercession; Prayer; Relationships; Trials; Trouble

In April 2001, in the midst of Israeli/Arab conflict, a motorcade carrying the Security Service Chief of Gaza came under bullet fire from Israeli troops. The frightened security official called Yasir Arafat from his car for help. Arafat in turn called the U.S. ambassador, who then called the U.S. secretary of state, Colin Powell. Colin Powell then phoned Ariel Sharon, the Israeli prime minister, who ordered the shooting to stop immediately. And it did. The Security Chief's connections eventually saved his life.

In a similar way, Christians have a divine connection to the ultimate power of the universe that can make a world of difference in any situation.

Citation: "Washington Whispers," U.S. News and World Report (4-30-01), p. 6; submitted by Kevin Short; Springfield, Missouri

AFFIRMATION

A FATHER WHO WON'T AFFIRM

Proverbs 25:11; Ephesians 6:4; 1 Thessalonians 5:11; Hebrews 3:13

Affirmation; Approval; Child-rearing; Criticism; Encouragement; Family; Fatherhood; Fathers; Faultfinding; Men; Parenting; Sports

In *We Are Still Married*, Garrison Keillor writes:

> The town ball club was the Lake Wobegon Schroeders, so named because the starting nine were brothers, sons of E. J. Schroeder. E. J. was ticked off if a boy hit a bad pitch. He'd spit and curse and rail at him. And if a son hit a homerun, E. J. would say, "Blind man coulda hit that one. Your gramma coulda put the wood on that one. If a guy couldn't hit that one out, there'd be something wrong with him, I'd say. Wind practically took that one out of here, didn't even need to hit it much"—and lean over and spit.

So his sons could never please him, and if they did, he forgot about it. Once, against Freeport, his oldest boy, Edwin Jim, Jr., turned and ran to the center-field fence for a long, long, long fly ball. He threw his glove forty feet in the air to snag the ball and caught the ball and glove. When he turned toward the dugout to see if his dad had seen it, E. J. was on his feet clapping, but when he saw the boy look to him, he immediately pretended he was swatting mosquitoes. The batter was called out, the third out. Jim ran back to the bench and stood by his dad. E. J. sat chewing in silence and finally said, "I saw a man in Superior, Wisconsin, do that a long time ago. But he did it at night, and the ball was hit a lot harder."

Citation: Garrison Keillor, We Are Still Married *(Penguin, 1990)*

ALCOHOL

U.S. ALCOHOL ABUSE STATISTICS

PROVERBS 23:19-21; EPHESIANS 5:18
Alcohol; Crime; Drugs; Drunkenness; Sin; Violence

A policy-research group called Drug Strategies has produced a report that calls alcohol "America's most pervasive drug problem" and then goes on to document the claim:

Alcohol-related deaths outnumber deaths related to drugs four-to-one. Alcohol is a factor in more than half of all domestic violence and sexual assault cases. In 1995, four out of every ten people on probation said they were drinking when they committed a violent crime, while only one in ten admitted using illicit drugs. Between accidents, health problems, crime, and lost productivity, researchers estimate alcohol abuse costs the economy $167 billion a year.

Citation: Anna Quindlen, "The Drug That Pretends It Isn't," Newsweek *(4-10-00), p. 88*

ATHEISM

THE BEAR AND THE ATHEIST

PSALM 27; ROMANS 1:18-22

Atheism; Creation; Crisis; Evolution; Gratitude; Ideologies and Belief Systems; Judgment; Prayer; Thankfulness; Thanksgiving; Unbelief

An atheist was walking through the woods admiring all the "accidents" that evolution had created. "What majestic trees! What powerful rivers! What beautiful animals!" he said to himself.

As he was walking alongside the river, he heard a rustling in the bushes behind him. Turning to look, he saw a 7-foot grizzly bear charge towards him. He ran away as fast as he could up the path.

He looked over his shoulder and saw the grizzly was closing. Somehow he ran even faster, so scared that tears came to his eyes. He looked again, and the bear was even closer. His heart was pounding, and he tried to run faster. He tripped and fell to the ground. He rolled over to pick himself up, but the bear was right over him, reaching for him with its left paw and raising its right paw to strike him.

At that instant the atheist cried, "Oh my God!"

Time stopped. The bear froze. The forest was silent. Even the river stopped moving.

As a bright light shone upon the man, a voice came out of the sky, "You deny my existence for all these years, teach others that I don't exist, and even credit creation to a cosmic accident. Do you expect me to help you out of this predicament? Am I to count you as a believer?"

The atheist looked directly into the light and said, "I would feel like a hypocrite to become a Christian after all these years, but perhaps you could make the bear a Christian?"

"Very well," said the voice.

The light went out. The river ran. The sounds of the forest resumed. Then the bear dropped his right paw, brought both paws together, bowed its head, and spoke: "Lord, for this food which I am about to receive, I am truly thankful."

Citation: Source unknown; submitted by David Holdaway; Stonehaven, Kincardinshire, Scotland

AUTHORITY

FIDEL CASTRO PLAYS BASEBALL

1 CORINTHIANS 3:10-15; 2 CORINTHIANS 5:10
Authority; Judgment; Law; Morality; Power

In Cuba, nothing is bigger than baseball, not even the cigars. Nothing, that is, except Castro. Recently, the 74-year-old dictator grabbed an aluminum bat and walked to the plate in an exhibition game against Venezuela. When Castro approached the batter's box, the president of Venezuela, Hugo Chavez, left his first-base position to take the mound. His first pitch didn't even reach the plate, and Castro kept his bat on his shoulder. The next pitch was a strike, but Castro missed. A couple more balls and an attempted bunt later, the two heads of state were locked into a full count. Castro watched the 3-2 pitch sail through the middle of the strike zone and listened as the umpire called him out. "No," Castro said, "that was a ball." And he took first base. No one argued. President Chavez said nothing. The opposing team said nothing, and the umpire said nothing. Later Castro joked, "Today just wasn't his [President Chavez's] day."

It is hard to get a batter out when he has the power to overrule the umpire's calls. Dictators can get away with that. The rest of us can't. In God's economy, dictators can't either. Everyone will face God's ultimate judgment, and when we do, his word will be final.

Citation: Yahoo! Sports (10-29-00); submitted by Jim Wilson

13

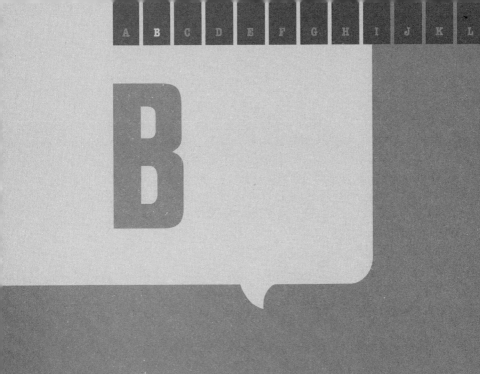

B

B

BIBLE

THE BIBLE'S BIG PICTURE

PSALM 119:18-19; LUKE 24:25-27

Bible; God, grace of; Inspiration of Scripture; Kingdom of God; Redemption; Salvation

In her book *Mystery on the Desert*, Maria Reiche describes a series of strange lines made by the Nazca in the plains of Peru, some of them covering many square miles. For years people assumed these lines were the remnants of ancient irrigation ditches.

Then in 1939 Dr. Paul Kosok of Long Island University discovered that their true meaning could only be seen from high in the air. When viewed from an airplane, these seemingly random lines form enormous drawings of birds, insects, and animals.

In a similar way, people often think of the Bible as a series of individual, unconnected stories. But if we survey the Scriptures as a whole, we discover that they form one great story of redemption—from the opening scenes of Genesis to the final chapter of Revelation. Weaving through all the diverse strands of the Bible is a divine story line, the overarching story of what God has been up to in the rescue and restoration of fallen human beings, from the first nanosecond of creation through the final cry of victory at the end of time.

Citation: Timothy George, "Big Picture Faith," Christianity Today *(10-23-00)*

BIBLE

THE LIVING WORD

Isaiah 55:11; 2 Timothy 3:16; Hebrews 4:12

Authority of Scripture; Bible; Evangelism; Religion, Islam; Word of God

A Christian university student shared a room with a Muslim. As they became friends, their conversation turned to their beliefs. The believer asked the Muslim if he'd ever read the Bible. He answered no, but then asked if the Christian had ever read the Koran.

The believer responded, "No, I haven't, but I'm sure it would be interesting. Why don't we read both together, once a week, alternating books?" The young man accepted the challenge, their friendship deepened, and during the second term he became a believer in Jesus.

One evening, late in the term, he burst into the room and shouted at the longtime believer, "You deceived me!"

"What are you talking about?" the believer asked.

The new believer opened his Bible and said, "I've been reading it through, like you told me, and just read that the Word is living and active!" He grinned. "You knew all along that the Bible contained God's power and that the Koran is a book like any other. I never had a chance!"

"And now you'll hate me for life?" queried the believer.

"No," he answered, "but it was an unfair contest."

Citation: Floyd Schneider, *Evangelism for the Fainthearted* (Kregel, 2000); quoted in Men of Integrity *(March/April 2001)*

BIBLE

LOVE LETTER FROM GOD

Isaiah 40:8; John 1:1-2; 1 Peter 1:22-25

Bible; Christ, love of; Christ, the word; God, love of; Love; Love, divine; Scripture; Word of God

M any years ago, a doting groom penned a love letter to his bride. Stationed at a California military base thousands of miles away from his wife, James Bracy's links to the lovely woman waiting for him to come home were their love letters.

But this letter didn't get delivered. Somehow it was lost, lodged between two walls in Fort Ord's mailroom in San Francisco. The letter was lost in the shadows, with its romantic affections of a youthful marriage, sealed with a kiss.

A half century later, James and Sallie Bracy had just finished celebrating their 50th wedding anniversary and were relaxing in the living room when "Once in a While," their song, began to play on the radio. Sallie remembered affectionately the 1950s song and how she used to get calls and letters from the man who owned her heart. They joked together knowing there would be no letter or phone call this time because James was at her side.

Meanwhile, a construction crew was dismantling the old post office at Fort Ord, and they discovered a long-forgotten letter from a young army corporal. The crew turned the letter over to Bob Spadoni, the postmaster in nearby Monterey. Spadoni began the process of delivering that letter, tracking down the Bracys through post office records and phone books.

Just a few days after hearing their song, the letter, dated January 28, 1955, was delivered to Sallie Bracy. The letter sent her heart aflutter, tears welled, and she again became a love-struck 22-year-old. "It meant a lot to me then," said Sallie. "It means even more now."

Many years ago God wrote his love letter to us. It's waiting to be delivered, to be opened at just the right time. It meant a lot then, and it means even more now.

Citation: Drew Zahn, assistant editor, Leadership Journal; *source:* Jefferson City News Tribune *(4-25-01)*

BIRTH, NEW

JOYS OF EVANGELISM

MATTHEW 28:18-20; JOHN 3:3; 1 CORINTHIANS 4:15

Birth, new; Conversion; Evangelism; Ministry; Outreach

Barbara was a member of the Faith ministry team in our church. Each night following an outreach service, Faith members gave guidance to those who ask for spiritual direction. On the very last night of the play "Heaven's Gates and Hell's Flames," Barbara went to our fellowship hall and greeted a family—a mom, dad, and two boys, ages 10 and 12. Both of the boys accepted Christ as their Savior as Barbara counseled them from the Bible and then led them in prayer. Afterward, the mom looked at Barbara and said, "You don't remember us, do you?"

Barbara looked at the boys and the mom, and finally recognized the mother as a patient in her busy OB/GYN practice. The mom hugged her with tears in her eyes and said, "You not only delivered both of our boys into the world years ago, but now you've also assisted in their spiritual birth."

Citation: David Mahfouz, pastor of First Baptist Church; Port Neches, Texas

BITTERNESS

LINGERING EFFECTS OF ANGER

PROVERBS 29:11; EPHESIANS 4:26

Anger; Attitudes and Emotions; Bitterness; Forgiveness; Resentment; Self-control

Author and church minister Ed Rowell writes:

> When I was young, a neighboring family came down with a devastating illness. Several of the children died, and the rest suffered permanent brain damage. What investigators discovered was that the father had found a truckload of discarded seed corn and fed it to the family hogs. The corn (not intended for animal feed) had been treated with something so bugs wouldn't eat it before it germinated. The hogs ate it, seemingly with no ill effects.
>
> But when the family hogs became the family breakfast, the family was poisoned. It seems that many substances—pesticides and heavy metals like lead and mercury—do not pass through the digestive system, but remain in the body, always. In tiny doses, the effects are minimal. But over time, the effects are horrible.
>
> That's what happens to many of us. . . . Every day we ingest minute amounts of conflict and disrespect. No big deal, we think. Just blow it off. But we don't. Instead it gets buried in our liver and 20 years

later, we go ballistic over some kid skateboarding in the parking lot and wonder, *Where did that come from?*

Citation: Ed Rowell, "Why Am I Angrier Than I Used to Be?" Leadership Journal (Summer 2000), pp. 79-80

BITTERNESS

MOVING FORWARD MEANS LEAVING BEHIND

PSALM 37:37; MATTHEW 18:21-22; PHILIPPIANS 3:13; COLOSSIANS 3:13

Bitterness; Forgiveness; Hatred; Revenge

After the Civil War, in an incident recounted by Charles Flood in *Lee: The Last Years,* Robert E. Lee visited a woman who took him to the remains of a grand old tree in front of her home. There she cried bitterly that its limbs and trunk had been destroyed by Union artillery fire. She waited for Lee to condemn the North or at least sympathize with her loss. But Lee—who knew the horrors of war and had suffered the pain of defeat—said, "Cut it down, my dear madam, and then forget it."

In the late 1990s, Pete Peterson was appointed U.S. ambassador to Vietnam. Peterson had served six years as a prisoner of war in the dreaded "Hanoi Hilton" prison camp. When asked how he could return to the land where he'd endured years of starvation, brutality, and torture, he replied, "I'm not angry. I left that at the gates of the prison when I walked out in 1972. I just left it behind me and decided to move forward with my life."

When you're tempted to get even with those who hurt you, remember that you can't go back, you can't stay where you are, but by God's grace, you can move forward one step at a time.

Citation: Ray Pritchard, Something New Under the Sun

BLAME

BLAMING GOD FOR MESSES

GENESIS 1; 1 CORINTHIANS 14:33

Blame; Creation; Disorder

My husband and I are always talking to our son about all the wonderful things God has made. We ask him questions like "Who made the sun?" and "Who made the rain?"

One evening, I looked at the toys scattered on the floor and asked, "Who made this mess?"

After thinking for a few minutes, my son said, "God did!"

Citation: Shawne B.; Warsaw, Indiana, "Life in Our House," Christian Parenting Today *(March/April 2000)*

BUSINESS

DOING BUSINESS GOD'S WAY

MATTHEW 25:34-40

Business; Character; Giving; Ministry; Money; Obedience; Sabbath; Work

Truett Cathy has answered the question "What would Jesus do?" The founder of Chick-fil-A restaurants is a successful businessman, but for many, he is even better known—and respected—for letting his faith guide his business operation. Here are a few examples:

Mr. Cathy's restaurants have been closed on Sundays since 1948. The 79-year-old CEO of the nearly 1,000 Chick-fil-A restaurants doesn't mind losing millions of dollars of business to honor the Lord's Day.

At his first restaurant in 1948 he hired Eddie J. White, a 12-year-old African American. This was an unpopular choice during a time of segregation. He also mentored an orphan, Woody Faulk, since he was 13. Today Woody is vice president of product development at Chick-fil-A.

Cathy developed a successful foster home system called WinShape Homes. There are now eleven homes in the U.S. and one in Brazil. His daughter Trudy and son-in-law John were Southern Baptist missionaries at the Brazil home for ten years. His Camp WinShape and the WinShape Foundation provide scholarships for kids and college students.

One of his favorite truisms is "It's easier to build boys and girls than to mend men and women." Chick-fil-A Kids Meals don't come with promotional toys from the latest popular movie. Instead he offers VeggieTales books, audiocassettes of Focus on the Family's "Adventures in Odyssey," and other character-building materials.

Woody Faulk gives a good summary of Cathy's character: "A lot of people look on Truett as Santa Claus, but he's not. He'll meet you halfway so that you can learn a lesson from the process. He's the personification of James 1:22: 'Do not merely listen to the word, and so deceive yourselves. Do what it says.' I sincerely owe my life to that man."

Citation: Tom Neven, "A Doer of the Word," Focus on the Family magazine (September 2000); submitted by Jerry De Luca; Montreal West, Quebec, Canada

BUSYNESS

IF ONLY I'D KNOWN

MATTHEW 24:32-51; MATTHEW 25:1-13; LUKE 14:15-24
Busyness; Choices; Distractions; Family; Fatherhood; Fathers; Parenting; Priorities; Return of Christ; Time

On June 4, 2001, 12-year-old Little League pitcher Robert Knight pitched the game of his life. As batter after batter came to the plate for the opposing team in suburban Detroit, each player did his best to make his parents proud. Each tried, and failed, again and again, to hit a pitch off the 5-foot-3-inch, 100-pound Robert Knight.

Knight threw a perfect game—no, a PERFECT game. All 18 batters he faced in the six-inning game struck out! The final batter to face Knight had worked the count to 3 and 0, but Knight came back to strike him out as well.

"I could tell the other team didn't really want to come up to bat anymore after a while," said Mr. Perfect.

As the last strike was called, everyone from Knight's team ran out and celebrated with him. Parents clapped and yelled, but not Knight's parents. They were not at the game.

It's not that they didn't care. Robert's dad had driven his other son to another game, and his mom was at a softball game of her own down the street. When Mrs. Knight did arrive to pick up her son, Robert's coach told her, "Oh, this wasn't the game for you to miss."

Don't you hate it when you are so busy that you miss something really good?

Citation: Michael Herman,;Glen Ellyn, Illinois; source: ESPN.com (6-6-01)

C

CALLING

WILLIAM CAREY'S DREAM

PSALM 37:4; 1 CORINTHIANS 1:26-31

Calling; Desire; Desire, spiritual; Discipline; Evangelism; Goals; Mission; Missions; Outreach; Passion; Passion, spiritual; Self-discipline

Some people thought he was a nut. He was just a shoemaker, after all, and an average one at that. But in the evenings, after work, he studied Greek, Hebrew, and a variety of modern languages. He devoured *Captain Cook's Voyages* to expand his horizons, which, because of his poverty, kept him bound to a small, forgotten English village. Some people said his time would have been better spent getting a second job to support his growing family.

But the young man's passion wasn't a curious, self-satisfying hobby. Early in life he had become concerned about the millions of unbelievers outside of Europe, and he was trying to figure out what could be done to bring them the gospel.

With God's help, he slowly figured it out. He ended up going to India to serve as the first Protestant missionary in the modern era. His passion inspired a generation of men and women—the likes of Adoniram Judson, Hudson Taylor, and David Livingstone (among others)—to take up the cause of missions as well.

Because one impoverished shoemaker named William Carey followed his God-given passion, large parts of the world that had little or no access to the gospel have large populations of people today who confess Christ as Lord.

Citation: Ruth Tucker, From Jerusalem to Irian Jaya: A Biographical History of Christian Missions *(Zondervan, 1983), pp. 114-115; submitted by Mark Galli, managing editor of* Christianity Today

CALLING

A WORKING MAN'S DUAL CALLING

Acts 18:1-3; 1 Corinthians 12:1-31; Ephesians 4:11-13

Calling; Christian Life; Gifts; Purpose; Work

Max DePree, CEO of Herman Miller, Inc., describes a simple, but profound, incident that altered the culture of his organization:

In the furniture industry of the 1920s, the machines of most factories were not run by electric motors but by pulleys from a central driveshaft. The millwright was the person on whom the entire activity of the operation depended. He was the key person.

One day, the millwright died.

My father, being a young manager at the time, did not know what to do when a key person died, but thought he ought to go visit the family. He went to the house and was invited to join the family in the living room.

The widow asked my father if it would be all right if she read aloud some poetry. Naturally, he agreed. She went into another room, came back with a bound book, and for many minutes read selected pieces of beautiful poetry. When she finished, my father commented on how beautiful the poetry was and asked who wrote it. She replied that her husband, the millwright, was the poet.

It is now nearly 60 years since the millwright died, and my father and many of us at Herman Miller continue to wonder: Was he a poet who did millwright's work, or was he a millwright who wrote poetry?

Citation: Peter Grazier in "Work and Spirituality" on teambuildinginc.com; reprinted in Homiletics *(September 2001), pp.13-14*

CARING

TEEN'S SACRIFICE SAVES BABY

Matthew 22:37-40; Mark 12:29-31; Luke 10:27; John 15:13; Acts 2:42-47; Romans 12:10; Ephesians 5:2

Caring; Community; Compassion; Conversion; Giving; Handicaps; Help from God; Love; Mercy; Money; Sacrifice; Sickness; Teenagers; Youth

Jeff Leeland had just accepted a teaching position at Kamiakin Junior High in Seattle, Washington. The family had endured months of Jeff's driving to and from work before the family could relocate from their previous home.

As winter struggled toward spring in 1992, Jeff and Kristi heard the devastating news: "Your baby boy has cancer. Michael needs a bone-marrow transplant." The good news was that Michael's six-year-old sister, Amy, was a perfect match for the transplant. But Jeff's insurance company wouldn't pay for it. A tiny clause in the contract coldly stated that Jeff had to be on the job for at least a year before they would cover a transplant. He had been teaching in the new job for only six months.

By March, Michael's need for a transplant became urgent. If he couldn't receive the new marrow soon, his illness would progress quickly, and he would die. The Leelands needed to raise an impossible sum of $200,000 by May.

Fellow teacher Joe Kennedy told his class about Mr. Leeland's situation. Dameon, a seventh-grade boy who walked with a limp and struggled in special education classes, heard about Mr. Leeland's son, Michael, and made a visit to Jeff's house.

"Mr. Leeland, don't make a big deal out of this . . . if your baby's in trouble, I want to help out." Dameon, the kid others teased, reached out his hand and stuffed 12 five-dollar bills into the hand of a teacher who had made a difference in his life. It was the boy's life savings.

Word got out about "Dameon's gift." Some kids organized a walk-a-thon. Others contacted a local newspaper. Others held a car wash. "Teenagers," Jeff says, "are preadults in limbo-land, waiting around for something important to do." Michael became important.

The Kamiakin kids' wave of compassion poured out across Seattle. One week after Dameon's gift, Michael's fund grew to $16,000. On Friday, May 22, a man walked into the bank with a check for ten thousand dollars. By late May, area TV stations picked up the story. The response from the news stories was overwhelming. By May 29, Michael's fund grew to $62,000. The Leelands were boosted with hope when the hospital moved Michael's transplant back by two weeks.

On Friday, June 5, the fund had grown to $143,000. Monday, June 8: $160,000. Tuesday, June 9: $185,000. When a TV news broadcast pronounced victory for Michael, the Kamiakin Junior High kids went crazy with happiness. Only four weeks after Dameon's gift of $60, the Michael Leeland Fund totaled over $220,000.

Michael got the marrow transplant. He lived. Dameon, the boy who gave sacrificially so another could live, accepted Jesus Christ as his Savior after becoming close with Michael's family. Having struggled for years with physical problems of his own, Dameon died from complications after he got an infection in one of his legs.

Michael Leeland lives to tell Dameon's story. Dameon, the unlikely hero, gave his all to save the life of another. And in the process, he received life everlasting.

Citation: Adapted from Jeff Leeland, One Small Sparrow *(Multnomah, 2000) and from a phone interview with Jeff Leeland; Sisters, Oregon; submitted by Clark Cothern; Tecumseh, Michigan*

■

CHANGE

NECESSITY OF WRITTEN WORD

ECCLESIASTES 12:11-14; PROVERBS 8

Change; Culture; Humanity; New Things

Marshall McLuhan said the printed word is "obsolete." To prove it he wrote fifteen books.

Citation: Saturday Review, quoted in "Reflections," Christianity Today (4-24-00)

■

CHANGE

READING THE CULTURAL WAVES

1 CHRONICLES 12:32

Change; Decisions; Leadership; Leadership of the Church; Planning; Vision

Travel back 50 years to the mahogany-paneled office of Sewell Avery, then chairman of Montgomery Ward & Co. Avery was responsible for Ward's failure to open a single new store from 1941 to 1957. Instead, the big retailer piled up cash—and then sat on it. Ward's amassed $607 million, earning them a dubious Wall Street nickname: "the bank with the department store front."

So why didn't Avery join in the nation's postwar expansion by following Americans to the suburbs? He held firmly to the belief and vision that a depression had followed every major war since the time of Napoleon. "Who am I to argue with history?" Avery demanded. "Why build $14-a-foot buildings when we soon can do it for $3-a-foot?"

On the other side of Chicago, Ward's rival, Sears, Roebuck & Co., had a different idea. In 1946, Sears gambled its future and began a costly expansion into suburbia. Had another depression occurred, Sears would have been financially devastated. Instead, Sears doubled its revenues while Ward's stood still. Sears never looked back, and Ward's never caught up. In fact, Ward's eventually went bankrupt.

How could corporate planning go so wrong? Montgomery Ward's postwar troubles sprang from its firm adherence to an idea from a different time and culture. Because Sewell Avery thought a depression would follow World War II, and because he failed to see that middle-America was moving to the suburbs, he misread the cultural waves and consequently his business wiped out.

Christian leaders also, and not just business executives, need to read the waves of cultural change.

Citation: Rick Ezell, Hitting a Moving Target *(Zondervan, 1999), pp. 34-35; original story in John McCormick, "You Snooze You Lose," Newsweek (7-21-97), #50; submitted by Jeff Arthurs*

CHILDLIKENESS
LEARNING FROM CHILDLIKENESS
MATTHEW 18:1-6; LUKE 18:16-17
Attitudes; Childlikeness; Children; Maturity; Youth

When I look at a patch of dandelions, I see a bunch of weeds that are going to take over my yard. Kids see flowers for Mom and blowing white fluff you can wish on.

When I look at an old drunk and he smiles at me, I see a smelly, dirty person who probably wants money, and I look away. Kids see someone smiling at them, and they smile back.

When I hear music I love, I know I can't carry a tune and don't have much rhythm, so I sit self-consciously and listen. Kids feel the beat and move to it. They sing out the words, and if they don't know them, they make up their own.

When I feel wind on my face, I brace myself against it. I feel it messing up my hair and pulling me back when I walk. Kids close their eyes, spread their arms, and fly with it, until they fall to the ground laughing.

When I pray, I say "thee" and "thou" and "grant me this" and "give me that." Kids say, "Hi, God! Thanks for my toys and my friends. Please keep the bad dreams away tonight. Sorry, I don't want to go to heaven yet. I would miss Mommy and Daddy."

When I see a mud puddle, I step around it. I see muddy shoes and clothes and dirty carpets. Kids sit in it. They see dams to build, rivers to cross, and worms to play with.

I wonder if we are given kids to teach or to learn from? No wonder God loves the little children!

Citation: From the Internet; submitted by Debi Zahn; Sandwich, Illinois

---

CHRIST, AS SHEPHERD

IRA SANKEY DELIVERED FROM SNIPER

PSALM 20:1; PROVERBS 18:10; JOHN 17:11

Christ, as Shepherd; Deliverance; Enemies; Mercy; Music; Protection

When Ira Sankey was at the height of his ministry, traveling on a steamer in the Delaware River, he was recognized by some passengers. They'd seen his picture in the newspaper and knew he was associated with evangelist D. L. Moody. When they asked him to sing one of his own compositions, Sankey said he preferred the hymn by William Bradbury, "Savior, Like a Shepherd Lead Us." He suggested that everyone join in the singing. One of the stanzas begins, "We are thine, do thou befriend us; be the guardian of our way."

When he finished, a man stepped out of the shadows and inquired, "Were you in the army, Mr. Sankey?"

"Yes, I joined up in 1860."

"Did you ever do guard duty at night in Maryland, about 1862?"

"Yes, I did."

"Well, I was in the Confederate army," said the stranger. "I saw you one night at Sharpsburg. I had you in my gunsight as you stood there in the light of the full moon. Then just as I was about to pull the trigger, you began to sing. It was the same hymn you sang tonight," the man told an astonished Sankey. "I couldn't shoot you."

Citation: I. M. Anderson, Moody Monthly *(02-86); quoted in* Men of Integrity *(March/April 2001)*

CHRIST, AS SHEPHERD

OUR COMFORTING SHEPHERD

PSALM 23; 1 PETER 5:7

Christ, as Shepherd; Circumstances and Faith; Comfort; Jesus Christ; Peace; Trust

During the recent uprisings in the Middle East, Ron and Joke Jones, who serve with the Christian and Missionary Alliance in Israel, communicated the following in their prayer letter:

The result of the fighting and killing has left a profound sense of discouragement that hovers over the country. Several times we have come into closer contact with this conflict than our comfort zone allowed.

Yesterday a friend shared with us something she observed that was a delightful reminder of God's care for us. She watched a shepherd caring for his flock near the area where guns are fired. Every time the shots rang out the sheep scattered in fright. The shepherd then touched each of them with his staff and spoke calmly to them, and the sheep settled down immediately because they trusted the shepherd. And then another shot sounded, and the same routine happened again. Each time, the sheep needed the shepherd to orient them again and to reassure them they were safe.

We are like those sheep, and our Shepherd reaches out and touches us with his staff, speaking words of calm and comfort.

Citation: Greg Asimakoupoulos, writer; Naperville, Illinois

CHRIST, BURDEN BEARER

JESUS UNDERSTANDS OUR PAIN

John 14:26; Acts 1:8; Hebrews 4:14-16

Christ, burden bearer; Christ, cross of; Christ, humanity of; Christ, incarnation of;
Dependence on God; Gospel; Hearing God; Holy Spirit; Inspiration; Jesus Christ;
Preaching

Author and speaker Jill Briscoe recalls:

In Croatia I was asked to speak to a church gathering for about
200 newly arrived refugees. Refugees from this area of the world are
mostly women because the men are either dead or in camp or fighting.
This group of Muslims, Croats, and a few Serbs had fled to a seminary
on the border of a battered Croatian town. The town was still in danger
of sniper fire and bombing, but the church had escaped because there
were apartment buildings between it and the guns. Attackers had tried
to fire shells over the apartment buildings to the seminary, but they
hadn't managed to do it, so it became the refugee receiving and feeding place.

We worked all day visiting with the refugees. At night a service was held
in this huge, old church, and I had to speak. I didn't know what to say.
Everything I had prepared seemed totally inadequate, so I put my notes
away and prayed, "God, give me creative ideas they can identify with."

I told them about Jesus, who as a baby became a refugee. He was
hunted by soldiers, and his parents had to flee to Egypt at night, leaving
everything behind. I could tell the people began to click with what I was
saying. I kept praying like crazy.

I continued telling them about Jesus' life, and when I got to the cross, I
said, "He hung there naked, not like pictures tell you." They knew what
that meant. Some of them had been stripped naked and tortured.

At the end of the message, I said, "All these things have happened to
you. You are homeless. You have had to flee. You have suffered unjustly.
But you didn't have a choice. He had a choice. He knew all this would
happen to him, but he still came." And then I told them why.

Many of them just knelt down, put their hands up, and wept. I said,
"He's the only one who really understands. How can I possibly under-

stand, but he can. This is what people did to him. He's the suffering God. You can give your pain to him."

Citation: Jill Briscoe, "Keeping the Adventure in Ministry," Leadership Journal (Summer 1996)

■

CHRIST, DEATH OF

MISSION TO DIE

Matthew 16:21; Luke 9:22; 1 John 3:16; 1 John 4:9-10

Atonement; Christ, death of; Cross; Death; God, love of; Jesus Christ; Sacrifice; Suffering

In *The God of the Towel*, Jim McGuiggan writes:

In 490 B.C. as Xerxes was advancing into Greece, he came to Thermopylae, a small pass in central Greece. Herodotus tells us that by the time he got there, he had something like six million troops on land and sea. Gathered there to stop the advance of the powerful Persian monarch was a mere handful of Greeks headed up by 300 Spartans led by the Spartan king Leonidas.

When Persian troops came to check the pass, they saw 300 warriors brushing their long hair and doing calisthenics and other such things. Back they went to their master to report that some fools with weapons were playing games in the ravine. Demaratus, a Greek physician and counselor to the Persian court, assured the king they weren't playing games—they were performing a death ritual.

These men had come to die!

Many an unmarried man had volunteered, but Leonidas insisted on taking with him men who had living sons. They never meant to come back!

Love of Sparta motivated these men—love of humanity moved this God of ours. This God came to earth to die! In doing this, God was demonstrating his own love for us.

Citation: Jim McGuiggan, The God of the Towel (Howard, 1997)

CHRIST, ONE WITH THE FATHER
GANDHI CAN'T COMPARE TO CHRIST

John 12:44-45; 1 John 2:3-6
Christ, deity of; Christ, greatness of; Christ, one with the Father; Christ, only Savior; Christ, uniqueness of; Fatherhood of God; Knowing God; Religion; Religions, compared

Author Michael Green writes:

Only Jesus fully understands God the Father. Great people have discovered and taught many true and noble things about God. Nobody has known him with the intimacy of Jesus, who could call him Abba, "dear daddy."

When that holy man, Mahatma Gandhi, was dying, one of his relatives came to him and asked, "Babaki, you have been looking for God all your life. Have you found him yet?"

"No," was the reply. "I'm still looking." The humility, the earnestness, the sheer goodness of a great teacher like Gandhi shine through a remark like that. But it stands in the most stark contrast with Jesus' claim, "No one knows the Father except the Son."

Citation: Michael Green, *The Message of Matthew (IVP, 2000), p. 141; submitted by Owen Bourgaize; Guernsey, United Kingdom*

CHRIST, THE WORD
THE TRUTH ABOUT READING

John 1
Christ, the Word; Knowledge and Knowing; Study; Truth; Understanding

Reading ought to be an act of homage to the God of all truth. We open our hearts to words that reflect the reality he has created or the greater reality which he is. . . . Christ, the incarnate Word, is the Book of life in whom we read God.

Citation: Thomas Merton, quoted in "Reflections," Christianity Today (4-24-00)

CHRISTAIN LIFE

GOLFER PAYNE STEWART CREDITS GOD

PSALM 145:1-7; 1 PETER 3:15-16

Christian Life; Sports; Success; Testimony; Witnessing

A few nights following Payne Stewart's second PGA Open victory (less than six months before he died), friends gathered to pay tribute to the champ. The focal point of the party was a big-screen replay of the final-day TV coverage. Seeing the tape for the first time, Payne watched images of himself sinking the winning putt and moments later giving credit to God.

At the party, Stewart's pastor, J. B. Collingsworth, noticed Payne walking away trying to hide the tears welling up in his eyes. When he faced his pastor, the tears began to flow.

Collingsworth recalls, "I put my arm around him and said, 'Payne, I just want you to know I appreciate what God's doing with your heart.' He looked at me as hard as he could, tears now streaming down his face. He said, 'J. B., I'm not going to be a Bible-thumper. I'm not going to stand up on some stump. But I want everybody to know—it's Jesus.' "

Citation: Larry Guest, The Payne Stewart Story *(Stark Books, 2000), pp. 50-51; submitted by Greg Asimakoupoulos; Naperville, Illinois*

CHRISTMAS

CHRISTMAS GIVING

MATTHEW 2:1-12; MATTHEW 6:1-4; 2 CORINTHIANS 8; 2 CORINTHIANS 9

Christian Life; Christmas; Family; Gifts; Giving; Happiness; Love; Ministry

It's just a small, white envelope stuck among the branches of our Christmas tree. No name, no identification, no inscription. It has peeked through the branches of our tree for the past 10 years or so.

It all began because my husband, Mike, hated Christmas—oh, not the true meaning of Christmas but the commercial aspects of it: overspending, the frantic running around at the last minute, the gifts given in desperation.

Knowing he felt this way, I decided one year to bypass the usual shirts, sweaters, ties. . . . I reached for something special just for Mike.

Our son Kevin was wrestling at the junior level at the school he attended. Shortly before Christmas, there was a nonleague match against a team sponsored by an inner-city church. These youngsters, dressed in sneakers so ragged that shoestrings seemed to be the only things holding them together, presented a sharp contrast to our boys in their spiffy blue-and-gold uniforms and sparkling new wrestling shoes.

As the match began, I was alarmed to see that the other team was wrestling without headgear. It was a luxury the ragtag team obviously could not afford.

We ended up walloping them. As each of their boys got up from the mat, he swaggered around in his tatters with false bravado, a kind of street pride that couldn't acknowledge defeat.

Mike shook his head sadly. "I wish just one of them could have won," he said. "They have a lot of potential, but losing like this could take the heart right out of them." That's when the idea for his present came.

That afternoon, I went to a local sporting goods store and bought an assortment of wrestling headgear and shoes and sent them anonymously to the inner-city church. On Christmas Eve, I placed an envelope on the tree, the note inside telling Mike what I had done and that this was his gift from me. His smile was the brightest thing about Christmas. Each Christmas, I followed the tradition—one year sending a group of mentally handicapped youngsters to a hockey game, another year giving a check to a pair of elderly brothers whose home had burned to the ground the week before Christmas.

The envelope became the highlight of our Christmas. It was always the last thing opened on Christmas morning, and our children would stand with wide-eyed anticipation as their dad lifted the envelope from the tree to reveal its contents. As the children grew, the envelope never lost its allure.

The story doesn't end there. We lost Mike due to cancer. When Christmas rolled around, I was so wrapped up in grief that I barely got the tree up. But on Christmas Eve I placed an envelope on the tree, and in the morning it was joined by three more.

Each of our children had placed an envelope on the tree for their dad. The tradition has grown and someday will expand even further with our grandchildren standing around the tree with wide-eyed anticipation, watching as their fathers take down the envelopes.

Mike's spirit, like the Christmas spirit, will always be with us.

Citation: Source unknown; submitted by Charles Middleton

■

CHRISTMAS

HENRI NOUWEN DEFINES CHRISTMAS

MATTHEW 1; MATTHEW 2; LUKE 1; LUKE 2; 2 CORINTHIANS 1:18-20
Christmas; God, sovereignty of; Hope; Incarnation; Providence; Salvation;

Songs, good feelings, beautiful liturgies, nice presents, big dinners, and sweet words do not make Christmas. Christmas is saying yes to something beyond all emotions and feelings. Christmas is saying yes to a hope based on God's initiative, which has nothing to do with what I think or feel. Christmas is believing that the salvation of the world is God's work and not mine.

Citation: Henry Nouwen, New Oxford Review *(November 1986); submitted by Greg Asimakoupoulos*

■

CHRISTMAS

KEEPING CHRIST IN CHRISTMAS

MATTHEW 1; MATTHEW 2; LUKE 2
Advent; Birth of Christ; Christmas; Distractions; Priorities; Traditions; Worship

Evangelist Luis Palau tells of a wealthy European family that decided to have their newborn baby baptized in their enormous mansion. Dozens of guests were invited to the elaborate affair, and they all arrived dressed to the nines. After depositing their elegant wraps on a bed in an upstairs room, the guests were entertained royally.

Soon the time came for the main purpose of their gathering: the infant's baptismal ceremony. But where was the baby? No one seemed to know. The child's governess ran upstairs and returned with a desperate look on her face. Everyone searched frantically for the baby. Then someone recalled having seen him asleep on one of the beds. The baby was on a bed all right—buried beneath a pile of coats, jackets, and furs. The object of that day's celebration had been forgotten, neglected, and nearly smothered.

The baby whose birthday we celebrate at Christmas is easily hidden beneath the piles of traditions and cultural observances of the season. We need to enter every Advent season asking, "Where's the baby?"

Citation: Greg Asimakoupoulos; Naperville, Illinois

■

CHURCH

BLAME ME

Matthew 5:13-16; Romans 12:5
Blame; Church; Community; Responsibility

Several months ago I was on a TV show to discuss with other panel members recent problems plaguing the Jackson, Mississippi, community. The city council was in disarray because the council president and another councilman were headed off to jail. The council president had been caught making shady deals with a strip club in relation to a rezoning ordinance. The panel moderator, a news lady named Katina Rankin, looked at me and asked, "Matt, whose fault is all of this?"

Suddenly, I became agitated. I prepared to tell her in dramatic on-air fashion that we are a nation of laws and that the council president trampled on those laws. If we were looking to place blame, there was only one place to put it—smack-dab in his lap as he sat in his well-deserved jail cell.

That is what I was going to say. But I never got the words out. One of the panelists sitting next to me was a gentleman named John Perkins—author, teacher, community developer, and national evangelical leader. Before I could respond, Perkins answered, "It's my fault."

All heads turned his way.

He elaborated. "I have lived in this community for decades as a Bible teacher. I should have been able to create an environment where what our council president did would have been unthinkable because of my efforts. You want someone to blame? I'll take the blame. All of it."

Citation: The Clarion-Ledger (8-09-00); submitted by Matt Friedeman; Jackson, Mississippi

CHURCH ATTENDANCE

EXCUSES FOR MISSING CHURCH

ROMANS 12:4-5; ROMANS 12:10; HEBREWS 10:25

Attendance; Attitudes; Church; Church Attendance; Excuses

Why I stopped going to ball games:

1. Whenever I go to a game, they ask for money.
2. The other fans don't care about me.
3. The seats are too hard.
4. Coach never visits me.
5. The referee makes calls I don't agree with.
6. Some of the games go into overtime and make me late for dinner.
7. The band plays songs I don't know.
8. I have other things to do at game time.
9. My parents took me to too many games when I was growing up.
10. I know more than the coaches do anyway.
11. I can be just as good a fan at the lake.
12. I won't take my kids to a game either. They must choose for themselves which teams to follow.

Citation: Mike and Amy Nappa, A Heart Like His *(Barbour, 1999), pp.182-183*

CIRCUMSTANCES AND FAITH

PURPOSE OF PAIN

ROMANS 8:28; PHILIPPIANS 1:19

Apologetics; Attitudes and Emotions; Circumstances and Faith; Evil, explanations for; Faith; God, goodness of; Goodness, divine; Pain; Suffering; Trust; Wisdom

In *The Case For Faith*, Lee Strobel records a dialogue between himself and author/philosopher Peter Kreeft:

"How can a mere finite human be sure that infinite wisdom would not tolerate certain short-range evils in order for more long-range good that we cannnot foresee?" [Kreeft] asked.

I could see his point but needed an example. "Elaborate a bit," I prodded.

Dr. Kreeft (a philosophy professor for 38 years) thought a moment. "Look at it this way," he said. "Imagine a bear in a trap and a hunter who, out of sympathy, wants to liberate him. He tries to win the bear's confidence, but he can't do it, so he has to shoot the bear full of drugs. The bear, however, thinks this is an attack and that the hunter is trying to kill him. He doesn't realize this is being done out of compassion.

"Then, in order to get the bear out of the trap, the hunter has to push him further into the trap to release the tension on the spring. If the bear were semiconscious at that point, he would be even more convinced that the hunter was his enemy out to cause him suffering and pain. But the bear would be wrong because his understanding is too limited."

Kreeft let the illustration soak in for a moment. "Now," he concluded, "how can anyone be certain that's not an analogy between us and God? I believe God does the same to us sometimes, and we can't comprehend why he does it any more than the bear can understand the motivations of the hunter. As the bear could have trusted the hunter, so we can trust God."

Citation: Lee Strobel, The Case for Faith *(Zondervan, 2000), p. 32; submitted by Rich Scott; Wheaton, Illinois*

COMFORTER

GOD AT OUR SIDE

PSALM 16:8; JOHN 14:27; 2 CORINTHIANS 7:6; 2 TIMOTHY 4:17; HEBREWS 13:5-6
Advocate; Comfort; Comforter; Encouragement; Friendship of God; Ministry; Security in God; Support

One of the most moving passages in English literature comes toward the end of Charles Dickens's *Tale of Two Cities,* a story of the French revolution. Each day, a grim procession of prisoners made its way on the streets of Paris to the guillotine. One prisoner, Sidney Carton, a brave man who had once lost his soul but had now found it again, was now giving his life for his friend. Beside him there was a young girl. They had met before in the prison, and the girl had noticed the man's gentleness and courage. She said to him, "If I may ride with you, will you let me hold your hand? I am not afraid, but I am little and weak, and it will give me more courage."

So they rode together, her hand in his; and when they reached the place of execution, there was no fear in her eyes. She looked up into the quiet composed face of her companion and said, "I think you were sent to me by heaven."

In all the dark valleys of life, God our Father, the God of all comfort, in the person of the Lord Jesus Christ, is at our side.

Citation: Owen Bourgaize; Guernsey, United Kingdom

COMFORTER

JESUS HOLDS ME

MATTHEW 11:28-30; MATTHEW 19:13-15; 2 CORINTHIANS 1:3-8

Children; Comfort; Comforter; Cross; Drugs; Drunkenness; Family; Jesus Christ; Resurrection

For several weeks running the number one song on country music charts has been a ballad sung by John Michael Montgomery called "The Girl." The lyrics tell the sad story of a little girl who hid behind the couch while her drug addict mother and alcoholic father continually fought. They never went to church or spoke of the Lord (except in vain). The parents eventually died in a murder/suicide.

The state placed the child in a foster home where there were "kisses and hugs every day." They took the little girl to Sunday school, where she saw a picture of Jesus hanging on a cross. With a smile on her face the girl asked the teacher the identity of the man in the picture. "I don't know his name," the girl said, "but I know he got off [the cross] . . . because he was there in my old house. He held me close to his side as I hid behind our couch the night that my parents died."

Citation: Greg Asimakoupoulos; Naperville, Illinois; "The Girl" produced by Warner Brothers

COMMANDMENTS

OBEYING OUR COMMANDING OFFICER

Matthew 12:50; Matthew 28:18-20; John 15:10-14

Attitudes and Emotions; Commandments; Obedience

My friend's father, an Army sergeant, tried for 25 years to quit smoking. After multiple failed attempts, he went in for his yearly medical exam with an Army doctor. The physician told him that his health was being severely harmed by smoking and that he should stop. The sergeant confessed he knew he should stop and, in a tone of despair, related his multiple attempts to stop smoking over many years.

The physician looked at him and said, "What are these two bars on my lapel?"

The sergeant replied, "They mean you are a captain."

"Yes," said the captain, "And they also mean I outrank you, and I am giving you a direct order to stop smoking."

My friend's father went home and never smoked another cigarette. He could not quit on his own, even after years of trying, but he could quit when he understood the power of a direct order from a superior officer. He was thoroughly indoctrinated by the United States Army and not willing to violate an order.

As believers in Christ, our Commander in Chief has given us many commands in the New Testament. When we take them as seriously as this sergeant took his order to quit smoking, we'll be surprised how God can transform our lives.

Citation: David Gibson; Idaho Falls, Idaho

COMMITMENT

COMMITMENT MEANS WORK

Galatians 6:9; Colossians 4:17

Body, human; Commitment; Consequences; Dedication; Duty; Exercise; Fatherhood; Laziness; Parenting; Promises; Responsibility; Teenagers; Work

Though skeptical of his teenage son's newfound determination to build bulging muscles, one father followed his teenager to the store's weight-lifting department, where they admired a set of weights.

"Please, Dad," pleaded the teen, "I promise I'll use 'em every day."

"I don't know, Michael. It's really a commitment on your part," the father said.

"Please, Dad?"

"They're not cheap either," the father said.

"I'll use 'em, Dad, I promise. You'll see."

Finally won over, the father paid for the equipment and headed for the door. After a few steps, he heard his son behind him say, "What! You mean I have to carry them to the car?"

Citation: Pastor Tim's Clean Laugh List; submitted by Mark Moring, managing editor of Campus Life

COMMUNITY

CHIEF JUSTICE STANDS BY LAUNDRYMAN

MATTHEW 23:1-12; ROMANS 12:16; JAMES 2:1-9

Church; Community; Humility; Pride; Unity

When Charles Evans Hughes was appointed Chief Justice of the Supreme Court of the United States, he moved to Washington and transferred his membership to a Baptist church there. His father had been a Baptist minister, and Hughes had been a lifelong witness to his own faith in Christ.

It was the custom in that Baptist church to have all new members come forward during the morning service and be introduced to the congregation. On this particular day, the first to be called was a Chinese laundryman, Ah Sing, who had moved to Washington from San Francisco and kept a laundry near the church. He stood at the far side of the pulpit. As others were called, they took positions at the extreme opposite side. When a dozen people had gathered, Ah Sing still stood alone.

Then Chief Justice Hughes was called, and he significantly stood next to the laundryman. A Christian who only associates with people of the same intellectual, academic, or professional interests is not living up to what Scripture mandates.

Citation: Donald Gray Barnhouse, God's Covenants, God's Discipline, God's Glory (Scripture Truth); reprinted in Men of Integrity *(3.3), p. 55*

COMMUNITY

HEALTHFUL COMMUNITY

HEBREWS 10:24-25

Church; Church Attendance; Church Involvement; Community; Fellowship; Individualism; Solitude; Spiritual Disciplines; Spiritual Formation

Dietrich Bonhoeffer said, "Let [the person] who cannot be alone beware of community. Let [the person] who is not in community beware of being alone."

Citation: *Parker J. Palmer,* The Courage to Teach *(Jossey-Bass, 1998), p. 65; submitted by Jeffrey Arthurs; Portland, Oregon*

■

COMPASSION

CARING FOR THE HURTING

MATTHEW 25:31-40; 1 CORINTHIANS 13

Caring; Compassion; Empathy; Mercy; Pity; Sympathy

Patricia L. Miller, a former hospital staff person, writes:

While at work in the emergency room, I learned to stop crying at the pain around me. Each day it seemed I was becoming more insensitive to people and their real needs. Five years of emergency-room exposure had taken its toll.

Then God intervened.

I was taking information for registering a young woman who had over-dosed on drugs and had attempted suicide. Her mother sat before me as I typed the information into the computer. The mother was unkempt and bleary eyed. She had been awakened in the middle of the night by the police to come to the hospital. She could only speak to me in a whisper.

Hurry up, I said to myself, as she slowly gave me the information. My impatience was raw as I finished the report and jumped to the machine to copy the medical cards. That's when God stopped me—at the copy machine. He spoke to my heart so clearly: *You didn't even look at her.* He repeated it gently: *You didn't even look at her.*

I felt his grief for her and for her daughter, and I bowed my head. *I'm sorry, Lord. I am so sorry.*

I sat down in front of the distraught woman and covered her hands with mine. I looked into her eyes with all the love that God could flood through me and said, "I care. Don't give up."

She wept and wept. She poured her heart out to me about her years of dealing with a rebellious daughter as a single mom. Finally, she looked up and thanked me. Me . . . the coldhearted one with no feelings.

My attitude changed that night. My Jesus came right into the workplace in spite of rules that tried to keep him out. He came in to set me free to care again. He gave himself to that woman through me. My God, who so loved the world, broke that self-imposed barrier around my heart. Now he could reach out, not only to me in my pain, but to a lost and hurting woman.

Citation: Patricia L. Miller, adapted from Pentecostal Evangel *(10-15-00), pp. 9-11*

COMPASSION

LOVING THE UNLOVABLE

LUKE 10:30-37; PHILIPPIANS 4:13

Compassion; Experiencing God; Giving; Grace; Love; Mercy; Strength

One day Francis of Assisi was riding on horseback down the road that went by a leper hospital situated far from Assisi, for then, as in biblical times, lepers were a rejected lot. Francis, at the time, was not yet the saint of history; he was still caught between the lure of wealth and glory (he assisted in his father's successful cloth business, and he longed to become a gallant knight) and the life of discipleship (he had recently sensed God leading him into a life of spiritual service). As he rode along, he was absorbed in his thoughts.

We pick up the story as recorded by historian Arnoldo Fortini:

"Suddenly the horse jerked to the side of the road. With difficulty Francis pulled him back by a violent jerk at the reins. The young man looked up and recoiled in horror. A leper stood in the middle of the road a short distance away, unmoving and looking at him. He was no different from the others: the usual wan specter with stained face, shaved head, dressed in gray sackcloth. He did not speak and showed no sign of moving or of getting out of the way. He looked at the horseman fixedly, strangely, with an acute and penetrating gaze.

"An instant that seemed eternity passed. Slowly Francis dismounted, went to the man, and took his hand. It was a poor emaciated hand, blood-stained, twisted, inert, and cold like that of a corpse. He put a mite of charity in it, pressed it, carried it to his lips. And suddenly, as he kissed the lacerated flesh of the creature who was the most abject, the most hated, the most scorned, of all human beings, Francis was flooded with a wave of emotion, one that shut out everything around him, one that he would remember even on his deathbed.

"It was an early step in Francis's conversion, which took many months. But he was learning that to follow Christ may require doing some things that may naturally repulse us. What Francis didn't know at the time was that something greater was prompting him, allowing him to do that which, humanly speaking, he was incapable of doing."

Citation: Arnoldo Fortini, Francis of Assisi *(Crossroad, 1992), translated by Helen Moak, pp. 211-212, submitted by Mark Galli, managing editor,* Christianity Today

---

COMPASSION

TOUCHING THE HURTING

MATTHEW 25:40; JOHN 15:13
Compassion; Empathy; Love; Ministry; Mothers; Suffering; Sympathy; Understanding

Len Sweet in *Postmodern Pilgrims* recounts a letter a physician wrote to a church-related magazine:

Today I visited an eight-year-old girl dying of cancer. Her body was disfigured by her disease and its treatment. She was in almost constant pain. As I entered her room, I was overcome immediately by her suffering—so unjust, unfair, unreasonable. Even more overpowering was the presence of her grandmother lying in bed beside her with her huge body embracing this precious, inhuman suffering.

I stood in awe, for I knew I was on holy ground. . . . The suffering of innocent children is horrifying beyond words. I will never forget the great, gentle arms and body of this grandmother. She never spoke while I was there. She was holding and participating in suffering that she could not relieve, and somehow her silent presence was relieving it. No words could express the magnitude of her love.

Citation: Leonard Sweet, Postmodern Pilgrims *(Broadman & Holman, 2000), p.16; submitted by Merle Mees; Topeka, Kansas*

■

COMPETITION
COMPETITION SPIKES HORMONES

ROMANS 8:37; 2 CORINTHIANS 2:14

Ambition; Anger; Competition; Ego; Gender Differences; Men; Winning and Losing

H*arper's* Index offers some insight into men and competition:

Average percentage points by which a male sports fan's testosterone level rises when his team wins: 20

Average points by which it falls when his team loses: 20

Citation: Harper's *(October 1998)*

■

COMPROMISE
NATURAL DRIFT FROM HOLINESS

1 CORINTHIANS 10:12

Backsliding; Compromise; Holiness; Self-control; Spiritual Disciplines; Tolerance

P*eople* do not drift toward holiness. Apart from grace-driven effort, people do not gravitate toward godliness, prayer, obedience to Scripture, faith, and delight in the Lord.

We drift toward compromise and call it tolerance; we drift toward disobedience and call it freedom; we drift toward superstition and call it faith. We cherish the indiscipline of lost self-control and call it relaxation; we slouch toward prayerlessness and delude ourselves into thinking we have escaped legalism; we slide toward godlessness and convince ourselves we have been liberated.

Citation: D. A. Carson, quoted in "Reflections," Christianity Today *(7-31-00)*

CONFESSION

CONFESSION PREPARES THE HEART

MATTHEW 13:3-23; 1 JOHN 1:9

Confession; Heart; Preparation; Spiritual Disciplines

Max Lucado writes:

Confession does for the soul what preparing the land does for the field. Before the farmer sows the seed, he works the acreage, removing the rocks and pulling the stumps. He knows that seed grows better if the land is prepared. Confession is the act of inviting God to walk the acreage of our hearts. "There is a rock of greed over here, Father; I can't budge it. And that tree of guilt near the fence? Its roots are long and deep. And may I show you some dry soil, too crusty for seed?" God's seed grows better if the soil of the heart is cleared.

Citation: Max Lucado, In the Grip of Grace *(Word, 1996); submitted by Van Morris; Mount Washington, Kentucky*

CONFESSION

GUILTY PLEA BRINGS FREEDOM

PSALM 51; LUKE 18:9-14; ROMANS 10:9-10; 1 JOHN 1:9

Confession; Forgiveness, divine; Freedom; Grace; Guilt; Salvation and Lostness

The banner headline across the top of one *Chicago Tribune* read, "Guilty Plea Sets Inmate Free." The picture showed the freed man embracing his sister, and the article told how a man imprisoned for eight years cut a deal with the state's attorney's office in which the time served satisfied his sentence.

What struck me was that headline. My first reaction was, "Another criminal gets off with a plea bargain." Then I realized that was what happened to me: "Guilty Plea Sets Inmate Free." Freedom is not in a plea of innocence but in the admission of guilt. My story is different, but the headline fits perfectly.

Citation: Lee Eclov; Lake Forest, Illinois; source: Chicago Tribune *(8-2-00)*

CONTENTMENT

WEALTH IRRELEVANT TO CONTENTMENT

PHILIPPIANS 4:11-13; 1 TIMOTHY 6:6-10

Attitudes; Contentment; Coveting; Desires; Greed; Happiness; Money; Peace

Contentment comes not so much from great wealth as from few wants.

Citation: Epictetus, circa A.D. 100; submitted by David Holdaway; Stonehaven, Kincardinshire, Scotland

CONVENIENCE

CHOOSING CONVENIENCE

1 CORINTHIANS 13:4-7; EPHESIANS 5:25

Convenience; Expedience; Love; Marriage; Relationships; Selfishness; Self-sacrifice

In her column, Ann Landers recently passed along a joke she credited to Curmudgeon's Corner. It goes like this:

Emily Sue was going into labor, and her husband, Bubba, called 911. The operator told Bubba she would send someone out right away. "Where do you live?" asked the operator.

Bubba replied, "Eucalyptus Drive."

The operator asked, "Can you spell that for me?"

There was a pause, and then Bubba said, "How about I take her over to Oak Street, and you pick her up there?"

Citation: Monterey County Herald (2-21-01), quoted in Freshministry e-letter (March 2001); submitted by John Wilson

CONVICTION

SEEING YOURSELF IN A SERMON

Isaiah 66:2; Acts 7:51; Ephesians 6:19-20; Hebrews 4:12

Bible; Conviction; Disobedience; Preaching; Scripture; Sermon; Sin, avoidance of; Sin, conviction of

Following the Sunday morning service, the pastor stood at the back of the church, shaking hands with the worshipers as they left. As one man shook hands, he looked intently at the pastor and said, "Powerful sermons, Pastor. Thoughtful, well researched. I can always see myself in them . . . and I want you to knock it off."

Citation: From a cartoon by Lee Johnson, The Best Cartoons from Leadership Journal, *Volume 1 (Broadman & Holman, 1999)*

CONVICTIONS

STANDING FOR WHAT'S RIGHT

2 Timothy 1:8; 2 Timothy 3:12

Christian Life; Compromise; Convictions; Courage; Evil; Sacrifice

Martin Niemoeller, a World War I hero in Germany, was imprisoned for eight years by Hitler. He spent time in prisons and concentration camps, including Dachau. Hitler realized if Niemoeller could be persuaded to join his cause then much opposition would collapse, so he sent a former friend of Niemoeller's to visit him, a friend who supported the Nazis.

Seeing Niemoeller in his cell, the onetime friend said, "Martin, Martin! Why are you here?"

Niemoeller replied, "My friend! Why are you not here?"

Citation: Rev. Amos S. Creswell, I've Told You Twice, *(Paignton, Devon, United Kingdom: Vigo Press, 1995); submitted by Owen Bourgaize; Guernsey, United Kingdom*

COURAGE

FOR CHRIST AND HIS KINGDOM

1 Corinthians 10:24; 1 Corinthians 10:33; Philippians 2:4-8
Courage; Crisis; Family; Heroes; Prayer; Sacrifice; Self-sacrifice; Unselfishness; Violence; War

The week before September 11, 2001, America's "Tuesday of Terror," 32-year-old Todd Beamer and his wife, Lisa, had spent a romantic getaway in Italy. The couple, both 1991 graduates of Wheaton College, returned home Monday rested and relieved to be reunited with their boys David, 3, and Andrew, 1.

But extended family time would have to wait. The next morning Todd, an executive with Oracle, had to be at a sales reps meeting in Northern California. He kissed Lisa, who was five months pregnant with their third child, good-bye and headed to the Newark, New Jersey, airport, where he boarded United Flight 93 for San Francisco.

About 90 minutes into the westbound flight, the Boeing 757 was approaching Cleveland when three hijackers onboard identified themselves to the 34 passengers and 7 crew and proceeded to take control of the cockpit and cabin. The plane, now piloted by the would-be terrorists, made a sharp turn to the south.

Todd reached for the GTE Airfone in the back of one of the seats and was connected to a GTE supervisor on the ground. He explained to her what was happening and indicated that he and the other passengers would not likely survive. He presumed the pilot and copilot were already seriously injured or dead.

The GTE employee explained to Todd what had already happened at the World Trade Center and Pentagon. Upon hearing this news, Todd must have realized that the hijackers were intent on crashing the plane into another prominent building near Washington D.C. (the direction they were now headed). Even though the hijacker nearest Todd had a bomb belted around his middle, the former Wheaton College baseball player told the GTE representative that he and a few others were determined to do whatever they could to disrupt the terrorists' plan.

He then asked the person on the other end of the phone to call his wife and report their entire conversation to her (including how much he loved her). Before hanging up, this committed Christian and devoted family man, who taught Sunday school each week, asked the GTE employee to pray the Lord's Prayer with him. With the sound of passengers screaming in the background, she complied. When they concluded the prayer, Todd calmly said, "Help me, God. Help me, Jesus."

The GTE employee then heard Todd say, apparently to the other three businessmen he'd alluded to earlier: "Are you ready, guys? Let's roll!" With that the phone went dead.

Within a few minutes, Flight 93 was nose-diving into a rural field 80 miles southeast of Pittsburgh, where it left a crater 40 feet deep as it disintegrated upon impact. Because Todd Beamer was committed to Jesus Christ and his kingdom, he was willing to do whatever was necessary to put the needs of others above his own fear of danger and imminent death. Thanks to him and the three other businessmen who joined with him, the intended target in the nation's capital was not reached, and who knows how many lives were saved because of that. No one on the ground was killed.

According to Todd's wife, Lisa, "His example of courage has given me, my boys (and my unborn baby) a reason to live."

That's what can happen when we, like Jesus Christ, put the needs of others ahead of our own.

Citation: Greg Asimakoupoulos; Naperville, Illinois; source: Chicago Tribune *(9-17-01),* San Francisco Chronicle *(9-17-01)*

■

COURTSHIP

MADONNA'S VIEW OF COURTSHIP

1 CORINTHIANS 7:32-40
Courtship; Dating; Marriage; Relationships; Romance

According to pop singer/actress Madonna: "You really have to get to know someone. Courtship, the whole idea of courtship, is such a boring, dated thing, but I am a big fan of it. I think most of the relationships I've had that have not worked out, or had started really passionately and then crashed and burned, were because I didn't spend enough time getting to know the person."

Citation: Liz Smith, "Madonna Grows Up," Good Housekeeping *(April 2000), p. 180*

COVETING

SEE WHAT YOU HAVE

1 Kings 17:1-16; Matthew 6:25-34; 1 Timothy 6:6-11

Coveting; Covetousness; Daily Bread; Greed; Help, divine; Help from God; Money; Needs; Provision; Supply

If Danny Simpson had known more about guns, he might not have needed to rob the bank. But in 1990, in Ottawa, Canada, this 24-year-old went to jail, and his gun went to a museum. He was arrested for robbing a bank of $6,000 and then sent to jail for six years. He had used a .45 caliber Colt semiautomatic, which turned out to be an antique made by the Ross Rifle Company, Quebec City, in 1918.

The pistol is worth up to $100,000—much more than Danny Simpson had stolen. If he had just known what he carried in his hand, he wouldn't have robbed the bank.

In other words, Danny already had what he needed.

Citation: Arnell Motz, pastor of International Evangelical Church; Addis Ababa, Ethiopia; source: The Province *(of Vancouver, British Columbia) (9-19-90)*

CREATION

MAN CAN'T DUPLICATE CREATION

Genesis 1; Psalm 19

Creation; Creator, God; God, evidence of; Wisdom of God

Biosphere 2 was an attempt to set up an isolated living environment that would supply all the factors necessary for sustaining life. It was to be a self-contained microcosm of life on earth, containing soil, air, water, plants, and animals.

Biosphere 2 originally consisted of an airtight enclosure covering 3.15 acres in Arizona. Despite an investment of about $200 million from 1984 to 1991, a multimillion-dollar operating budget, almost unlimited technological support and heroic effort, it proved impossible to sustain eight human beings with adequate food, water, and air for two years.

Just 1.3 years after enclosure in 1991, oxygen levels had fallen to the point that oxygen had to be added from the outside. Nineteen of twenty-five vertebrate species placed in the unit became extinct. All the species that could pollinate the plants became extinct, as did most insects. Water and air pollution became acute, and temperature control was a problem.

With all the intelligence put into the design of Biosphere 2, it couldn't be made to work, yet the wonderfully integrated ecosystems of Earth supposedly just happened without intelligent design!

Citation: "Lessons from Biosphere 2," Creation Ex Nihilo (June 1997), p. 8; submitted by Aaron Goerner; New Hartford, New York

CREATION

RANDOM CREATION? DO THE MATH

GENESIS 1:26-31; PSALM 139:14; ECCLESIASTES 11:5; ROMANS 1:19-20
Bible; Creation; Evolution; Ideologies and Belief Systems; Science; Truth

A chance of 1 out of 1,000,000,000,000,000 (quadrillion, 10 with 14 zeros) is considered a virtual impossibility. But when DNA codiscoverer Francis Crick calculated the possibility of a simple protein sequence of 200 amino acids (much simpler than a DNA molecule) originating spontaneously, his figure was 10 with 26 zeroes after it.

Those who remember one fad of the past will appreciate British scientist Fred Hoyle's view of the odds against evolved life. "Anyone acquainted with the Rubik's Cube," he wrote, "will concede the impossibility of a solution being obtained by a blind person moving the cube faces at random."

Mr. Hoyle's best-known analogy, however, has a tornado in a junkyard taking all the pieces of metal lying there and turning them into a Boeing 747. It might be possible for two pieces to be naturally welded together, and then two pieces more in a later whirlwind, but production of even a simple organic molecule would require all of the pieces to come together at one time.

Citation: Marvin Olasky, "Things Unseen," World (4-14-01)

CRISIS

DISGUISED OPPORTUNITY

Matthew 19:26; Romans 8:28

Circumstances and Faith; Crisis; Doubt; Miracles; Opportunity

We are all faced with innumerable opportunities brilliantly disguised as impossible situations.

Citation: Chuck Swindoll, quoted by Bob Reccord, Forged by Fire: How God Shapes Those He Loves *(Broadman & Holman, 2000), p. 118*

CRITICISM

LINCOLN'S DETRACTORS RECANT

Matthew 10:17-20; Acts 5:27-39

Character; Compromise; Conflict; Convictions; Criticism; Leadership; Persecution; Rewards

The influential *London Times* was one of Abraham Lincoln's fiercest European critics during the Civil War. After he announced the Emancipation Proclamation, freeing the slaves, he was condemned by the paper as "a sort of moral American pope," destined to be "Lincoln the Last." But three years later, after Lincoln's assassination, the paper realized his greatness, eulogizing, "Abraham Lincoln was as little a tyrant as any man who ever lived. He could have been a tyrant if he pleased, but he never uttered so much as an ill-natured speech."

In the Christian life, there will be times when we must take an unpopular stand—at work, at school, even at church—and stubbornly stick to principle. We will be called all manner of names, but if we're in God's will, we will be vindicated, certainly in the next life, but sometimes in this one.

Citation: Mark Galli, managing editor of Christianity Today; *source: Thomas Bailey and David Kennedy,* The American Pageant, *ninth edition (D.C. Heath, 1991), p. 472*

CROSS

PARABLE OF CHRIST'S SACRIFICE

John 3:16; Romans 5:6-8; Romans 6:23; 2 Corinthians 5:21; 2 Corinthians 8:9; 1 John 3:16
Children; Christ, cross of; Christ, death of; Christ, substitute for humanity; Cross; Easter; Giving; Grace; Jesus Christ; Love; Mercy; Redemption; Sacrifice; Salvation

The mother of a nine-year-old boy named Mark received a phone call in the middle of the afternoon. It was the teacher from her son's school.

"Mrs. Smith, something unusual happened today in your son's third-grade class. Your son did something that surprised me so much that I thought you should know about it immediately." The mother began to grow worried.

The teacher continued, "Nothing like this has happened in all my years of teaching. This morning I was teaching a lesson on creative writing. And as I always do, I tell the story of the ant and the grasshopper:

"The ant works hard all summer and stores up plenty of food. But the grasshopper plays all summer and does no work. Then winter comes. The grasshopper begins to starve because he has no food. So he begs, 'Please Mr. Ant, you have much food. Please let me eat, too.' "

Then I said, "Boys and girls, your job is to write the ending to the story."

"Your son, Mark, raised his hand. 'Teacher, may I draw a picture?'

" 'Well, yes, Mark, if you like, you may draw a picture. But first you must write the ending to the story.'

"As in all the years past, most of the students said the ant shared his food through the winter, and both the ant and the grasshopper lived. A few children wrote, 'No, Mr. Grasshopper. You should have worked in the summer. Now I have just enough food for myself.' So the ant lived and the grasshopper died.

"But your son ended the story in a way different from any other child, ever. He wrote, 'So the ant gave all of his food to the grasshopper; the grasshopper lived through the winter. But the ant died.'

"And the picture? At the bottom of the page, Mark had drawn three crosses."

Citation: Brad Walden, senior minister at Tates Creek Christian Church; Lexington, Kentucky; true story told by Mark's grandfather at Westwood Cheviot Church of Christ; Cincinnati, Ohio

D

DATING

COLLEGE WOMEN MISS COURTSHIP

COLOSSIANS 3:5-9; 2 TIMOTHY 2:22
Courtship; Dating; Relationships; Sex; Sexual Immorality; Women

Scholars from the Institute for American Values conducted a survey, "Hooking Up, Hanging Out, and Looking for Mr. Right," that asked 1,000 college women about courtship in the new millennium. The survey found that courtship—dating a male with the hopes of finding a lifelong mate—has been replaced by "hooking up." Hooking up with a male partner usually is fueled by alcohol and entails engaging in sexual activity. Forty percent of the women surveyed admitted to hooking up with men, and one in ten disclosed they'd done so at least six times.

Elizabeth Marquardt, coauthor of the report, says, "[The women] wish they could really get to know a guy without necessarily having a sexual relationship." This survey was conducted after the National Marriage Project at Rutgers University released a report in 1999 that concluded that Americans are marrying far less, and those who do marry are less happy.

Citation: "Lack of Courtship Rules Leaves College Women in a Muddle," Washington Post (7-30-01); submitted by Melissa Parks; Des Plaines, Illinois

DEATH

DEATH WITHOUT HOPE

1 Corinthians 15:12-32; 1 Thessalonians 4:13-18

Afterlife; Death; Despair; Funerals; Hopelessness; Life and Death

Philip Yancey describes a unique funeral custom conducted by African Muslims. Close family and friends circle the casket and quietly gaze at the corpse. No singing. No flowers. No tears.

A peppermint candy is passed to everyone. At a signal, each one puts the candy in his or her mouth. When the candy is gone, each participant is reminded that life for this person is over. They believe life simply dissolves. No eternal life. No hope.

Citation: Philip Yancey, Where Is God When It Hurts? *(Zondervan, 1997); submitted by Van Morris; Mount Washington, Kentucky*

DEDICATION

COSTLY DEVOTION

Romans 12:10; 1 Peter 1:22

Dedication; Devotion; Evangelism; Family; Help, human; Love; Loyalty; Outreach; Persistence; Redemption; Relationships; Sacrifice

One day in the spring of 2001, Ken Waters awakened in his own bed for the first time in 19 years. Nineteen years ago Ken Waters was sentenced to life in prison after being convicted in a Massachusetts courtroom of first-degree murder. Devastated, his sister, Bette Anne Waters, was convinced of her brother's innocence and refused to accept the outcome of the trial. A single mother of three, Bette went to law school for the express purpose of overturning her brother's conviction.

After studying recent convictions overturned by DNA evidence, Bette scoured the courthouse to see if any DNA evidence was available from her brother's trial. She knew it was a long shot because most evidence is destroyed after 10 years. Her heart was pounding as she awaited the response from the courthouse clerk. Within minutes she was informed that the DNA evidence was still intact.

There was only one more question. Would the DNA evidence exonerate her brother? The testing that followed clearly showed this was not Ken Waters' DNA. Waters was a free man.

It was an emotional scene as Ken's mother and sister, Bette Anne, wept and embraced him. Though costly, Bette's devotion helped free her brother. It was worth every bit of sacrifice.

Citation: David Slagle; Lawrenceville, Georgia; source: The Today Show *(3-15-01)*

■

DELIVERANCE

GOD PROTECTS PRISONER

PSALM 135:7; JEREMIAH 10:13; JEREMIAH 51:16; MARK 4:41; ACTS 5:27-32; ACTS 16:22-34

Boldness; Deliverance; Experiencing God; God, sovereignty of; Help from God; Martyrdom; Nature; Overcoming; Persecution; Protection

Aberra Wata worked with Christian youth in the southern part of Ethiopia during the time of Communist rule (1974–1991). He reported the following story to fellow missionary John Cumbers:

Word came from the commandant that the Party leaders had studied my report about the work among the Christian young people. The authorities decided I had to be executed because of my "treasonous" words.

"The only way you can overturn this sentence," said the commandant, "is for you to deny that you are one of the believers."

What could I say? I told the commandant, "If they execute me, I will be immediately with the Lord."

The commandant replied, "That's what I expected you to say."

As I awaited execution in prison, my Savior gave me songs to sing I had never heard before. He turned me into a composer. [My fellow prisoners and I] reveled in the joys of praise to our God. The guards kept trying to silence us, but with the threat of execution hanging over us, why should we keep quiet? Seven men had come to Christ in that prison, and we all sang together.

One particular guard took delight in mocking us, yelling at us, and insulting us. He would put filthy words to the tunes we sang. One night he patted his revolver and promised, "Tomorrow morning at this time you won't be in the land of the living."

Just after midnight that evening a tremendous storm burst on the town and the prison. Huge hailstones fell, wrecking several roofs, including the one where the insulting guard was sleeping. He became terrified, pulled out his revolver, and shot at random into the darkness, using up all the bullets he had promised would finish us off the next day.

One by one the roofs were taken off the commandant's house and the offices of the chief judge, the administrator, and his deputy. The prisoners in cells three, four, and five got a soaking from the rain too. We were in cell one and were kept dry. There were a lot of wet and unhappy people in Yavello that night.

At nine o'clock the next morning, while expecting the cruel guard to fulfill his promise to shoot us, we observed a remarkable sight. That same guard was pushed into our cell, without his uniform, by the commandant, who was whipping him with his belt. Other people in the background were yelling, "We told this man to leave the believers alone, but he refused, and so God has sent this terrible punishment on the town and prison. He deserves to be given some of his own medicine."

After some time the guard was released and given back his uniform. He told us, "I know that the Lord was with you. I know the way I should have treated you, but Satan persuaded me otherwise. Please forgive me." We did, and several more men came to Christ in the prison.

Citation: John Cumbers, SIM missionary in Ethiopia during the Communist years

■

DENIAL

MAKING LIGHT OF POISON

PSALM 1:1-3; ROMANS 6:23; HEBREWS 9:27-28; 1 JOHN 1:8
Danger; Denial; Sin; Stubbornness

Fallon, Nevada, is the arsenic capital of America. According to the *Chicago Tribune*, the Environmental Protection Agency found that Fallon's water system delivers more arsenic to its customers than any other large town water system. Folks there even joke about it: "Arsenic? It only bothers you if you're not used to it."

Tim Miller, who has lived in Fallon all his life, jests, "Arsenic is no biggie. I'll die of something. It's called life. Once you're born, you start dying."

The arsenic levels remain high, not because people like drinking arsenic, but because they don't want to pay for the solution—a $10-million treatment plant. Said one official, "This is Nevada. They don't want to feel government is intruding in their lives."

Talking about sin often gets about the same response. It's not that we wouldn't like to get rid of it, but we don't like anyone—even God—telling us what we have to do. "Sin is no biggie," folks seem to say. "I'll die of something. It's called life."

Citation: Lee Eclov; Lake Forest, Illinois; source: Chicago Tribune (4-18-01)

DENIAL
MASQUERADE OF INNOCENCE
Exodus 20:15; Luke 12:2-3; John 3:19-20
Deception; Denial; Excuses; Guilt; Sin; Stealing

A woman was working one night in a HoneyBaked Ham store. The store was equipped with security cameras, and she was watching the small, black-and-white monitors when she saw a woman come in the store, walk down the handicapped ramp, and go between two shelves. To the clerk's amazement, this woman grabbed a ham off the shelf and stuffed it up her dress. With the ham wedged between her thighs, the woman waddled toward the door.

The clerk was stunned and wondered what she should do. Should she yell out? follow the woman?

Just then, the ham dropped out from between the woman's legs. It hit the metal handicapped ramp with a loud bang, and then rolled and clanged to the bottom.

The thief didn't miss a beat. She quickly turned her head and yelled out, "Who threw that ham at me? Who threw that ham at me?" Then she ran out of the store.

Citation: Kevin A. Miller, vice president, Christianity Today International

DEPENDENCE ON GOD
AVOIDING UNCERTAINTY

Exodus 16:3; Numbers 13:1-33; Numbers 14:1-45; Proverbs 26:11

Change; Dependence on God; Faith; Habits; Obedience; Risk

Most people prefer the certainty of misery to the misery of uncertainty."

Citation: Virginia Satir, therapist; submitted by Kevin A. Miller, vice president, Christianity Today International

DEPENDENCE ON GOD
FORGETTING SOMEONE?

Deuteronomy 8:10-18; Daniel 4:30; Romans 1:21; Romans 11:36;
1 Thessalonians 5:18

Acknowledging God; Depending on God; Gratitude; Ingratitude; Money; Pride; Provision; Self-sufficiency; Thanksgiving; Work

Percentage of senior corporate executives with a high net worth (defined as having a net worth of $1 million or more, not including primary residence) who credit their current financial status to:

Hard work—99
Intelligence and good sense—97
Higher-than-average I.Q. —83
Being the best in every situation—62
Luck—32

Citation: 2000 Phoenix Wealth Management Survey; USA Today Snapshots (11-13-00), B1

DEPENDENCE ON GOD
GOD PROVIDES BIG AND SMALL

Luke 11:9-13; 2 Corinthians 9:6-11; Ephesians 3:20

Daily Bread; Dependence on God; Experiencing God; Faith; Help from God; Money; Needs; Prayer; Prayer, answers to; Provision

In the mid 1980s, my family moved to northern Saskatchewan to start a church. As a church planter, part of my support was funded by the local mission. Most months were difficult financially.

One week in April, when the ground was still frozen and snow-covered, we were down to only a few dollars in the bank. Our usual reaction to that need was to look for our own solution. This time, however, in a stroke of faith, I went before God and told him that we needed eggs, bread, and milk. I would wait upon him.

That afternoon, a man came to my little fix-it shop with a leaky tea-kettle. He said, "I know I could get another, but it's my favorite kettle. Please fix it." In a matter of minutes the job was done, and I didn't even charge him for it. But he pulled out a $10 bill and insisted that I take it—just enough to buy a gallon of milk, a dozen eggs, and a loaf of bread.

As he left, with a bit of pride in my faith decision, I thanked God, to which he replied: "Don't you wish you had asked for a half a beef?"

Citation: Len Sullivan; Tupelo, Mississippi

DEPENDENCE ON GOD
HERSHISER'S SOURCE OF SUCCESS

MATTHEW 23:12; LUKE 14:11; LUKE 18:14; ROMANS 12:3
Christian Life; Dependence on God; Humility; Prayer; Pride; Spiritual Disciplines; Spiritual Formation; Strength; Success

For two months in 1988, Orel Hershiser was perhaps the best pitcher ever. From late August through the World Series, he had an ERA of 0.60 and led the Dodgers to an improbable world championship. A Christian for only a few years, Hershiser spoke of his Savior in interviews and knelt on the mound in thanks after one World Series victory.

But this wasn't the first time Hershiser had thrown so well. While pitching in the minor leagues at San Antonio a few years earlier, he had also fashioned a 0.60 ERA going into June.

"I got caught up in the scouting reports, what I read in the papers, and the phone calls from the Dodgers," he recalls. "I stopped praying. And I stopped listening to God. I started going out with the guys and not really having a focus on what I was supposed to be doing."

By the time he was done with his next three pitching assignments, Hershiser's ERA had ballooned to 8.60.

"It was like God had come down from heaven and hit me over the head and said, 'You dummy. Remember who got you here. Remember where your abilities come from.' "

Citation: Dave Branon and Joe Pellegrino, "Safe at Home" (Moody, 1992)

■

DESIRE

HEARING WHATEVER WE WANT

COLOSSIANS 3

Appetites; Communication; Desire; Hope

Josh, 4, was visiting his grandfather and me. I told him he could have either cereal, pancakes, or waffles for breakfast.

He thought a moment, looked up at me, and asked, "Did you say cookies?"

Citation: Barb Clark; Lakeland, Minnesota, "Kids of the Kingdom," Christian Reader (July/August 2000)

■

DESIRES

PREFERRING MOM'S APPLE PIE

EXODUS 20:1-6; JEREMIAH 2:13; MATTHEW 22:37; MARK 11:1-26; MARK 12:30; JAMES 4:4; 1 JOHN 2:15-17

Desires; Devotion; Hope; Idolatry; Love for Christ; Pleasure, sinful; Ten Commandments; World; Worldliness

When I was growing up, whenever we went out to dinner as a family, and the possibility of ordering dessert came up, my father would say to me, "Don't order the apple pie."

Now, my father was not a cruel man; he was not trying to keep me from ordering dessert. He wanted to protect me from disappointment. You see, my mother makes the best apple pie in the whole world, and my father had learned from experience that no apple pie could ever compare to Mom's apple pie.

In the same way, we do ourselves a disservice by substituting anything for Christ himself.

Citation: Aaron Baker; Chicago, Illinois; submitted by Linda Gehrs

■

DEVOTION

PRICE OF COMMITMENT

MATTHEW 16:24-26; ROMANS 6; GALATIANS 2:20; PHILIPPIANS 1:21; PHILIPPIANS 2:1-8; PHILIPPIANS 3:10

Death; Death to sin; Devotion; Purpose; Sacrifice

Adventurer Robert Young Pelton was confronted with the price of commitment while in Afghanistan. "When I was being shelled on a front line north of Kabul, I asked a 23-year-old Taliban fighter, 'Why don't we dig trenches to escape the bombardment?'

"He looked at me and asked, 'If you didn't come here to die, why are you here?' "

Citation: Robert Young Pelton, The Adventurist: My Life in Dangerous Places *(Doubleday; 2000); submitted by Lee Eclov; Lake Forest, Illinois*

■

DIRECTION

WRONG WAY REGALS: INSTINCT WITHOUT DIRECTION

PSALM 16; MATTHEW 18:15-18; ROMANS 3; 1 CORINTHIANS 5; GALATIANS 6:1-2; PHILIPPIANS 1:9-11; JAMES 5:19-20

Community; Correction; Direction; Error; Mistakes; Sin

Roy Regals was a lineman for the University of California in 1929 when they went up against Georgia Tech at the Rose Bowl. The game was scoreless when he picked up a fumble from the other team, and headed for the end zone—the wrong end zone. A teammate chased him and tackled him with one yard to go, but on the next play, Regals's quarterback got sacked in the end zone for a two-point safety. When the game was over, his team had lost by one point. Thus, Roy Regals has been known ever after as Wrong Way Regals.

Regals later said he had heard his teammate behind him yelling, "You're going the wrong way," but thought, *What's wrong with him?*

One author said of Regals: "He had instincts without direction."

We're all like that. Sometimes we have the right instincts, but we go in the wrong direction, and it's dangerous.

Citation: Lee Eclov, pastor of Village Church of Lincolnshire; Lake Forest, Illinois; from his sermon "Safety Zone"

■

DISEASE, SEXUALLY TRANSMITTED

STDS IN THE UNITED STATES

EPHESIANS 5:3-4

Consequences; Disease, sexually transmitted; Sex; Sexual Immorality; Teenagers

The American Social Health Association recently published these statistics about sexually transmitted diseases:

One in five people in the United States has a sexually transmitted disease.

Two-thirds of all STDs occur in people 25 or younger.

One in four new STD infections occur in teenagers.

At least one in four Americans will contract an STD at some point in their lives.

Human papillomavirus is the most common STD in the United States.

More than 5 million people are infected with human papillomavirus each year.

At least 15 percent of all infertile American women are infertile because of tubal damage caused by pelvic inflammatory disease, the result of an untreated STD.

Citation: The Wheaton Sun, (3-30-01), p. 32; source: American Social Health Association, Research Triangle Park, North Carolina

DISCIPLESHIP

"DIFFERENT" APPROACH TO EVANGELISM

MATTHEW 28:18-20; 2 TIMOTHY 2:2

Discipleship; Evangelism; Ministry; Missions; Witnessing

Leroy Eims tells about visiting a foreign mission field and talking with a veteran missionary:

He told me a story that still haunts me; I can't get it out of my mind. He had gone overseas some 15 years before we met and began the usual programs. About the time he arrived on the field, he met a young man named Johnny, who was involved in something quite different.

Johnny was a committed disciple of Jesus Christ, but he was going about his ministry in all the wrong ways according to the "book." In contrast to the typical missionary approach, Johnny was spending the bulk of his time meeting with a few young men in that country. The veteran missionary tried to get Johnny straightened out, but the young man kept on with his "different" approach. The years passed, and the veteran missionary now had to leave the country of his service due to new visa restrictions.

As he sat across the coffee table from me in his home, he told me, "Leroy, I've got little to show for my time here. Oh, there is a group of people who meet in our assembly, but I wonder what will happen to them when I leave. They are not disciples. They have been faithful in listening to my sermons, but they do not witness. Few of them know how to lead another person to Christ. They know nothing about discipling others. And now that I am leaving, I can see I've all but wasted my time here.

"Then I look at what has come out of Johnny's life. One of the men he worked with is now a professor at the university. This man is mightily used of God to reach and train scores of university students. Another is leading a witnessing and discipling team of about 40 young men and women. Another is in a nearby city with a group of 35 growing disciples around him. Three have gone to other countries as missionaries and are now leading teams who are multiplying disciples. God is blessing their work. I see the contrast between my life and Johnny's, and it is tragic. I was so sure I was right. What he was doing seemed so insignificant, but now I look at the results, and they are staggering."

Citation: Discipleship: Great Insights from the Most Experienced Disciple Makers, *edited by Billie Hanks and William Shell (Zondervan, 1993), pp. 73-74; submitted by David Holdaway; Stonehaven, Kincardinshire, Scotland*

■

DISCOURAGEMENT
MOTHER TERESA FELT ABANDONED BY GOD

PSALM 27:13-14; JEREMIAH 14:19-22; EPHESIANS 4:11; HEBREWS 2:18
Calling; Devotion; Discouragement; Doubt; Experiencing God; Faith; God, faithfulness of; God, sovereignty of; Temptation; Trials

Archbishop of Calcutta Henry D'Souza knows that at times in her life, Mother Teresa felt abandoned by God.

He said that in one letter, she wrote that she had been walking the streets of Calcutta searching for a house where she could start her work. At the end of the day, she wrote in her diary, "I wandered the streets the whole day. My feet are aching, and I have not been able to find a home. And I also get the Tempter telling me, 'Leave all this, go back to the convent from which you came.' "

She found her home, and the rest is history. The Missionaries of Charity feeds 500,000 families a year in Calcutta alone, treats 90,000 leprosy patients annually, and educates 20,000 children every year.

Citation: Kevin A. Miller, vice president, Christianity Today International; source: CNN

■

DIVORCE
STAY MARRIED FOR KIDS' SAKE

MATTHEW 19:3-12; MARK 10:10-12
Child-rearing; Children; Divorce; Family; Marriage; Parenting

Children don't need their parents to like each other. They don't even need them to be especially civil. They need them to stay together, for better or for worse. That's the conclusion of therapist Judith Wallerstein in her book *The Unexpected Legacy of Divorce*.

This imperative comes with asterisks, of course, but fewer than one might think. Physical abuse, substance addiction, and other severe pathologies cannot be tolerated in any home. Absent these, however, Wallerstein stands firm: at least where the children's welfare is concerned, a lousy marriage beats a great divorce.

Citation: Walter Kirn, "Should You Stay Together for the Kids?" Time (9-25-00); submitted by Greg Asimakoupoulos; Naperville, Illinois

DIVORCE

UGLINESS OF DIVORCE

MALACHI 2:16; MATTHEW 19:1-6; 1 CORINTHIANS 7:10-11
Conflict; Divorce; Marriage; Relationships

The Chicago *Sun-Times* recently carried the story of a local couple in the midst of a hostile divorce. Six months into their case, their baby boy was born.

His mother named him a day later, only to find her husband had gone to court to bar her from naming the child. Shortly thereafter, they began legal mediation to see if they could agree on a name.

The *Sun-Times* article concluded with the overseeing judge urging the couple to work things out, saying, "I would hate to see this thing turn ugly."

Citation: Ken Cavanagh; Wheaton, Illinois; source: Abdon M. Pallasch, "Wife Won't Have to Pump Milk," Chicago Sun-Times (12-14-00), p. 26

DOCTRINE, FALSE

BLIND TO FALSE DOCTRINE

DEUTERONOMY 18:10-13; COLOSSIANS 2:8; 1 TIMOTHY 6:20
Astrology; Doctrine, false; Occult

Pastor Wilkins sat behind his desk, a look of utter disbelief upon his face. Standing in front of him was church member Mrs. Trent.

"According to my horoscope," she said, "this is a good week to preach against false doctrine."

Citation: *Adapted from an original cartoon by Jonny Hawkins,* The Best Cartoons from Leadership Journal, *Volume 1 (Broadman & Holman, 1999)*

DOUBT

SECONDHAND DOUBTERS

2 PETER 3:3-4; JUDE 1:18

Atheism; Doubt; Ideologies and Belief Systems; Skepticism

We hear so much criticism from skeptics about what they often brand as "secondhand faith." It is implied that many people believe in God only because of the context of their birth or family or determined conditions.

If the criticism is justified, and undoubtedly it sometimes is, why do we not show the same distrust of secondhand doubt? If it is possible for a person's belief to be merely an echo of someone else's faith, are there not hypocrites in doubt also?

Citation: *Ravi Zacharias,* Jesus Among Other Gods *(Word, 2000); submitted by Van Morris; Mount Washington, Kentucky*

DYING TO SELF

FACING PERSECUTION FOR RIGHTEOUSNESS

PSALM 41:12; PROVERBS 11:3; MATTHEW 5:10; MATTHEW 16:24-26; GALATIANS 2:20;
PHILIPPIANS 3:7-17

Character; Circumstances and Faith; Convictions; Dishonesty; Dying to Self; Honesty; Integrity; Persecution; Work

George Galatis was an engineer at Millstone Nuclear Power Station in Waterford, Connecticut, when he discovered something was wrong. Spent fuel-rod pools threatened to release radioactivity throughout the plant. The pools were not designed to serve as nuclear dumps. Federal guidelines required the Millstone plant to move only one-third of the rods into the pools, but Galatis found all of the hot fuel had been dumped into them. On other occasions, alarms would sound as the fuel was unloaded just 65 hours after a shutdown, far sooner than the mandated period of 250 hours. Supervisors winked at the routine violations, knowing they were saving millions in shortcuts.

Fearing the violations could threaten thousands of lives, Galatis told his colleague George Betancourt they should contact the Nuclear Regulatory Commission (NRC). Betancourt agreed but was concerned for his colleague's future. "You do that," he said, "and you're dog meat."

When Galatis urged plant managers to stop the hazardous practices, they refused. Since many of his supervisors were churchgoers, he was baffled.

"This was not splitting hairs," Galatis says. "These were not technical issues. These were moral issues." Galatis warned his supervisors what could happen: eventual shutdown, decommissioning of the plants, and criminal investigations.

But after two years, nothing had changed—except the workplace atmosphere in which Galatis found himself. When he sat down in the cafeteria, coworkers left. When he entered a meeting, the room fell silent. Coworkers spread rumors that he was an alcoholic, and his performance evaluation suffered.

Galatis began an intense search for God's guidance. He awoke at 4 A.M. to pray and read Scripture. During lunch breaks, he drove to a secluded place to pray and search the Bible. It was during one of these prayer times that Galatis believed God whispered to him, "Will you die for me?"

Though he feared for his safety, Galatis realized there were many ways of dying: his livelihood, his reputation, and his family were at stake. Previous whistle-blowers' families had brooked intense emotional strain. Northeast Utilities, owner of the nuclear plants, would likely hire one of the nation's top law firms to fight him. How many men in their mid-40s can lose high-paying jobs and start a second career?

After months of prayer and study, he concluded that no matter how much he was badgered, God would not allow him to be devastated. He decided to contact the NRC. They offered him no refuge.

When Galatis further petitioned the NRC to suspend Millstone's license, his cause became public and the pressure on him increased. Coworkers confronted him in the hallways and in his office. Some called him a fool; others said he was a troublemaker. He was subtly intimidated and harassed for months, and coworkers often told him, "Shut up and keep your job."

After four years of battling Millstone and co-worker pressure, Galatis finally obtained a severance agreement and left. The NRC never suspended Millstone's license, but three reactors were shut down for repairs at a cost of over $1 billion. A criminal investigation was launched. Millstone reactor 1 will never reopen. The Millstone 2 and 3 plants did not reopen until years later.

Galatis is now 47 and attends Gordon-Conwell Theological Seminary, with hopes of becoming a pastor.

Citation: Adam Bowles, "A Cry in the Nuclear Wilderness," Christianity Today, *Vol. 44, no. 11 (10-2-00), p. 66*

E

E

EARTH

EARTH CREATED TO SUSTAIN LIFE

GENESIS 1; PSALM 95:1-5; ISAIAH 45:18
Creation; Earth; God, creator; Life

Dr. Seth Shostak, an astronomer with the SETI Institute, points out in his course "The Search for Intelligent Life in Space" what conditions favor the development of life in the universe:

The system's star ("sun") must not be a giant star, because these burn out too quickly before life can fully develop.

The system's star must not be a dwarf star, because such a star locks in the close planets, meaning "one side of the planet forever faces its sun, resulting in horrific weather and unlikely venues for life."

The system's star cannot be a double star, because the unusual gravitational forces created by a double-star sun might not allow stable planetary systems.

The system's star must not be a young star, because stars less than 1 billion years old have not had enough time, so astronomers think, for life to develop.

Ideally, the planet would have a large moon, which creates active tides.

The planet should have tectonic activity, which causes metals to be pushed up to the surface, since metals are valuable to technological civilization.

The planet should have a large planet farther out in its solar system, which by its great gravitational pull cleans the inner solar system of deadly asteroids and comets.

The planet should not have a highly elliptical orbit, which is unsuitable for incubating life.

For life to live on the surface, the planet must have an atmosphere. "Very small planets lose their air, and very large planets tend to sport poisonous atmosphere. Earth-sized planets are ideal."

And it just so happens that all these conditions fit our earth!

Citation: From "The Search for Intelligent Life in Space" course outline (The Teaching Company Limited Partnership, 1999); submitted by Kevin A. Miller, vice president, Christianity Today International

■

EASTER
PSALM OF LAUGHTER FOR EASTER
ACTS 2:24-32; ROMANS 5:9-11
Easter; Experiencing God; Jesus Christ; Laughter

Let's celebrate Easter with the rite of laughter.

Christ died and rose and lives.

Laugh like a woman who holds her first baby.

Our enemy death will soon be destroyed.

Laugh like a man who finds he doesn't have cancer, or he does, but now there's a cure.

Christ opened wide the door of heaven.

Laugh like children at Disneyland's gates.

This world is owned by God, and he'll return to rule.

Laugh like a man who walks away uninjured from a wreck in which his car was totaled.

Laugh as if all the people in the whole world were invited to a picnic and then invite them.

Citation: Joseph Bayly, Psalms of My Life (David C. Cook, 2000)

EDUCATION

GOOD CHOICES BY THE SPIRIT

Romans 7; Romans 8:6-11; Galatians 5:22

Change; Education; Holy Spirit; Lifestyle; New Life; Self-control

In the 1990s, a group of Washington children participated in an eight-year antismoking-campaign program. The results were not impressive. Of the group that went through the program, 25.4 percent now smoke regularly. And of the control group—those who did not participate in the study—25.7 percent now smoke regularly. The education campaign hardly made any difference at all.

Our society believes education is the answer to our culture's problems. And for some of them, it is. But for many, it is not. People don't need new ideas or new techniques but a new power within to change bad behavior or to resist temptations. It is by the Spirit that we gain self-control (Gal. 5:22); it is when we live by the Spirit that we gain life and peace (Rom. 8:6).

Citation: Mark Galli, managing editor, Christianity Today; *source: "Harper's Index,"* Harper's *(March 2001)*

ENCOURAGEMENT

JESSE OWENS VALUES GERMAN'S ENCOURAGEMENT

1 Thessalonians 5:14-15; Hebrews 3:12-13

Encouragement; Overcoming; Peace; Racism; Reconciliation

Jesse Owens seemed sure to win the long jump at the 1936 Olympic games in Berlin, Germany. Just the year before, he had set three world records in one day. He was the record holder for the running broad jump with 26 feet 8 ¼ inches—a record that would stand for 25 years.

As he walked to the long-jump pit, however, Owens saw a tall, blue-eyed, blond German taking practice jumps in the 26-foot range. Owens was nervous. He was aware of the tension created with his presence. He knew the Nazis' desire was to prove Aryan "superiority," especially over the blacks.

The pressure was overwhelming, and on his first jump Owens inadvertently leaped from several inches beyond the takeoff board. Rattled, he fouled on the second attempt, too. He was only one foul away from being eliminated.

At this point, the tall German approached Owens and introduced himself as Luz Long. Then an amazing event took place. The black son of a sharecropper and the white model of Nazi manhood chatted in view of the entire stadium. What were they talking about?

Since the qualifying distance was only 23 feet 5 ½ inches, Long suggested making a mark several inches before the takeoff board and jumping from there, just to play it safe. Amazing! At the beginning of World War II, this model of Germany's strength was providing technical assistance and words of encouragement to a foe both on and off the field.

Owens qualified easily. In the finals, he set an Olympic record and earned the second of four gold medals during the 1936 Olympics. The first person to congratulate Owens was Luz Long—in full view of Adolf Hitler.

Owens never saw Long again, for Long was killed in World War II. "You could melt down all the medals and cups I have," Owens later wrote, "and they wouldn't be plating on the 24-carat friendship I felt for Luz Long."

Citation: Ken Sutterfield, The Power of an Encouraging Word *(New Leaf, 1997), pp. 105-106*

■

ENCOURAGEMENT
LASTING EFFECTS OF ENCOURAGEMENT

ROMANS 12:6-8; EPHESIANS 4:29; 1 THESSALONIANS 5:11; HEBREWS 3:13
Affirmation; Christian Life; Communion; Discipleship; Encouragement; Failure; Kindness; Mentoring; Prayer

Dr. Larry Crabb recalls an incident in the church he attended as a young man. It was customary in this church that young men were encouraged to participate in the Communion services by praying out loud. Feeling the pressure of expectation, the young Crabb (who had a problem with stuttering) stood to pray. In a terribly confused prayer, he recalls "thanking the Father for hanging on the cross and praising Christ for triumphantly bringing the Spirit from the grave."

When he was finished, he vowed he would never again speak or pray out loud in front of a group.

At the end of the service, not wanting to meet any of the church elders who might feel constrained to correct his theology, Crabb made for the door. Before he could get out, an older man named Jim Dunbar caught him.

Having prepared himself for the anticipated correction, Crabb instead found himself listening to these words: "Larry, there's one thing I want you to know. Whatever you do for the Lord, I'm behind you one thousand percent."

Crabb reflects in his book: "Even as I write these words, my eyes fill with tears. I have yet to tell that story to an audience without at least mildly choking. Those words were life words. They had power. They reached deep into my being."

Citation: Larry Crabb, Encouragement: The Key to Caring *(Zondervan, 1984); submitted by Alan Wilson; Nyon, Switzerland*

ENCOURAGEMENT
TOM HANKS ENCOURAGES FELLOW ACTOR

ROMANS 15:1-2; 1 CORINTHIANS 10:24; PHILIPPIANS 2:3-4
Encouragement; Excellence; Help, human; Mentoring; Teamwork; Unselfishness; Work

Frank Darabont, director of *The Green Mile,* reflects on Tom Hanks's selfless commitment to helping rising actor Michael Duncan achieve his best:

Fifteen, twenty years from now, what will I remember [about filming *The Green Mile*]? There was one thing—and I'll never forget this: When [Tom] Hanks was playing a scene with Michael Duncan. . . .

As we're shooting, [the camera] is on Michael first, and I'm realizing that I'm getting distracted by Hanks. Hanks is delivering an Academy Award-winning performance, *off-camera,* for Michael Duncan—to give him every possible thing he needs or can use to deliver the best possible performance.

"He wanted Michael to do *so* well. He wanted him to look *so* good. I'll never forget that."

In 1999 Michael Clarke Duncan was nominated for an Academy Award in the Best Actor in a Supporting Role category. Tom Hanks, however, was not nominated.

Citation: Excerpted from the behind-the-scenes documentary "Walking the Mile" (Warner Home Video, 1999); submitted by Rich Tatum; Wheaton, Illinois

ENDURANCE

ENDURANCE PREPARES US FOR ADVERSITY

Romans 5:3-4; James 1:2-4; 1 Peter 1:6-7

Adversity; Endurance; Hardship; Perseverance; Trials

After college and marriage, I found it easy to put on weight and get out of shape. A year ago, I became committed to working hard to take the "sag" out of my sagging waistline. Day after day, I worked hard on cardio-vascular exercise and weight training, seeming to get nowhere. Straining. Sweating. Sucking wind. Questioning my sanity.

But then after several months, it was as though a quantum leap occurred. Weight began to drop off. Muscle began to get toned. And endurance increased significantly. Medical friends tell me that during the constancy of working out, regardless of how I felt, a whole new freeway system of small blood vessels and capillaries was forming within my body. Then came the day when they decided it was time for a "grand opening." Suddenly, more blood came flooding into the muscle tissue, and the resultant benefits seemed to be exponential.

Likewise, when we're walking through the depths of trials, God is building up a secondary support system of endurance, that we might be even more prepared for the next time adversity comes our way.

Citation: Bob Reccord, Forged by Fire *(Broadman & Holman, 2000), p. 24*

EUTHANASIA

KEVORKIAN PREYED ON VULNERABLE

Exodus 20:13

Death; Ethics; Euthanasia; Evil; Issues; Murder; Suicide

Jack Kevorkian preyed on the vulnerable, says a study of the 69 suicides Kevorkian assisted in Oakland County, Michigan. Seventy-five percent would have lived for at least another six months. The vast majority— 67 percent—were divorced, widowed, or never married, suggesting they had no social or family support. Only 35 percent were in pain, and 7 percent—five patients—had no evidence of disease at all. The findings, by Oakland County medical examiner and longtime Kevorkian critic L. J. Dragovic, were published in the letters section of *The New England Journal of Medicine.* Kevorkian is serving a 10- to 15-year sentence for second-degree murder.

Citation: *Christianity Today Online Weblog (12-8-00)*

EVANGELISM
FISHER OF MEN

MATTHEW 4:19; MARK 1:17
Evangelism; Mission; Outreach

Jens Oveson was fishing for salmon in central Norway's Gaula River when he was swept away by a strong current. Kjell Wilhelmsen, 55, spotted the man's struggle. Wilhelmsen had fished the river for 25 years and knew where the current would carry Oveson. Wilhelmsen ran across a bridge, waiting for Oveson as the current carried him downriver.

Wilhelmsen later told a newspaper, "He seemed paralyzed. Only his face and the tips of his boots were above water. I decided to start casting."

His homemade lure hooked Oveson's rubber waders on the first cast of about ten yards. But Oveson weighed nearly 250 pounds. Wilhelmsen used every trick he knew to reel in the big man without breaking his light line. He landed the half-conscious Dane and hauled him onto the shore. Oveson survived the ordeal.

Citation: *"Fisherman Hooks Drowning Dane to Save His Life,"* The Wenatchee World *(7-20-01); submitted by Jay Caron; Wenatchee, Washington*

EVANGELISM

GOD CONVERTS OTHERS THROUGH US

MATTHEW 28:19; MARK 1:17; ACTS 28:30-31; ROMANS 10:14-15; 1 CORINTHIANS 4:1-12
Conversion; Convert; Evangelism; Example; Missions; Witness

When William Carey, the "father of modern missions," first tried to convince fellow Baptists that the Great Commission required them (not just the early disciples) to go out into all the world and make disciples, he was met with fierce resistance. At one meeting, an older pastor interrupted Carey's impassioned pleas, saying, "Young man, sit down. When God pleases to convert the heathen, he will do it without your aid or mine."

So anxious was the man to protect the sovereignty of God, he failed to appreciate one fact repeated time and again throughout the history of the church: When God pleases to do anything on earth, he uses your aid and mine; he uses people.

Thankfully, William Carey would have none of this man's bad theology, and he ended up going to India as a missionary, and as a result, inspired hundreds and thousands of other 19th-century British and American Christians to do the same. Today, millions in China, Africa, and Latin America claim Jesus as their Lord because God used some person, missionary or friend, to bring them the good news of Jesus Christ.

Citation: Ruth Tucker, From Jerusalem to Irian Jaya: A Biographical History of Christian Missions *(Zondervan, 1983), p. 115; submitted by Mark Galli, editor* Christianity Today

EVANGELISM

ONLY JESUS CAN FIX THE WORLD

ISAIAH 9:6-7; ISAIAH 11:1-16; LUKE 10:25-37; JOHN 3:16-17; 1 TIMOTHY 1:15
Christ; Evangelism; Justice; Kingdom of God; Messiah; Peace; Redemption; Salvation; Savior

One Sunday morning, a man woke up around 5 A.M., his wife and children still asleep. Glad to have time to himself, he went downstairs, brewed some coffee, and began to read the morning paper. Three sentences into an article, he saw his five-year-old daughter descending the stairs.

He said, "Honey, go back to bed."

"But I'm not sleepy," she insisted.

Determined to read his paper, he again urged her to go back to bed. Again, she told him she was not tired.

Looking down at the newspaper, he conceived a plan. In the paper was a picture of the world, which he cut into several pieces. Handing his daughter some Scotch tape, he instructed her, "Go sit in the dining room, and see if you can put the world back together."

His daughter accepted the challenge, and he went back to the kitchen to finish his coffee and read the paper. After only a few sips of his coffee, though, his daughter came bounding into the kitchen. "Here, Daddy, I'm finished!" she said, showing him the picture of the world put back together.

Amazed, he asked, "Sweetie, how did you do that so fast?"

She replied, "It was easy, Daddy. On the back side of the page was a picture of a man. When you make the man right, you make the world right."

In a similar way, only Jesus can bring order to this world.

Citation: Source unknown; submitted by Steve Ellis; Florence, Kentucky

EVANGELISM
WINNING A CHILD TO JESUS
MATTHEW 19:13-15; MARK 4:3-20; ROMANS 10:14-15

Children; Discipleship; Evangelism; Fruitfulness; Outreach; Preaching; Youth

Winning a child to Christ is, of course, infinitely valuable in itself, but sometimes we are winning even more, as the following story shows:

Edward Kimball, a shoe-shop assistant and a Sunday school teacher in Chicago, loved boys. He spent hours of his free time visiting the young street urchins in Chicago's inner city, trying to win them for Christ. Through him, a young boy named D. L. Moody got saved in 1858. Moody grew up to be a preacher.

In 1879 Moody won to the Lord a young man by the name of F. B.

Meyer, who also grew up to be a preacher. Meyer won a young man by the name of J. W. Chapman to Christ. Chapman, in turn, grew up to be a preacher and brought the message of Christ to a baseball player named Billy Sunday.

As an athlete/evangelist, Sunday held a revival in Charlotte, North Carolina, that was so successful that another evangelist by the name of Mordecai Ham was invited to Charlotte to preach. It was while Ham was preaching that a teenager named Billy Graham gave his life to Jesus.

It all started with winning a child to Jesus.

Citation: Bill Wilson, Streets of Pain *(Word, 1992), pp. 123-24; submitted by Cora Reimer; Milton Keynes, England*

Citation: Bill Wilson, Streets of Pain *(Word, 1992), pp. 123-24; submitted by Cora Reimer; Milton Keynes, England*

EXAMPLE

HOSPITABLE MARRIAGE SETS EXAMPLE

GENESIS 1:26-31; GENESIS 2:4-25; ACTS 18:24-26; EPHESIANS 5:22-32

Example; Marriage; Ministry

Not long ago we became acquainted with a husband and wife who frequently open their home for short- and long-term hospitality. They've housed children of missionaries as well as people released from psychiatric hospitals. One man stayed with them for nearly two years. "It has caused certain difficulties," the husband admits, "but there's also tremendous joy in it."

What's the effect on their four kids? Do they feel neglected or put out? Their oldest daughter says, "I think I've really learned a lot from the people who have lived with us. I think I've learned love and acceptance and care.

"I can remember one time when Randy and I were little. It was late at night, and we heard this pounding on the door, and we went to the top of the steps. There was a woman there, and tears were just running down her face. As we were sitting at the top of the stairs, I saw Mom open the door and let this woman in. She put her arms around her. I guess this woman's husband had just left her, and she was hysterical.

"And as a child," she says, "I saw Christ's love. I think I've learned through Mom and Dad just to love, accept, and care for people."

Citation: Kevin and Karen Miller, More Than You and Me, Touching Others Through the Strength of Your Marriage, *(Focus on the Family, 1994), p. 30*

Citation: Kevin and Karen Miller, More Than You and Me, Touching Others Through the Strength of Your Marriage, *(Focus on the Family, 1994), p. 30*

EXAMPLE

MONEY MORE IMPORTANT THAN LIFE?

Matthew 6:19-21; 1 Timothy 6:8-9

Example; Fathers; Greed; Money; Values

When I was 13, my dad owned his own business—a tiny shack where he sold chicken, ribs, hamburgers, hot dogs, and fries. One day the oil that the chicken was fried in caught fire. In a few minutes the whole place exploded in flames. My dad bolted from the store before the flames could engulf him.

Then my mom and I arrived on the scene, and we all stood outside watching the fire burn away my dad's business. All of a sudden, my dad realized he had left his money in the metal cash register inside the building, and I watched in disbelief as he ran back into the inferno before anyone could stop him.

He tried to open the metal register, but the intense heat had already sealed the drawer shut. Knowing that every penny he had was locked in front of him about to go up into flames, he picked up the scalding metal box and carried it outside. When he threw the register on the ground, the skin on his arms and chest came with it. He had escaped the fire safely once, untouched. Then he voluntarily risked his life and was severely injured. The money was that important.

That was when I learned that money is obviously more important than life itself. From that point on, earning money—lots of money—not only became what drove me professionally, but also became my emotional priority.

Citation: Suze Orman, 9 Steps to Financial Freedom *(Random House, 2000), p. 3; submitted by Aaron Goerner*

EXCUSES

EXCUSES: ANY WILL DO?

Zechariah 7:11-12; Philippians 4:15-19

Excuses; Generosity; Motives; Selfishness

Zig Ziglar writes:

My brother, the late Judge Ziglar, loved to tell the story of the fellow who went next door to borrow his neighbor's lawn mower. The neighbor explained that he could not let him use the mower because all the flights had been canceled from New York to Los Angeles.

The borrower asked him what canceled flights from New York to Los Angeles had to do with borrowing his lawn mower. "It doesn't have anything to do with it, but if I don't want to let you use my lawn mower, one excuse is as good as another."

Citation: Zig Ziglar, Something Else to Smile About *(Thomas Nelson, 1999); submitted by Bonne Steffen; Wheaton, Illinois*

EXPERIENCE
DISCERNING THE DETAILS
PROVERBS 14:33; PHILIPPIANS 1:10; 1 TIMOTHY 4:8; HEBREWS 5:13-14; 1 JOHN 4:1
Dedication; Discernment; Experience; Spiritual Disciplines; Spiritual Perception; Sports

The floor of the Princeton gym was being resurfaced, so Princeton basketball standout (and later U.S. senator) Bill Bradley had to put in several practice sessions at the Lawrenceville School. His first afternoon at Lawrenceville, he began by shooting 14-foot jump shots from the right side. He got off to a bad start, and he kept missing them. Six in a row hit the back rim of the basket and bounced out.

He stopped, looking discomfited, and seemed to be making an adjustment in his mind. Then he went up for another jump shot from the same spot and hit it cleanly. Four more shots went in without a miss, and then he paused and said, "You want to know something? That basket is about an inch and a half low."

Some weeks later, I went back to Lawrenceville with a steel tape, borrowed a stepladder, and measured the height of the basket. It was nine feet, ten and seven-eighths inches above the floor, or one and one-eighth inches too low.

Citation: John McPhee, A Sense of Where You Are *(Farrar Straus & Giroux, 1965); submitted by Kevin Miller; Wheaton, Illinois*

EXPERIENCING GOD

GOD'S VOICE THROUGH ANOTHER

PSALM 8:2; MATTHEW 7:7-11

*Blessing; Children; Encouragement; Experiencing God; Hearing God; Identity in
Christ; Prayer; Prayer, answers to*

Two days ago I was kneeling in prayer in the front room of our house
at 6:30 in the morning. I'd just confessed sins and was asking God for a
blessing that day, needing to feel loved by him.

Our little boy Timothy, who is 22 months old, had just gotten up, and
I noticed out of the corner of my eye that he had sneaked quietly into the
front room. He's always quiet in the morning when I'm praying because
his mom tells him to be, but this time he ambled straight over to me, put
a hand on my clasped hands, and said, "Hi, special one. Hi, special one.
Hi, special one."

Never once had he called me that before. Six times he called me
"special one." He said it enough for me actually to get it—that God was
speaking to me and giving me a blessing.

Citation: Bill White, outreach and college pastor, Emmanuel Church; Paramount, California

F

FAITH

ONE MORE PRAYER

MATTHEW 7:7; MATTHEW 17:20; MATTHEW 21:21-22; JAMES 1:5-8
Faith; Perseverance; Prayer; Supplication

Nineteenth-century preacher and author A. B. Simpson gives a wonderful example of the power of accumulative prayer. In the city of Rangoon, Burma, resided the largest and finest bell in the East. It was the pride of the great Buddhist Temple, Shwee-da-gone. During one war the bell sank in a river. Over the years, various engineers tried but failed to raise it. At last, a clever priest asked permission to try, but only if the bell was given to his temple.

The priest had his assistants gather an immense number of bamboo rods. One by one the rods were fastened to the bell at the bottom of the river. After thousands of them had been fastened, the bell began to move. When the last bamboo rod was attached, the buoyancy of the accumulated rods lifted the bronze bell from the mire of the river bottom to the stream's surface.

A. B. Simpson writes:

Faith can lift the heaviest of burdens and the highest of mountains. Every whisper of believing prayer is like one of the little bamboo rods. For a time they seem to be in vain, but there comes a last breath of believing supplication, and lo, the walls of Jericho fall, the mountain becomes a plain, and the host of Amalek is defeated.

Citation: A. B. Simpson, Herald of His Coming *(January 1994); submitted by Cregg Puckett; Florence, Mississippi*

FAITH

PRAYING IN FAITH

Matthew 21:22; Mark 11:24; John 20:29
Belief; Circumstances and Faith; Faith; Prayer

Television interviewer and journalist Larry King describes three farmers who gather daily in a field during a horrible drought. The men are down on their knees, looking upward, and praying the skies will open and pour forth a much-needed rain. Unfortunately, the heavens are silent, and the petitioners become discouraged, but they continue to meet every morning to lift up their request to God.

One morning an uninvited stranger approaches and asks the men what they are doing. They respond, "We're praying for rain."

The newcomer looks at each of them and shakes his head, "No, I don't think so."

The first farmer says, "Of course we're praying. We are down on our knees pleading for rain. Look around; see the drought. We haven't had rain in more than a year!"

The outsider continues to nod his head and advises them their efforts will never work. The second farmer jumps in and says, "We need the rain; we aren't asking only for ourselves, but for our families and livestock."

The man listens, nods, and says he still isn't impressed. "You're wasting your time," he says.

The third farmer can't take any more, and in anger he says, "Okay, what would you do if you were in our shoes?"

The visitor asks, "You really want to know?"

The three landowners answer, "We really want to know! The future of our farmlands is at stake."

The guest announces, "I would have brought an umbrella!"

Citation: Larry King, Powerful Prayers *(Renaissance Books, 1998), p. 243; submitted by Louis Lapides; Thousand Oaks, California*

FAMILY

CAL RIPKEN: LOVING HIS CHILDREN

PSALM 66:8; PROVERBS 27:5; 1 CORINTHIANS 13:1-7; EPHESIANS 5:1-2

Affirmation; Family; Fatherhood; Fathers; Feelings; Love; Men; Relationships; Words

Baseball ironman Cal Ripken, Jr. said:

Growing up, "I love you" wasn't spread around too much in our household. Not that it wasn't meant. I could tell every time my dad told me he loved me without saying it. It's just the way things were then.

That part is different in my family. I want my kids to hear it. I tell them, "I love you no matter what," which means, "Whether you're good or bad, happy or sad. It doesn't matter whatever you are. I love you. Unconditionally. Always." It all goes back to security and telling them you'll always be there for them. Maybe you run the risk of telling them you love them so often that it loses meaning. I'll risk it.

Citation: Mark Hyman, Dad's Magazine *(June/July 2000); submitted by Dave Goetz; Wheaton, Illinois*

FAMILY

DECLINE OF THE TRADITIONAL FAMILY

PROVERBS 22:6; MATTHEW 5:27-28; LUKE 17:1-2; 1 CORINTHIANS 7:2-9

Children; Divorce; Family; Fathers; Marriage; Men; Morality; Mothers; Parenting; Values

The U.S. Census Bureau has come out with several findings in regard to the American family in the 1990s:

Households headed by unmarried partners grew by almost 72 percent during the decade.

Households headed by single mothers or fathers increased by 25 percent and 62 percent, respectively. And for the first time ever, nuclear families dropped below 25 percent of all households.

Thirty-three percent of all babies were born to unmarried women, compared to only 3.8 percent in 1940.

Cohabitation increased by close to one thousand percent from 1960 to 1998.

Citation: Interview with Dr. James Dobson, "The Family in Crisis," Focus on the Family (August 2001), pp. 2-4; source: U.S. Census Bureau Current Population Survey; submitted by Jerry De Luca; Montreal West, Quebec, Canada

■

FAMILY

GRANDPARENTS DOING MORE PARENTING

PSALM 68:5; PSALM 82:3; JAMES 1:27

Children; Family; Orphans; Parents; Social Trends; Society

Abandonment, incarceration, drugs, death, mental illness—these are some of the reasons 4 million American kids are no longer living with their parent(s). In more than 2.5 million families, this responsibility has been assumed by one or both grandparents. These "skipped generation households" have increased by more than 50 percent in the last 10 years. In almost one-third of these families the parents are completely absent. In other cases, parents are occasionally present but are emotionally or financially incapable of taking care of their kids.

"Contrary to the stereotype of the inner-city welfare mom who's raising her teenage daughter's baby, the majority of grandparent caregivers are white, between the ages of 50 and 64, and live in nonmetropolitan areas." There are more than 700 support groups nationwide that lobby government for legal rights and financial support for grandparent caregivers. Because their guardianship is often informal, grandparents also have problems getting medical care for the kids and enrolling them in school.

The first housing facility designed for grandparent-headed households opened in Boston in 1998. Twenty-six families now live in the home. Carl Bowman shares an apartment with his wife and 9-year-old grandson. "I don't know where we'd be without this place," he says. "We're all in the same boat here. We all help one another."

Citation: Lynette Clemetson, "Grandma Knows Best," Newsweek (6-12-00), pp. 60-61; submitted by Jerry De Luca; Montreal West, Quebec, Canada

FAMILY

QUALITY AND QUANTITY TIME

EPHESIANS 5:16; EPHESIANS 6:4

Children; Family; Fatherhood; Parenting

During morning devotions with his two young daughters, our family friend, Bill Cage, realized he hadn't been spending as much time with his girls as he wanted. After apologizing he said, "You know, it's not always important the quantity of time we spend together, as it is the quality of time we spend together."

Kristen, 6, and Madison, 4, didn't quite understand.

Bill further explained, "Quantity means how much time, and quality means how good the time is we spend together. Which would you rather have?"

Not missing a beat, Kristen replied, "Quality time. And a lot of it!"

Citation: Pat Ferguson; Virginia Beach, Virginia

FATHERHOOD OF GOD

A FATHER'S LOVE

MATTHEW 7:9-11; LUKE 15:1-10; REVELATION 3:20

Bondage; Call; Fatherhood; Fatherhood of God; Fathers; Freedom; God, love of; Lostness; Love; Love, divine; Parenting; Pursuing Sinners; Redeemer; Redemption; Salvation; Savior

In *Surprised by Children*, Harold Myra writes:

One afternoon my older brother Johnny and I were walking home from school when we suddenly found ourselves surrounded by four older boys we didn't know. Johnny was a good fighter, but they pushed us into a field, threw ropes around us, and shoved us down on the ground.

"What did we do?" we demanded. "We didn't do anything to you."

They laughed, tying us up, tangling us together, cinching the knots tight. They thoroughly enjoyed themselves, taunting us and pulling on the ropes.

Then the bullies left us in the secluded field—just left us trussed up. We yelled at them to free us, but they were soon gone.

At first a wave of relief rolled over me. They're gone! Now we can squirm free. We yanked at the ropes, thinking we could surely get loose somehow. But we couldn't. We strained and strained, feeling panic building as it started to get dark.

We lay there as the light slowly vanished. The moon and stars appeared. We wondered how anyone could find us in the dark and how long this could go on.

At long, long last, under the evening sky, we heard our father's voice. He had searched all along the way to school and found us in the field.

Citation: Harold Myra, Surprised by Children *(Zondervan, 2001)*

FATHERHOOD OF GOD

GOD LOVES THE SINNER

ROMANS 8:15-16; ROMANS 15:7; 1 CORINTHIANS 1:26-31; 1 CORINTHIANS 6:9-11; 1 CORINTHIANS 13:7-8; COLOSSIANS 1:21-22; HEBREWS 4:14-16; 1 JOHN 1:3-9; 1 JOHN 2:1-2
Acceptance; Fatherhood of God; God, love of; Grace; Love

Recently my 21-month-old, who had just learned to say "Daddy," had been struggling with asthma and an ear infection for two weeks. He coughed and sneezed continually, and his nose ran like a faucet. Each night when I came home, he ran to meet me at the door, smiling, coughing, nose running, yelling, "Daddy! Daddy!"

I was not repulsed by his runny nose or close-range sneezes in the least (he "slimed" every shirt I own!). I love him deeply and enjoy his love for me.

I'm reminded that though I am sick with sin, God loves me deeply and desires that I run to him as a son crying, "Abba, Father."

Citation: David Slagle; Lawrenceville, Georgia

FATHERS

ARE FATHERS NECESSARY?

PROVERBS 22:6; MARK 10:14; EPHESIANS 6:4

Child-rearing; Crime; Divorce; Family; Fatherhood; Fathers; Marriage; Parenting

In *How Now Shall We Live?* Chuck Colson notes the disturbing realities that plague children who grow up without a father:

Children in single-parent families are five times more likely to be poor, and half the single mothers in the United States live below the poverty line.

Children of divorce suffer intense grief, which often lasts for many years. Even as young adults, they are nearly twice as likely to require psychological help. Children from disrupted families have more academic and behavioral problems at school and are nearly twice as likely to drop out of high school. Girls in single-parent homes are at a much greater risk for precocious sexuality and are two and a half times more likely to have a child out of wedlock.

Crime and substance abuse are strongly linked to fatherless households. Statistics show that 60 percent of rapists grew up in fatherless homes, as did 72 percent of adolescent murderers, and 70 percent of all long-term prison inmates. In fact, most of the social pathologies disrupting American life today can be traced to fatherlessness.

Citation: Charles Colson, How Now Shall We Live? *(Tyndale, 1999); U.S. Department of Health and Human Services, National Center for Health Statistics; submitted by Mike Penninga; British Columbia, Canada*

FATHERS

STATISTICS ON FATHERLESSNESS

PROVERBS 22:6; MARK 10:14; EPHESIANS 6:4

Child-rearing; Crime; Divorce; Family; Fatherhood; Fathers; Marriage; Parenting

Girls without a father in their life are two and a half times as likely to get pregnant and 53 percent more likely to commit suicide. Boys without a father in their life are 63 percent more likely to run away and 37 percent more likely to abuse drugs. Both girls and boys without a father are twice as likely to drop out of high school, twice as likely to end up in jail, and nearly four times as likely to need help for emotional or behavioral problems.

Source: U.S. Dept. of Health and Human Services press release, "HHS Launches 'Be Their Dad' Parental Responsibility Campaign" (March 26, 1999)

According to a study of white families, daughters of single parents are 53 percent more likely to marry while still teenagers, 11 percent more likely to have children as teenagers, and 92 percent more likely to dissolve their own marriages.

Source: Cited in Irwin Garfinkel & Sara McLanahan, *Single Mothers and Their Children* (Urban Institute Press, 1989)

Premarital pregnancy, out-of-wedlock childbearing, and absent fathers are the most common predictors of child abuse.

Source: Selwyn M. Smith, Ruth Hanson, and Sheila Noble, "Social Aspects of the Battered Baby Syndrome," in Joanne V. Cook and Roy T. Bowles (eds.), *Child Abuse: Commission and Omission* (Butterworths, 1980)

Citation: Statistics compiled from various Web sites by Rich Tatum, Web site manager, Christianity Today International

■

FEAR

FEAR LEADS TO DEATH

MATTHEW 6:25-34; PHILIPPIANS 4:6-7; 2 TIMOTHY 1:7; 1 PETER 5:7
Anxiety; Fear; Stress; War; Worry

During the Gulf War of 1991, Iraq launched a series of Scud missile attacks against Israel. Many Israeli citizens died as a result of these attacks. After the war was over, Israeli scientists analyzed the official mortality statistics and found something remarkable. Although the death rate had jumped among Israeli citizens on the first day of the Iraqi attacks, the vast majority of them did not die from any direct physical effects of the missiles. They died from heart failure brought on by fear and stress associated with the bombardment.

Psychological studies conducted on Israelis at the time showed that the most stressful time was the first few days leading up to the outbreak of war on January 17 and peaking on the first day of the Scud missile attacks. There was enormous and well-founded concern about possible Iraqi use of chemical and biological weapons. The government had issued to the entire Israeli population gas masks and automatic atropine syringes in case of chemical attack, and every household had been told to prepare a sealed room.

After the first Iraqi strike turned out to be less cataclysmic than feared, levels of stress declined markedly. As in other wars, the people adapted to the situation with surprising speed. Then as the fear and anxiety subsided, the death rate also declined. There were 17 further Iraqi missile attacks over the following weeks, but Israeli mortality figures over this period were no higher than average.

It was fear and the psychological impact of the missiles, not the physical impact, that claimed the majority of victims.

Citation: Paul Martin, The Sickening Mind *(HarperCollins, 1997), pp. 3-4; submitted by David Holdaway; Stonehaven, Kincardinshire, Scotland*

■

FEAR

FEAR OVERWHELMS THE OVERCONFIDENT

LUKE 22:31-34; 1 CORINTHIANS 10:11-13; EPHESIANS 6:10-18; 2 TIMOTHY 1:7
Attitudes and Emotions; Confidence; Fear; Panic; Preparation; Self-confidence; Spiritual Warfare

On July 21, 1861, raw Yankee recruits marched toward the Confederate Army camping at Bull Run, 30 miles southwest of Washington. The Union soldiers were overconfident and acted like they were headed toward a sporting event.

Congressmen, ladies, and all sorts of spectators trailed along with lunch baskets to observe the fun. But the courage of the Confederates (who stood their ground like a stone wall—giving their leader, Thomas J. Jackson, his nickname) and the arrival of Confederate reinforcements threw the Union forces into a panic—even though the Union had superior forces!

One observer wrote, "We called to them, tried to tell them there was no danger, called them to stop, implored them to stand. We called them cowards, denounced them in the most offensive terms . . . but all in vain; a cruel, crazy, mad, hopeless panic possessed them."

Fear and panic have a way of doing that—overwhelming us emotionally even though we have the spiritual resources to deal with the situation. We are better able to face into fearful situations—and stop a "cruel, crazy, mad, hopeless panic" from possessing us—if we prepare ourselves soberly for the challenges life will hand us.

Citation: Mark Galli, managing editor of Christianity Today, *from Thomas Bailey and David Kennedy,* The American Pageant, *ninth edition (D.C. Heath, 1991), pp. 450-452*

■

FEAR, OF GOD

TENSION OF LOVING AND FEARING GOD

DEUTERONOMY 6:13; PSALM 147:11; ROMANS 3:18; 2 CORINTHIANS 5:11; 1 PETER 1:17-18; 1 PETER 2:17

Awe; Experiencing God; Fear of God; God, love of; Knowing God; Reverence; Worship

Jerry Bridges, in his book *The Joy of Fearing God*, describes the healthy tension between loving and fearing God:

In the physical realm there are two opposing forces called "centrifugal" and "centripetal." Centrifugal force tends to pull away from a center of rotation, while centripetal force pulls toward the center.

A stone whirled about on the end of a string exerts centrifugal force on the string, while the string exerts centripetal force on the stone. Take away one and the other immediately disappears.

These two opposing forces can help us understand something of the fear of God. The centrifugal force represents the attributes of God such as his holiness and sovereignty that cause us to bow in awe and self-abasement before him. They hold us reverently distant from the one who, by the simple power of his word, created the universe out of nothing. The centripetal force represents the love of God. It surrounds us with grace and mercy and draws us with cords of love into the Father's warm embrace. To exercise a proper fear of God we must understand and respond to both these forces.

Citation: Jerry Bridges, The Joy of Fearing God *(WaterBrook Press, 1997); submitted by Van Morris; Mount Washington, Kentucky*

FELLOWSHIP

LOYAL TO TEAMMATES

JOHN 13:34-35; ROMANS 12:10; GALATIANS 6:2

Church; Community; Encouragement; Failure; Fellowship; Loyalty; Suffering;
Winning and Losing

On Saturday, October 7, 2000, the number-one-ranked college football team in the nation, the Florida State Seminoles, played the University of Miami Hurricanes.

In 1991 and 1992, Florida State, with realistic dreams of a national championship, played the Hurricanes. In both games it came down to an FSU field goal in the final seconds. Both field goals went "wide right" of the goal posts, and FSU lost both games to Miami.

This year, FSU had those same dreams of a national championship. And for the third time, they had to go through Miami.

After being down 17-0 at the half, FSU was behind only 27-24 with 5 seconds left in the game. Enter Matt Munyon, FSU's walk-on freshman kicker. He had already missed a simple 23-yard kick earlier. Now he would attempt to boot a 49-yard field goal to send the game into overtime.

Keith Cottrell, senior punter and placekick holder, described what happened. "He hit it clean. There was no 'chunk' to it. There was no duckhook to it. When it passed the line of scrimmage, I thought it had a chance. It just banana'd about halfway there."

It barely missed. It went "wide right." History had repeated itself.

Cottrell said, "I've been with Matt from the beginning of this season, when everybody cussed him before he even kicked the ball." Cussed him, in general, because Munyon is not Sebastian Janikowski, the All-American kicker from Florida State's National Championship team of the previous year.

Cottrell said, "It's very important for me, as a senior, as a teammate, and as a brother in Christ, to be there for him, through the good times and the bad."

Citation: Adapted from Gary Long, "Teammates Stick by Munyon," Miami Herald
(10-8-00); submitted by Eugene A. Maddox; Interlachen, Florida

FORGIVENESS BONDS US TO JESUS

JEREMIAH 31:34; MICAH 7:18-20; LUKE 7:36-48; HEBREWS 10:22-23; 1 JOHN 1:9

Feelings; Forgiveness; Freedom; Grace; Love for Christ; Mercy; Repentance; Thanksgiving

Recently I went to purchase an airline ticket online for my wife, Susan, to fly from Chicago to Dallas to help her sister make a move. I've done it before, and it's a snap. I picked the time, checked "one passenger," "one-way," the airline, even the seat assignment. Then I checked that I understood this was nonrefundable and nontransferable, and that my credit card would be charged. I clicked on "Yes, I'm sure. This will complete my transaction."

Then I noticed the ticket was for me, not Susan. I panicked. I didn't want to fly to Dallas, and I didn't want to swallow $152! Heart pounding, I called American Airlines. "Sorry," the guy said after conferring with his supervisor. "There's nothing we can do." I was sick.

"Try calling Travelocity," he said. I did, and a voice said, "Due to the large volume of calls you may have to wait." Aaargh! Ten minutes of funeral music.

Then Jacob came on the line. "Jacob," I said, "I made a terrible mistake, and I'm hoping you can help me." I explained what had happened.

"No problem," Jacob said. "I'll delete your transaction here, and you can go online and redo your reservation."

"Really, Jacob?" I said, "Just like that? No penalty or anything?"

"No problem," Jacob said.

"Jacob, you are a gift from God! You made my day," I gushed. If he had been there, I surely would have hugged him.

If your debt is great enough, having it erased by someone is a bonding experience! When you're forgiven much, you love much. Face your sin, and you will fall in love with Jesus.

Citation: Lee Eclov; Lake Forest, Illinois

FORGIVENESS

FORGIVENESS SOFTENS A MURDERER

Psalm 32:1-11; Proverbs 25:21-22; John 3:16; Romans 5:6-8; Ephesians 2:1-9

Forgiveness; Justice; Love; Mercy; Revenge

Albert Tomei is a justice of the New York State Supreme Court. A young defendant was convicted in Judge Tomei's court of gunning down another person execution-style. The murderer had a bad record, was no stranger to the system, and only stared in anger as the jury returned its guilty verdict.

The victim's family had attended every day of the two-week trial. On the day of sentencing, the victim's mother and grandmother addressed the court. When they spoke, neither addressed the jury. Both spoke directly to the murderer. They both forgave him.

"You broke the Golden Rule—loving God with all your heart, soul, and mind. You broke the law—loving your neighbor as yourself. I am your neighbor," the older of the two women told him, "so you have my address. If you want to write, I'll write you back. I sat in this trial for two weeks, and for the last sixteen months I tried to hate you. But you know what? I could not hate you. I feel sorry for you because you made a wrong choice."

Judge Tomei writes: "For the first time since the trial began, the defendant's eyes lost their laser force and appeared to surrender to a life force that only a mother can generate: nurturing, unconditional love. After the grandmother finished, I looked at the defendant. His head was hanging low. There was no more swagger, no more stare. The destructive and evil forces within him collapsed helplessly before this remarkable display of humaneness."

Citation: "Touching the Heart of a Killer," New York Times (3-7-97); submitted by Rubel Shelly; Nashville, Tennessee

FORGIVENESS

HOLOCAUST VICTIM FORGIVES CAPTOR

MATTHEW 6:14-15; MATTHEW 18:21-35; EPHESIANS 4:30-32; COLOSSIANS 3:13

Emotions; Feelings; Forgiveness; Hatred; Help from God; Injustice; Obedience

Corrie ten Boom and her family secretly housed Jews in their home during WWII. Their "illegal" activity was discovered, and Corrie and her sister Betsie were sent to the German death camp Ravensbruck. There Corrie would watch many, including her sister, die.

After the war she returned to Germany to declare the grace of Christ:

It was 1947, and I'd come from Holland to defeated Germany with the message that God forgives. It was the truth that they needed most to hear in that bitter, bombed-out land, and I gave them my favorite mental picture. Maybe because the sea is never far from a Hollander's mind, I liked to think that that's where forgiven sins were thrown.

"When we confess our sins," I said, "God casts them into the deepest ocean, gone forever. And even though I cannot find a Scripture for it, I believe God then places a sign out there that says, 'NO FISHING ALLOWED.'"

The solemn faces stared back at me, not quite daring to believe. And that's when I saw him, working his way forward against the others. One moment I saw the overcoat and the brown hat; the next, a blue uniform and a cap with skull and crossbones. It came back with a rush—the huge room with its harsh overhead lights, the pathetic pile of dresses and shoes in the center of the floor, the shame of walking naked past this man. I could see my sister's frail form ahead of me, ribs sharp beneath the parchment skin. Betsie, how thin you were! That place was Ravensbruck, and the man who was making his way forward had been a guard—one of the most cruel guards.

Now he was in front of me, hand thrust out: "A fine message, Fräulein! How good it is to know that, as you say, all our sins are at the bottom of the sea!" And I, who had spoken so glibly of forgiveness, fumbled in my pocketbook rather than take that hand. He would not remember me, of course—how could he remember one prisoner among those thousands of women? But I remembered him. I was face-to-face with one of my captors and my blood seemed to freeze.

"You mentioned Ravensbruck in your talk," he was saying. "I was a guard there." No, he did not remember me. "But since that time," he went on, "I have become a Christian. I know that God has forgiven me for the cruel things I did there, but I would like to hear it from your lips as well. Fräulein,"—again the hand came out—"will you forgive me?"

And I stood there—I whose sins had again and again to be forgiven—and could not forgive. Betsie had died in that place. Could he erase her slow terrible death simply for the asking? It could have been many seconds that he stood there—hand held out—but to me it seemed hours as I wrestled with the most difficult thing I had ever had to do.

For I had to do it—I knew that. The message that God forgives has a prior condition: that we forgive those who have injured us. "If you do not forgive men their trespasses," Jesus says, "neither will your Father in heaven forgive your trespasses." And still I stood there with the coldness clutching my heart.

But forgiveness is not an emotion—I knew that too. Forgiveness is an act of the will, and the will can function regardless of the temperature of the heart. "Jesus, help me!" I prayed silently. "I can lift my hand. I can do that much. You supply the feeling." And so woodenly, mechanically, I thrust out my hand into the one stretched out to me. And as I did, an incredible thing took place. The current started in my shoulder, raced down my arm, sprang into our joined hands. And then this healing warmth seemed to flood my whole being, bringing tears to my eyes.

"I forgive you, brother!" I cried. "With all my heart!" For a long moment we grasped each other's hands, the former guard and the former prisoner. I had never known God's love so intensely, as I did then. But even then, I realized it was not my love. I had tried, and did not have the power. It was the power of the Holy Spirit.

Citation: Corrie ten Boom, Tramp for the Lord *(Berkley, 1978), pp. 53-55; submitted by Eugene A. Maddox; Interlachen, Florida*

FORGIVENESS

LOVE YOUR ENEMIES

MATTHEW 5:43-48

Enemies; Forgiveness; Grace; Love for Enemies; Tragedy

In his recent book *How Small a Whisper,* Roger Carswell relates an amazing story of a Christian family's response to tragedy:

In May 1987, 39 American seamen were killed in the Persian Gulf when an Iraqi pilot hit their ship, the *USS Stark,* with a missile. Newspapers carried a picture of the son of one of these seamen, a shy five-year-old boy, John Kiser. He was standing with his hand on his heart as his father's coffin was loaded onto a plane to take him back to the U.S.A.

His mother said, "I don't have to mourn or wear black, because I know my husband is in heaven. I am happy, because I know he is better off." Later on, she and young John sent a letter and an Arabic New Testament to the pilot of the Iraqi plane, addressed to: "The man who attacked the *Stark,* Dad's ship, in the hope that it will show that even the son and the wife do not hold any grudge and are at the same time praying for the one who took the life of our father."

Citation: Roger Carswell, How Small a Whisper *(Kregel, 2000), p. 67; submitted by Greg Asimakoupoulos; Naperville, Illinois*

FREEDOM

LINCOLN FREES A SLAVE

PSALM 130:7-8; HOSEA 11:1-4; 1 CORINTHIANS 6:20; 1 CORINTHIANS 7:22-23; 1 PETER 2:16

Freedom; Grace; Liberty; Obedience

There is an old story that Abraham Lincoln went down to the slave block to buy a slave girl. As she looked at the white man bidding on her, she figured he was another white man going to buy her and then abuse her. He won the bid, and as he was walking away with his property, he said, "Young lady, you are free."

She said, "What does that mean?"

"It means you are free."

"Does that mean," she said, "that I can say whatever I want to say?"
Lincoln said, "Yes, my dear, you can say whatever you want to say."
"Does that mean," she said, "that I can be whatever I want to be?"
Lincoln said, "Yes, you can be whatever you want to be."
"Does that mean I can go wherever I want to go?"
He said, "Yes, you can go wherever you want to go."
The girl, with tears streaming down her face, said, "Then I will go with you."

Citation: Steve Brown, Preaching Today, #58

FREEDOM

THANKFUL FOR FREEDOM

Acts 21:39; Romans 13:1-7; 1 Peter 2:17

Citizenship; Complaining; Complaints; Freedom; Government; Gratitude; Happiness; Liberty; Thanksgiving

While I was attending graduate school in the early 1980s, I stopped for coffee in a Malibu, California, restaurant. Coming from a nonpolitical family, I knew nothing of political activists—but I met one that day in that restaurant.

He told everyone what a mess the United States had become. He ridiculed our government and our educational, industrial, and banking systems. He was on such a roll that he had everyone on his side except for two people: an old man and me. The activist shied away from me, seeing my Pepperdine hat, Ronald Reagan T-shirt, and *Wall Street Journal.* So he went after the old man.

As he approached, the old man continued slurping his soup and turned his back. The activist sat down at the old man's table and offered, "Mister, if you can tell me just one thing the United States has ever done for you, just one measly thing, I will leave you alone."

Finally, the old man looked up. He licked his spoon clean and set it down on the table. His red face indicated years of laboring in the sun. With a heavy Russian accent, he replied, "Ve hold zees truz to be self-evident, dat all men created equal, life, liberty, perzuit of happiness." Then he went back to the soup. The activist, defeated, could not argue against what the old man had experienced on both sides of Communism.

Citation: Michael Blakley; Milwaukee, Wisconsin

A B C D E F G H I J K L M
N
O
P
Q
R
S
T
U
V
W
X
Y
Z

G

GIVING

GIVING FOR TAX PURPOSES

PROVERBS 19:17; PROVERBS 22:9; 2 CORINTHIANS 8:7; 2 CORINTHIANS 9:6-11
Giving; Money; Motives; Tithing

The disciples were hard at work distributing the food that Jesus had blessed and multiplied to feed the thousands. Peter heard a voice behind him and turned to see the boy who had given Jesus the little meal that was now feeding so many.

"About my loaves and fishes," said the boy, "could I get a receipt for tax purposes?"

Citation: Adapted from an original cartoon by Doug Hall, The Best Cartoons from Leadership Journal, *Volume 1 (Broadman & Holman, 1999)*

■

GIVING

LIFE IS GIVING, NOT GETTING

MICAH 6:8; ACTS 20:35; 2 CORINTHIANS 9:7; 1 TIMOTHY 6:18-19
Generosity; Giving; Meaning of Life; Money; Work

We make a living by what we get. We make a life by what we give.

Citation: Winston Churchill, quoted in USA Today (11-10-00), p. 3B; submitted by Rubel Shelly; Nashville, Tennessee

■

GOD

CASE OF THE MISSING GOD

Psalm 19:1-4; Psalm 139:7-12; Matthew 28:20; Romans 1:18-20; Hebrews 13:5

Children; Discipline; Experiencing God; God; God, presence of; Parenting

A couple had two boys, 8 and 10, who were always getting into trouble. The parents were certain if any mischief occurred in the community that their two young sons were involved. They were at a loss as to what to do about their behavior.

Then the mother heard about a clergyman who'd been successful in disciplining children, so she brought the boys to him. The minister asked to see the boys individually, and the youngest went first. The clergyman sat the boy down and asked, "Where is God?" The boy made no attempt to answer. The question was repeated in a sterner voice but still no answer. Then the minister shook his finger at the boy and asked in an even sterner voice, "Where is God?" At that the boy ran from the room and into a closet and slammed the door.

His older brother followed him in and asked what happened. The younger brother replied, "We're in trouble this time. God is missing, and they think we did it!"

Citation: The Bridge; submitted by Owen Bourgaize; Guernsey, United Kingdom

■

GOD, CREATOR

CREATOR MAKES AND FIXES CREATIONS

Genesis 1; Exodus 15:26; Isaiah 64:8; Jeremiah 18:6

Creation; Deliverance; God, creator; God, power of; Healing; Power, divine; Redemption; Restoration; Salvation; Spiritual Formation

When we were missionaries in the Philippines, we vacationed in Baguio City in the mountains of Northern Luzon. While there, we visited the St. Louis Silver School, where silversmiths are trained. We admired exquisite workmanship in the workshop and gift shop, and took home a souvenir— a pure silver money clip embellished with a distinctive design. I carried that clip for the next 24 years. One day it finally broke as I slipped a few bills into it. I then took the two pieces of the money clip back to the silver school in Baguio. One workman, about my age, asked if he could help me. I explained my predicament and laid the pieces in his outstretched hand.

After examining the pieces for a minute or so, he looked up at me and said, "I designed this clip. I was the only one to make this design. I made all of these that were ever made."

I asked, "Can you fix it?"

He said, "I designed it. I made it. Of course I can fix it!"

Citation: Allen Dale Golding; La Mirada, California

■

GOD, CREATOR
GOD'S POWER IN CREATION

GENESIS 1:26-27; PSALM 139:13-16; COLOSSIANS 1:16
Creation; God, creator; Human Limitations; Power; Pride

Patrick O'Boyle recalls the late-1940s Hyde Park "Speakers' Corner" appearances of Frank Sheed, the Catholic author and publisher:

Sheed could be devastating with hecklers. Once, after Sheed had described the extraordinary order and design to be seen in the universe, a persistent challenger retorted by pointing to all the world's ills, and ended shouting, "I could make a better universe than your God!"

"I won't ask you to make a universe," Sheed replied. "But would you make a rabbit—just to establish confidence?"

Citation: Christianity Today (4-23-99), reprinted in "To Illustrate Plus," Leadership Journal (21.1), p. 69

■

GOD, FAITHFULNESS OF
GOD NEVER LEAVES US

DEUTERONOMY 31:6; PSALM 71; PSALM 139; MATTHEW 28:20; HEBREWS 13:5
Fatherhood of God; Fear; God, faithfulness of; Loneliness; Protection; Trials

One tribe of native Americans had a unique practice for training young braves. On the night of a boy's thirteenth birthday, he was placed in a dense forest to spend the entire night alone. Until then he had never been away from the security of his family and tribe. But on this night he was blindfolded and taken miles away. When he took off the blindfold, he was in the middle of thick woods. By himself. All night long.

Every time a twig snapped, he probably visualized a wild animal ready to pounce. Every time an animal howled, he imagined a wolf leaping out of the darkness. Every time the wind blew, he wondered what more sinister sound it masked. No doubt it was a terrifying night for many.

After what seemed like an eternity, the first rays of sunlight entered the interior of the forest. Looking around, the boy saw flowers, trees, and the outline of the path. Then, to his utter astonishment, he beheld the figure of a man standing just a few feet away, armed with a bow and arrow. It was the boy's father. He had been there all night long.

Can you think of any better way for a child to learn how God allows us to face the tests of life? God is always present with us. God's presence is unseen, but it is more real than life itself.

Citation: Leonard Sweet, SoulSalsa *(Zondervan, 2000), pp. 23-24; submitted by Mike Kjergaard; Hampton, Virginia*

GOD, GOODNESS OF

GEORGE MUELLER ON GOD'S GOODNESS

ROMANS 8:28

Death; God, goodness of; Sickness; Trust

Is God good even in the most painful times in life? In his book *The Pleasures of God,* John Piper shared the following account from the life of 19th-century British orphanage founder George Mueller to illustrate his point:

On February 6, 1870, George Mueller's wife, Mary, died of rheumatic fever. They had been married 39 years and four months. He was 64 years old.

Shortly after the funeral he was strong enough to preach a "funeral sermon" as he called it. What text would he choose when God had taken his beloved? He chose Psalm 119:68, "You are good, and do good." His three points were:

1. The Lord was good, and did good, in giving her to me.

2. The Lord was good, and did good, in so long leaving her to me.

3. The Lord was good, and did good, in taking her from me.

Under this third point, he recounts how he prayed for her during her illness:

"Yes, my Father, the times of my darling wife are in Thy hands. Thou wilt do the very best thing for her and for me, whether life or death. If it may be, raise up yet again my precious wife. Thou art able to do it, though she is so ill; but howsoever Thou dealest with me, only help me to continue to be perfectly satisfied with Thy holy will."

Citation: John Piper, The Pleasures of God *(Multnomah, 1991); submitted by Van Morris; Mount Washington, Kentucky*

■

GOD, INVISIBLE
NEED FOR A PERSONAL GOD

PSALM 23:1-4; MATTHEW 6:9; MATTHEW 28:20; 1 PETER 5:7

Agnosticism; Dependence on God; Faith; Fear; God; God, invisible; God, omnipresence of; Guidance; Help from God; Ideologies and Belief Systems; Prayer; Trust

Trisha MacFarland stopped alongside the trail on a family hike across the Appalachians. She needed to go to the bathroom. She lagged behind her family and stepped off into the woods. When she emerged . . . she was on the wrong trail . . . lost and alone.

This is the setting for Stephen King's novel *The Girl Who Loved Tom Gordon.* King writes:

Trisha sat down, closed her eyes and tried to pray for rescue. Now, however, praying was hard. Now, she discovered herself lost and without vocabulary. She said, "Our Father," and it came out of her mouth flat and uncomforting.

She couldn't remember discussing spiritual matters with her mother, but she asked her father not a month ago if he believed in God.

"God," said Larry MacFarland, "now I'll tell you what I believe in. I believe in the Subaudible."

"The what?"

"Do you remember when we lived on Fore Street? Do you remember how the electric baseboard units would hum? Even when they weren't heating?"

Trisha had shaken her head.

"That's because you got used to it," he said, "but take my word, Trisha, that sound was always there. Even in a house where there aren't baseboard heaters, there are noises. The fridge goes on and off. The traffic goes by outside. We hear those things all the time, so most of the time we don't hear them at all. They become . . . "

"Subaudible," she said.

"Pree-cisely. I don't believe in any thinking God that marks the fall of every bird, a God that records all of our sins in a big golden book and then judges us when we die. But I believe there has to be something. Some sort of insensate force for the good."

"The Subaudible," she said.

"You got it."

So, here's this girl, in the woods, lost and sensing that there must be something more. And then she remembers her baseball hero, the great closer of the Boston Red Sox, Tom "Flash" Gordon. He pulls out miraculous saves for the Bosox, and when he wins, he points his finger to the sky giving credit to a personal God who has revealed himself to the world in Jesus Christ.

Well into a 9-day trial of being bug-bitten, scared, cut, sick from drinking bad water and eating poisonous berries, she pleads to a personal God to bring her out of the woods.

"Please God, help me find the path," she thought and closed her eyes. It was the God of Tom Gordon that she prayed to, not her father's Subaudible. She needed a God that was really there, one you could point to when and if you got the save. "Please, God, please, help me. . . ."

Citation: Stephen King, The Girl Who Loved Tom Gordon *(Scribner, 1999); submitted by Randy L. Rowland; Seattle, Washington*

GOD, LOVE OF

GOD'S FAVOR TOWARD US

LUKE 2; JOHN 3:16-17; EPHESIANS 2:1-10

Birth of Christ; Christmas; Favor; God, love of; Grace; Love, divine; Salvation; Savior

There are many reasons God saves you: to bring glory to himself, to appease his justice, to demonstrate his sovereignty. But one of the sweetest reasons God saved you is because he is fond of you. He likes having you around. He thinks you are the best thing to come down the pike in quite a while. . . . If God had a refrigerator, your picture would be on it. If he had a wallet, your photo would be in it. He sends you flowers every spring and a sunrise every morning. Whenever you want to talk, he'll listen. He can live anywhere in the universe, and he chose your heart. And the Christmas gift he sent you in Bethlehem? Face it, friend. He's crazy about you!

Citation: Max Lucado, A Gentle Thunder *(Word, 1995); submitted by Greg Asimakoupoulos*

GOD, LOVE OF
GOD WEEPS FOR THE LOST

EXODUS 34:6-7; PSALM 86:15; EZEKIEL 18:23; LUKE 15:1-31; LUKE 19:10; 1 TIMOTHY 2:4; 2 PETER 3:9

Attributes of God; Deliverance; Fatherhood of God; Israel; Lostness

A Hasidic story tells of a great celebration in heaven after the Israelites are delivered from the Egyptians at the Red Sea and the Egyptian armies are drowned. The angels are cheering and dancing. Everyone in heaven is full of joy.

Then one of the angels asks the archangel Michael, "Where is God? Why isn't God here celebrating?"

Michael answers, "God is not here because he is off by himself weeping. You see, many thousands were drowned today."

Citation: Tony Campolo, Let Me Tell You a Story *(Word, 2000); submitted by Debi Zahn; Sandwich, Illinois*

GOSPEL
CAN'T HIDE GREAT NEWS

MATTHEW 28:18-20; JOHN 4:39-42; ACTS 4:18-20

Boldness; Evangelism; Gospel; Witnessing

While I was attending seminary, our two older children (ages 9 and 7) seemed to attract every other child in the mobile-home park for after-school games of hide-and-seek.

Our youngest, Carrie, was not quite 3—and (in the minds of the older siblings) always in the way. It was something you could count on; ten minutes into the games our little one would get pushed aside or skin a knee.

One afternoon she came through the front door crying for Mommy. She had gotten the worst again. My wife, Elizabeth, attempted to comfort her by giving her two freshly baked cookies. "Now, don't tell the big kids yet," she cautioned. "I haven't finished; I haven't got enough for everybody yet."

It took less than three seconds for Carrie to make it to the screen door, fling it wide, and announce to the big kids, "Cookies, I gots cookies!"

Great news should be shared with enthusiasm!

Citation: Russell Brownworth; Thomasville, North Carolina

■

GOSPEL

WITHHOLDING LIFE-SAVING TRUTH

Leviticus 19:17; Matthew 18:15-17; Luke 17:3; Acts 20:20; Ephesians 4:15; 2 Timothy 2:15
Evangelism; Gospel; Ministry; Preaching; Scripture; Truth

Recently, a Kansas City pharmacist was charged with diluting cancer treatment drugs, Gemzar and Taxol, in order to make a larger profit. So far there are 20 felony counts against the pharmacist, Robert Courtney. He admitted to diluting the drugs during a period of time spanning from November 2000 to March 2001.

This man held life-saving power in his hands and for the sake of personal gain diluted it to the point where it could not help people. We can do the same with God's life-saving truth.

Citation: Submitted by Michael W. Owenby; source: USA Today (8-28-01)

GRACE
GRACE OVERWHELMS U2

ROMANS 3; ROMANS 4; ROMANS 5:7-15; 2 CORINTHIANS 4:15; EPHESIANS 2:8-10
Christianity; Faith and Works; Grace; Ideologies and Belief Systems

Bono, lead singer of the band U2, recently said: "The most powerful idea that's entered the world in the last few thousand years—the idea of grace—is the reason I would like to be a Christian. Though, as I said to [U2 guitarist] The Edge one day, I sometimes feel more like a fan, rather than actually in the band. I can't live up to it. But the reason I would like to is the idea of grace. It's really powerful."

Citation: Bono of U2, quoted in an interview with Anthony DeCurtis (2-20-01); submitted by Dave Bootsma; Vernon, British Columbia, Canada

GRACE
HERE ONLY BY GRACE

ROMANS 12:16; ROMANS 14; ROMANS 15:1-7; 1 CORINTHIANS 1:26-31; 1 CORINTHIANS 3; 1 CORINTHIANS 4:6-13; 1 CORINTHIANS 8:1-13; EPHESIANS 2:8-9
Arrogance; Attitudes and Emotions; Church; Community; Factions; Grace; Pride; Weakness; Unity

After worrying for half an hour that we wouldn't get on an overbooked flight, my wife and I were summoned to the check-in desk. A smiling agent whispered that this was our lucky day. To get us on the plane he was bumping us up to first class. This was the first and only time we've been so pampered on an airplane—good food, hot coffee, plenty of elbow-room.

We played a little game, trying to guess who else didn't belong in first class. One man stuck out. He padded around the cabin in his socks, restlessly sampling magazines, playing with but never actually using the in-flight phones. Twice he sneezed so loudly we thought the oxygen masks would drop down. And when the attendant brought linen table-cloths for our breakfast trays, he tucked his into his collar as a bib.

We see misfits at church, too—people who obviously don't belong, people who embarrass us and cause us to feel superior. The truth is we don't belong there any more than they do.

Citation: Ken Langley; Zion, Illinois

GRACE, SALVATION BY

CAN'T EARN HEAVEN

LUKE 15:11-31; ROMANS 3:1-26; ROMANS 5:1-21; EPHESIANS 2:1-10; TITUS 3:3-7

Eternal Life; Favor; God, grace of; Good Works; Grace; Grace of God; Grace, salvation by; Heaven; Salvation

An old tale speaks of a man who died and faced the angel Gabriel at heaven's gates. The angel said, "Here's how this works. You need a hundred points to make it into heaven. You tell me all the good things you have done, and I will give a certain number of points for each of them. The more good there is in the work that you cite, the more points you will get for it. When you get to a hundred points, you get in."

"Okay," the man said, "I was married to the same woman for 50 years and never cheated on her, even in my heart."

Gabriel replied, "That's wonderful. That's worth three points."

"Three points?" said the man incredulously. "Well, I attended church all my life and supported its ministry with my money and service."

"Terrific!" said Gabriel, "that's certainly worth a point."

"One point?" said the man with his eyes beginning to show a bit of panic. "Well, how about this: I opened a shelter for the homeless in my city, and fed needy people by the hundreds during holidays."

"Fantastic, that's good for two more points," said the angel.

"TWO POINTS!" cried the man in desperation. "At this rate the only way I will get to heaven is by the grace of God."

"Come on in," said Gabriel.

Citation: Bryan Chapell, Holiness By Grace (Crossway, 2001), pp. 22-23; used by permission of Crossway Books, a division of Good News Publishers, Wheaton, Illinois 60187, www.crosswaybooks.org

GUIDANCE

GOD, OUR ULTIMATE TROUBLESHOOTER

PSALM 119:105; ISAIAH 55:3; ISAIAH 57:21; JOHN 10:10

Abundant Life; Bible; Consequences; Disobedience; Guidance; Happiness;
Obedience; Renewal; Sowing and Reaping

I was stumped. My old Macintosh laptop simply would not run the
MacBible software anymore. Though I had worked with it for hours,
nothing I did would help. My wife, wise woman that she is, had suggested
that I call the owners of the software for help, but *no,* I knew what I was
doing.

That morning, after having exhausted every last idea, I gave in and
called the MacBible Corporation. After speaking to a friendly voice, I was
assured that the person to whom I was being referred would know exactly
what to do. I wasn't convinced, but I called him anyway.

The name I had been given sounded familiar, and I soon learned why.
The person on the other end of the line was none other than the man who
wrote the MacBible software. He gave me a brief set of instructions; I took
them down and hung up the phone. In minutes, my computer software
program was up and running. I just had to go to the man who wrote the
program.

How many times in life do we try to work out our problems our own
way? Finally when all else has failed, we go to the one who designed us.
Soon, if we obey, we find ourselves once again at peace with God and
functioning as he planned.

Citation: Tim Quinn; Holland, Michigan

GUILT

WHAT CAN THE GUILTY SAY?

PSALM 63:11; ROMANS 3:19-20; ROMANS 14:11-12

Guilt; Judgment; Sin; Truth

While a seminary student at Regent College I had an assignment to attend and report on churches in various worship traditions outside my own. One evening I attended mass in a nearby and unfamiliar town.

After leaving St. Joseph's Catholic Church, I pulled out of a side street onto what *looked* like a county road. I managed to reach 40 miles per hour before being pulled over and ticketed for going 15 miles per hour over the city limit.

Since I was new to the town and because of my chosen route, I had not seen the 25 miles per hour limit. Therefore I decided to plead my case before a judge.

The court date came and I had my arguments and justification all worked out. I had rehearsed my little speech over and over in my head.

Finally, the court clerk read out my name with the charges. The judge, dressed in a black robe—representing his designated authority and power—said, "Mr. Mutchler, do you have anything you wish to say?"

Here it was, my chance to speak! Surely the judge would understand and side with me. But to my surprise, it hit me at that moment that I was, in fact, guilty, and my excuses would do nothing to change that. All I could say to his question was "No, sir."

That moment brought to life what Scriptures say to those who think they're going to argue their case before God.

Citation: Jon Mutchler; Ferndale, Washington

A B C D E F G H I J K L M N O P Q R S T U V W X Y Z

H

HEALING

AUGUSTINE TELLS OF MIRACULOUS HEALING

Exodus 15:26; Psalm 103:3; Matthew 8:17; John 11:38-44; James 5:13-16; 1 Peter 2:24
God, greatness of; God, power of; Healing; Help from God; Miracles; Power, divine; Signs and Wonders; Supernatural Occurrences

During his pastoral ministry, Augustine came to know a woman in Carthage named Innocentia. A devout woman and highly regarded, she tragically discovered that she had breast cancer.

A physician told her the disease was incurable. She could opt for amputation and possibly prolong her life a little, or she could follow the advice of Hippocrates and do nothing. Either way, death would not be put off for long.

Augustine reports: Dismayed by this diagnosis, "She turned for help to God alone, in prayer." In a dream, Innocentia was told to wait at the baptistry for the first woman who came out after being baptized, and to ask this woman to make the sign of the cross over the cancerous breast.

Innocentia did as she was told, and she was completely cured. When she told her doctor what had happened, he responded with a contemptuous tone, "I thought you would reveal some great discovery to me!" Then, seeing her horrified look, he backpedaled, saying, "What great thing was it for Christ to heal a cancer? He raised a man who had been dead for four days."

Citation: Bruce Shelley, "Miracles Ended Long Ago—Or Did They?" Christian History (Summer 2000)

HEALING

OLD WOUNDS RESURFACING

Matthew 18:23-35; Philippians 1:6

Anger; Emotions; Feelings; Forgiveness; Healing; Memories; Pain; Suffering

When my mother-in-law was first married, she was in a serious car accident that caused her to be thrown into the windshield (it was in the days before mandatory seat belts). She told us that for years following the removal of the glass from her face and the healing of the scars, she would periodically have a small piece of hidden glass rise to the surface of her skin. Although it didn't hurt her while it was lodged beneath her skin, the glass shard became very painful again as it moved toward the surface.

In a similar way, we all have tragedies, accidents, and times when we "hit the windshield" in life. We go through the healing process and fight through the pain that accompanies our struggle. It is easy to think all the "pieces of glass" are gone, only to have an event, a person, a holiday, or the like bring another piece to the surface, and it becomes painful all over again.

Complete healing often takes longer than we think.

Citation: Gary Sinclair; Mahomet, Illinois

HEALING

TEEN HEALED OF BROKEN NECK

Matthew 8:17; James 5:14-16

Experiencing God; Healing; Miracles; Supernatural Occurrences

On April 17, 2000, my son Nathan was in a near-fatal car accident. Investigators believe he lost control of the family convertible while trying to avoid a deer. Forty-five minutes later, Kevin Lindow, a young man with emergency medical skills, found Nathan at the scene of the crash and stabilized his neck while his mother called for help. When they arrived at the hospital, Nathan was suffering from a broken leg, spinal-cord damage, and numerous lacerations to his body. Doctors began treating him and found he was having trouble breathing due to a collapsed lung. To stabilize him, they decided to drug-induce a coma.

Nathan spent four days in that coma, and doctors at Marshfield Clinic estimated his odds for survival at 1-in-100. Then when they removed the drugs, he didn't come out of the coma. That night I prayed and read the Bible to Nathan, repeating the words Jesus said to Lazarus: "Come forth." I told him, "You've got to fight. You've got to wake up." And the next morning he did, acknowledging me later that afternoon. We were beside ourselves with joy.

But the spinal-cord damage was of major concern. Nathan had a fracture in the C-4 vertebra in his neck, the same part of the spinal cord that actor Christopher Reeve injured several years ago. The doctors gave Nathan a protective neck collar to help prevent against further separation of the vertebrae. He was in immediate danger of full or partial paralysis.

Nathan has the practice of reading his Bible and praying before going to bed at night. For two weeks, he prayed earnestly for healing. One night as he was lying still, falling asleep in bed, he noticed a popping sound in his neck. The next morning, physicians performed three sets of X rays to see if the vertebrae were continuing to separate. Instead, the X rays showed that the vertebrae had fused back together, stunning the nurses and doctors. There was no medical explanation.

Just three months after the accident, doctors cleared Nathan to resume his participation in athletics, including football, wrestling, and track and field.

Citation: Rev. James R. Christensen; Necedah, Wisconsin; adapted by Steve Gertz from the Pentecostal Evangel *(2-18-01), p. 11,* Daily Tribune, Wisconsin Rapids *(12-7-00), p. 1B, and the* Juneau County Star-Times *(9-13-00), p. A1*

HELP

INCONVENIENCE OF HELPING OTHERS

MATTHEW 7:12; LUKE 6:31; LUKE 10:30-37
Golden Rule; Help; Help, human; Servanthood; Service

As a general contractor, I frequently visit Home Depot. Actually, it has become one of my mission fields. I like to help people load their merchandise. Recently I was there and was on my way to my van when

I noticed a guy who realized he had left his lights on. He turned them off, expecting a dead battery. I jumped in my car and thought of helping him. Then I thought, *No*. It had been a bad day. I didn't sleep well the night before and was running behind schedule.

I prayed, *Lord, I don't need this right now. You know that I usually would help, but, God, not today! Let someone else do it. Yes, I know I have a set of jumper cables right behind my seat, but not today!* I slipped the key in the ignition, gave it a turn and . . . UUH . . . mm, UUH . . . mm, *click, click, click.* I looked down to see my light switch was on. Guess whose battery was dead now.

Citation: Rich McClean; Oakley, California

HOLY SPIRIT
EXPLAINING THE PARACLETE
ISAIAH 40:28-31; JOHN 14:16-18
Caring; Comfort; Help; Holy Spirit; Holy Spirit, ministry of; Power

The Karre language of equatorial Africa proved to be difficult for the translators of the New Testament, especially when it came to the word *paraclete.* How could they describe the Holy Spirit?

One day the translators came across a group of porters going off into the bush carrying bundles on their heads. They noticed that in the line of porters there was always one who didn't carry anything, and they assumed he was the boss, there to make sure that the others did their work. However, they discovered he wasn't the boss; he had a special job. He was there should anyone fall over with exhaustion; he would come and pick up the man's load and carry it for him. This porter was known in the Karre language as "the one who falls down beside us."

The translators had their word for *paraclete.*

Citation: Ian Coffey, "Deep Impact," Keswick '99 (OM Publishing); submitted by Owen Bourgaize; Guernsey, United Kingdom

HOMOSEXUALITY

SPITZER SAYS HOMOSEXUALS CAN CHANGE

1 CORINTHIANS 6:9-10
Homosexuality; Repentance; Sex

Robert L. Spitzer, the Columbia University psychiatry professor who convinced the American Psychiatric Association to remove homosexuality from its list of mental disorders in 1973, is now stirring controversy again by saying that homosexuals can change their orientation—if they want to. "The subjects' self-reports of change appear to be, by and large, valid, rather than gross exaggerations, brainwashing or wishful thinking," he summarizes. Spitzer interviewed 153 men and 47 women who said counseling had helped to change their sexual orientation from homosexual to heterosexual. ABCNews sums up the data: "66 percent of the men and 44 percent of the women reached what he called good heterosexual functioning—a sustained, loving heterosexual relationship within the past year, getting enough emotional satisfaction to rate at least a 7 on a 10-point scale."

Citation: Ted Olsen, "Gays can change, says Columbia University professor's study," Christianity Today Weblog (5-9-01)

HONESTY

HONESTY OVER SUCCESS

PSALM 41:12; PROVERBS 6:16-19; EPHESIANS 4:25
Character; Cheating; Honesty; Integrity

My *alma mater* has an honor code that is respected throughout the university. Freshmen pledge to do their own academic work with integrity and to report those who do not to the student-run honor council.

Student signatures remain on display in the lobby of the Sarratt Student Center throughout their four years at the university. Alongside the signatures is found not only a statement of the honor code itself, but also the often-quoted words of the man for whom the building is named.

Madison Sarratt, longtime dean of men at Vanderbilt University and a teacher in the mathematics department, died in 1978. He wrote:

"Today I am going to give you two examinations, one in trigonometry and one in honesty. I hope you will pass them both, but if you must fail one, let it be trigonometry, for there are many good [people] in this world today who cannot pass an examination in trigonometry, but there are no good [people] in the world who cannot pass an examination in honesty."

Former students of Sarratt's still speak of the effect those words have had on their adult lives.

Citation: Rubel Shelly; Nashville, Tennessee; source: Gaynelle Doll, "The Nature of Virtue," Vanderbilt Today, Vol. 37, no. 1 (Summer/Fall 1999), p. 4

■

HUMAN CONDITION

CHILD SUMMARIZES SINFULNESS

Isaiah 53:6; Romans 3:10-23

Children; Human Condition; Lostness; Parenting; Sin; Sinful Nature

I was sitting at my desk in my study after having scolded my 4-year-old daughter for misbehaving. I heard a gentle knock on the door. "Come in," I said.

Bethany entered and then matter-of-factly said, "Daddy, sometimes I am good, and sometimes I am bad. And that is just the way it is." Then she left the room just as summarily as she had come in, acting as if she had completely explained her misbehavior for all time.

I reflected on what my little girl had said, and later tried to explain to her that she had described the problem we all face. We all do bad things, and the Bible says even the good things we do are not good enough to meet God's standard of holiness. Sometimes we are good, and sometimes we are bad, and that is just the way it is.

Thank God, he has provided a Savior.

Citation: Tony Smith; Gainesville, Georgia

HUSBANDS

CAN'T REMEMBER ANNIVERSARY

Ephesians 5:25-33

Family; Husbands; Marriage; Time

My friend Margaret mentioned that her husband, George, never could remember their wedding anniversary on March 7. One year, when they were en route to Australia, at five minutes before midnight on March 6, George proudly looked at Margaret and said, "This year I remembered. Just five minutes."

At that moment the captain's voice announced, "We have crossed the International Date Line. It's now March 8."

Citation: Margaret Gunn; Mason, Michigan, "Lite Fare," Christian Reader (July/August 2000)

HYPOCRISY

ALWAYS AN EXAMPLE

Matthew 5:13-16; 1 Corinthians 11:1; 1 Timothy 4:16; James 1:22

Character; Christian Life; Example; Hypocrisy; Imitation of Christ; Preaching

At the 1993 annual meeting of the American Heart Association, 300,000 doctors, nurses, and researchers met in Atlanta to discuss, among other things, the importance a low-fat diet plays in keeping our hearts healthy. Yet during mealtimes, they consumed fat-filled fast food—such as bacon cheeseburgers and fries—at about the same rate as people from other conventions. When one cardiologist was asked whether or not his partaking in high-fat meals set a bad example, he replied, "Not me, because I took my name tag off."

Citation: Boston Globe (11-10-93); Stephen Nordbye; Charlton, Massachusetts

I

IDENTITY IN CHRIST

NAME SHOULDN'T BE SOLD

ACTS 11:26; 1 PETER 4:14-16

Character; Christian; Compromise; Convictions; Identity in Christ; Integrity; Money; Name

Mark Cuban, owner of the NBA's Dallas Mavericks, recently offered WGN Chicago Radio sports-talk host David Kaplan $50,000 to change his name legally to "Dallas Maverick."

When Kaplan politely declined, Cuban sweetened the offer. Cuban would pay Kaplan $100,000 and donate $100,000 to Kaplan's favorite charity if he took the name for one year.

After some soul-searching, and being bombarded by e-mails from listeners who said he was crazy to turn down the money, Kaplan held firm and told Cuban no. Kaplan explained: "I'd be saying I'd do anything for money, and that bothers me. My name is my birthright. I'd like to preserve my integrity and credibility."

"Christian" is the birthright of every follower of Jesus Christ. We have a responsibility to live every day in a way that brings honor to that name.

Citation: Gary Yates; Jamestown, Ohio; source: Skip Bayless, "Radio Host Prefers Class over Crass," Chicago Tribune (1-10-01)

IMPATIENCE

IMPATIENT FOR INVESTMENT RETURNS

Psalm 27:14; Isaiah 30:15-18; Matthew 19:29; Luke 6:38; Luke 18:28-29; Romans 5:3-5; Romans 8:25; 2 Corinthians 9:6-11; Galatians 6:9

Attitudes and Emotions; Giving; Harvest; Impatience; Money; Patience; Perseverance; Sowing and Reaping; Waiting on God

When our eldest daughter was old enough to understand what saving money was all about, my wife and I sat down with her and explained the value of money. We explained how you save, and when the piggybank was full, you take the money out and deposit it in a commercial bank so that it might draw interest. We thought we had done a thorough job. She seemed to understand and couldn't wait to open a savings account in our local bank by herself.

I called the banker in our little town and told him our daughter was on the way to open her savings account. We would stop in later and sign the necessary papers.

What a thrill! She got the president of the bank himself to wait on her. She handed over her savings, and he gave her a receipt and thanked her for her business. But she wouldn't leave. She just stood there like she was waiting on something else. "Is there anything else that I can help you with?" he asked.

"Yes," she said, "I want my interest."

Citation: Don Young, Sr.; Bern, Kansas

INCARNATION

CHRISTMAS: UNPREDICTABLE GOD

Philippians 2:6-11

Christmas; Incarnation

Frederick Buechner, in *The Hungering Dark*, writes:

Those who believe in God can never in a way be sure of him again. Once they have seen him in a stable, they can never be sure where he will appear or to what lengths he will go or to what ludicrous depths of self-humiliation he will descend in his wild pursuit of man. If the holiness and the awful power and majesty of God were present in this least auspicious of all events, this birth of a peasant's child, then there is no place or time so lowly and earthbound but that holiness can be present there too. And this means that we are never safe, that there is no place where we can hide from God, no place where we are safe from his power to break in two and re-create the human heart, because it is just where he seems most helpless that he is most strong, and just where we least expect him that he comes most fully.

Citation: Frederick Buechner, The Hungering Dark *(Harper San Francisco, 1985); submitted by Bill White; Paramount, California*

INCARNATION
PURPOSE OF INCARNATION

JOHN 17:11-26; GALATIANS 2:20; PHILIPPIANS 2:1-13
Christlikeness; Christmas; Incarnation; Jesus Christ; Sanctification

He became what we are that he might make us what he is.
Citation: Saint Athanasius; submitted by Aaron Goerner; New Hartford, New York

INFLUENCES
BE SHAPED BY THE GODLY

PROVERBS 27:17-19; TITUS 2:1-15
Discipleship; Friendship; Influences; Mentoring; Relationships

When you meet a man or woman who puts Jesus Christ first, knit that one to your soul.
Citation: Oswald Chambers, So I Send You/Workmen of God *(Discovery House, 1993), p. 35*

INFLUENCES

MUSIC INFLUENCES A TEEN KILLER

Romans 12:2; 1 Corinthians 15:33; Philippians 4:8

Culture, popular; Entertainment; Influences; Issues; Mind; Music; Thoughts

I used to think, *This ain't affecting me, you'd have to be weak-minded to let this stuff affect you,* and the whole time it affected me."

—Jamie Rouse commenting on how music affected his behavior without being aware of it. Jamie Rouse is the student who, on November 15, 1995, walked into his Lynnville, Tennessee, high school carrying a .22 caliber rifle and killed a teacher and a student.

Citation: Bob Waliszewski, "Confessions of a School Shooter," Plugged In, Vol. 6, no. 3, (March 2001); submitted by Darin Reimer; Saskatoon, Saskatchewan, Canada

INFLUENCES

TV WITCHES POPULARIZE OCCULT

1 Timothy 4:1; 2 Timothy 2:26

Entertainment; Influences; Occult; Satan; Television; Witchcraft

Great Britain's Pagan Federation, which represents druids and witches, is claiming that the TV shows *Buffy the Vampire Slayer* and *Sabrina the Teenage Witch* have fueled a rapidly growing interest in witchcraft among children. The organization averages 100 inquiries a month from kids who want to become witches. Last month it appointed its first-ever youth officer to counsel young people.

A spokesman for the Pagan Federation said his group is filling a spiritual need, picking up the baton dropped by the Christian Church.

Citation: Tracy Dawn, Plugged In (October 2000); submitted by Darin Reimer; Saskatoon, Saskatchewan, Canada

INSECURITY

MAX LUCADO'S PRAYER IN AFTERMATH OF TERRORISM

PSALM 27:1-14; PSALM 54:1-7; PHILIPPIANS 4:6-7

Dependence on God; Experiencing God; Fear; Innocence; Insecurity; Prayer; Security; Suffering; Terrorism; Tragedy; Trust

At the September 15, 2001, satellite broadcast of *America Prays*, author Max Lucado read the following prayer that he wrote in response to the September 11, 2001, terrorist attack on America:

Dear Lord, we're still hoping we'll wake up. We're still hoping we'll open a sleepy eye and think, *What a horrible dream.*

But we won't, will we, Father? What we saw was not a dream. Planes did gouge towers. Flames did consume our fortress. People did perish. It was no dream and, dear Father, we are sad. There is a ballet dancer who will no longer dance and a doctor who will no longer heal. A church has lost her priest; a classroom is minus a teacher. Cora ran a food pantry. Paige was a counselor, and Dana, dearest Father, Dana was only three years old. (Who held her in those final moments?)

We are sad, Father. For as the innocent are buried, our innocence is buried as well. We thought we were safe. Perhaps we should have known better. But we didn't.

And so we come to you. We don't ask you for help; we beg you for it. We don't request it; we implore it. We know what you can do. We've read the accounts. We've pondered the stories and now we plead, "Do it again, Lord. Do it again."

Remember Joseph? You rescued him from the pit. You can do the same for us. Do it again, Lord. Remember the Hebrews in Egypt? You protected their children from the angel of death. We have children, too, Lord. Do it again. And Sarah? Remember her prayers? You heard them. Joshua? Remember his fears? You inspired him. The women at the tomb? You resurrected their hope. The doubts of Thomas? You took them away. Do it again, Lord. Do it again.

You changed Daniel from a captive into a king's counselor. You took Peter the fisherman and made him Peter an apostle. Because of you, David went from leading sheep to leading armies. Do it again, Lord, for we need counselors today, Lord. We need apostles. We need leaders. Do it again, dear Lord.

Most of all, do again what you did at Calvary. What we saw here last Tuesday, you saw there that Friday. Innocence slaughtered. Goodness murdered. Mothers weeping. Evil dancing. Just as the smoke eclipsed our morning, so the darkness fell on your Son. Just as our towers were shattered, the very Tower of Eternity was pierced. And by dusk, heaven's sweetest song was silent, buried behind a rock.

But you did not waver, O Lord. You did not waver. After three days in a dark hole, you rolled the rock and rumbled the earth and turned the darkest Friday into the brightest Sunday. Do it again, Lord. Grant us a September Easter.

We thank you, dear Father, for these hours of unity. Christians are praying with Jews. Republicans are standing with Democrats. Skin colors have been covered by the ash of burning buildings. We thank you for these hours of unity.

And we thank you for these hours of prayer. The enemy sought to bring us to our knees and succeeded. He had no idea, however, that we would kneel before you. And he has no idea what you can do.

Let your mercy be upon our president, vice president, and their families. Grant to those who lead us wisdom beyond their years and experience. Have mercy upon the souls who have departed and the wounded who remain. Give us grace that we might forgive and faith that we might believe. And look kindly upon your church. For two thousand years you've used her to heal a hurting world. Do it again, Lord. Do it again. Through Christ, Amen.

Citation: Max Lucado, used by permission; submitted by Debi Zahn; Sandwich, Illinois

■

INTEGRITY

INTEGRITY WORTH MORE THAN PROFIT

DEUTERONOMY 23:23; PSALM 15; LUKE 12:32-34

Business; Character; Honesty; Integrity; Money

Author Larry Burkett writes:

[An] antique dealer [named] Roy bought what he thought might be

Jefferson's desk, which disappeared during the Civil War. But concluding it was simply a good reproduction, he included it in his auction. On auction day, a woman came in, loved the desk, and promised to pick it up and pay next day.

Before the auction, bidder Tom examined the desk. "Did you get a good price for that desk you have a hold on, Roy?"

"Just what I had in it—at least I will tomorrow."

"I'll give you twice what you paid right now!"

"You're crazy, Tom. That's not an original, just a good copy."

"No, Roy. Only the insides of the drawers have been replaced. The chestnut is 18th century; the craftsmanship is definitely original."

When the woman arrived next morning, Roy explained what he'd learned. "Then you won't sell it?" the woman asked dejectedly.

"Yes, I will," Roy replied. "I gave my word."

But after weighing the responsibility of owning a Jefferson desk, she told Roy she'd settle for a good reproduction. Roy sold the desk to a museum. He presented the woman with a beautiful reproduction—plus a check for $100,000. He realized his integrity was worth more than a short-term profit.

Citation: Larry Burkett, The Christian Businessman *(1-2-99)*

INTERPRETATION

UNDERSTAND THE AUTHOR'S MEANING

2 TIMOTHY 4:3-4; 2 PETER 1:20-21

Bible; Interpretation; Scripture

In his book *One Lord, One Faith,* author Rex Koivisto warns:

We cannot read into the [biblical] text some meaning if it conflicts with the writer's intended meaning.

[For example,] in the early 1960s the folk group Peter, Paul, and Mary sang a song about a young boy's imaginary world, which sadly falls aside as he grows into manhood. When I first heard that song in junior high, my friends told me it had a hidden meaning about marijuana. The "magic dragon" was supposed to be the marijuana, which, of course, you "puff" on. We bought into this secret meaning because it was not unlike contemporary musicians to hide counter-cultural messages in their songs. That, to us, was what the song meant.

But is that really what the song meant?

Peter, Paul, and Mary had a 30-year reunion tour. Late in the program, Peter Yarrow was about to lead the audience in singing "Puff," which had since become a popular American folk song. But he prefaced the song with a comment: "Many people thought this song was about drugs. But it never was. It was a simple song about a boy and his dragon, and the sorrows of leaving boyhood. I know. I'm Puff's daddy."

Citation: Rex Koivisto, One Lord, One Faith *(Bridge Point, 1993); submitted by Van Morris; Mount Washington, Kentucky*

J

JESUS CHRIST

ACCESS THROUGH JESUS' NAME

JOHN 14:6; 2 CORINTHIANS 5:18-19; EPHESIANS 2:18; 1 JOHN 2:1-2; 1 JOHN 3:21-23
Authority; Christ, authority of; Jesus Christ; Name; Prayer

I was traveling from Boston to Denver, and the departure area for my flight was buzzing with stern-looking men in dark suits talking into their lapels. I asked a flight attendant what was happening. She replied, "Just wait. You'll see."

After we settled into our economy-class seats, two of the dark-suited men arrived in first class, followed by former President Gerald Ford. I sat a few rows away! I thought, *I've never met a president before. I'll go intro-duce myself.*

But then I wondered, *Why would he want to meet me?* I didn't even vote for him!

Then I remembered that during my years in seminary, I had met President Ford's son, Mike. So I marched toward first class. Before the Secret Service men could stop me, I spoke boldly: "President Ford, I just wanted to meet you. I know your son, Mike."

We talked briefly, mostly about Mike. Mike's name gave me "author-ity" to approach the president.

Citation: Paul Borthwick, "In Jesus' Name, Amen," Christian Reader (January/February 2001), pp. 30-31

SKEPTIC CONVINCED OF CHRIST

JOHN 6:29; JOHN 20; 1 TIMOTHY 1:16; 1 JOHN 5:6-12; 1 JOHN 5:20

Agnosticism; Atheism; Belief; Christ, greatness of; Conversion; Doubt; Jesus Christ; Skepticism; Truth; Unbelief

After six years given to the impartial investigation of Christianity as to its truth or falsity, I have come to the deliberate conclusion that Jesus Christ is the Messiah of the Jews, the Savior of the world, and my personal Savior."

These were the words of Lew Wallace, Governor of New Mexico, over a century ago. He had started out to write a book against Jesus Christ and in the process was converted to Christianity. He told a friend how it happened:

I had always been an agnostic and denied Christianity. Robert C. Ingersoll, a famous agnostic, was one of my most intimate friends. He once suggested, "See here, Wallace, you are a learned man and a thinker. Why don't you gather material and write a book to prove the falsity concerning Jesus Christ, that no such man has ever lived, much less the author of the teachings found in the New Testament. Such a book would make you famous. It would be a masterpiece, and a way of putting an end to the foolishness about the so-called Christ."

The thought made a deep impression on me, and we discussed the possibility of such a book. I went to Indianapolis, my home, and told my wife what I intended. She was a member of the Methodist Church and naturally did not like my plan. But I decided to do it and began to collect material in libraries here and in the Old World. I gathered everything over that period in which Jesus Christ, according to legend, should have lived.

Several years were spent in this work. I had written nearly four chapters when it became clear to me that Jesus Christ was just as real a personality as Socrates, Plato, or Caesar. The conviction became a certainty. I knew that Jesus Christ had lived because of the facts connected with the period in which he lived.

I was in an uncomfortable position. I had begun to write a book to prove that Jesus Christ had never lived on earth. Now I was face-to-face with the fact that he was just as historic a personage as Julius Caesar, Mark Antony, Virgil, Dante, and a host of other men who had lived in olden days. I asked myself candidly, "If he was a real person (and there was no doubt), was he not then also the Son of God and the Savior of the world?" Gradually the consciousness grew that, since Jesus Christ was a real person, he probably was the one he claimed to be.

I fell on my knees to pray for the first time in my life, and I asked God to reveal himself to me, forgive my sins, and help me to become a follower of Christ. Towards morning the light broke into my soul. I went into my bedroom, woke my wife, and told her that I had received Jesus Christ as my Lord and Savior.

"O Lew," she said, "I have prayed for this ever since you told me of your purpose to write this book, that you would find him while you wrote it!"

Lew Wallace did write a very famous book. It was a masterpiece and the crowning glory of his life's work. He changed the book he was originally writing and used all his research to write another book.

Now every time I watch the epic film made from that book and see Charlton Heston racing those four magnificent white horses in that amazing chariot race, I wonder how many who have seen *Ben Hur,* with its moving references to Jesus, know it was written by a man who wanted to disprove that Jesus ever existed, and instead became convinced that he was the greatest man who ever lived!

Citation: David Holdaway, The Life of Jesus *(Sovereign World, 1997), pp. 42-43*

JOY

LAUGHTER IS GOOD MEDICINE

NEHEMIAH 8:10; PSALM 28:7; PSALM 126:2; PROVERBS 17:22; PHILIPPIANS 4:4
Attitudes and Emotions; Health; Joy; Laughter

The old axiom "Laughter is the best medicine" holds true when it comes to protecting your heart, according to a study conducted by the University of Maryland in Baltimore. Dr. Michael Miller, who conducted the study, says laughter releases chemicals into the bloodstream that relax the blood vessels. In addition, hearty laughter reduces blood pressure and heart rate.

Miller, who is the director of the Center for Preventive Cardiology at the university, interviewed 150 patients who had suffered heart troubles and 150 who had not. Each patient was asked questions to measure their response in typical day-to-day situations. The results showed that individuals with heart problems were 40 percent less likely to respond with laughter.

Citation: Reuters News Service and CBS radio news (11-15-00); submitted by Greg Asimakoupoulos

JUDGING OTHERS

HOLD YOUR JUDGMENT

PROVERBS 30:12-13; MATTHEW 7:1-5; LUKE 16:15; LUKE 18:9-14; ROMANS 2:1
Criticism; Faultfinding; Judging Others; Self-righteousness

A grocery store checkout clerk once wrote to advice-columnist Ann Landers to complain that she had seen people buy "luxury" food items—like birthday cakes and bags of shrimp—with their food stamps. The writer went on to say that she thought all those people on welfare who treated themselves to such nonnecessities were "lazy and wasteful."

A few weeks later Landers' column was devoted entirely to people who had responded to the grocery clerk. One woman wrote:

I didn't buy a cake, but I did buy a big bag of shrimp with food stamps. So what? My husband had been working at a plant for fifteen years when it shut down. The shrimp casserole I made was for our wedding-anniversary dinner and lasted three days. Perhaps the grocery clerk who criticized that woman would have a different view of life after walking a mile in my shoes.

Another woman wrote:

I'm the woman who bought the $17 cake and paid for it with food stamps. I thought the checkout woman in the store would burn a hole through me with her eyes. What she didn't know is the cake was for my little girl's birthday. It will be her last. She has bone cancer and will probably be gone within six to eight months.

You never know what other people are dealing with.

Citation: Terrie Williams, The Personal Touch *(Warner Books, 1994); submitted by Danny Smith*

JUDGING OTHERS

WOODEN WON'T TRASH KNIGHT

MATTHEW 7:1-2; JAMES 3:5-12

Attitudes and Emotions; Criticism; Faultfinding; Forbearance; Grace; Judging Others; Mercy; Self-control; Tongue

John Wooden, former basketball coach at UCLA, was the antithesis of many of today's coaches. He seldom left his seat on the Bruins bench during a UCLA game. "I tried to teach players that if they lose their temper or get out of control, they will get beat," he says. "Modeling was better than words. I liked the rule we used to have that a coach couldn't leave the bench. I'm sorry they did away with that."

Wooden set records that may never be broken in college basketball. From 1948 to 1975, he had a win-loss record of 885-203—a phenomenal career winning percentage of .813. He had an 88-game winning streak at UCLA. Players such as Kareem Abdul-Jabbar, Bill Walton, and Walt Hazzard played under him.

Pressed in an interview to be critical of former Indiana University coach Bobby Knight, Wooden would only say, "I think Bob Knight is an outstanding teacher of the game of basketball, but I don't approve of his methods. But I'm not a judge, and I'm not judging Bob Knight. There is so much bad in the best of us and so much good in the worst of us, it hardly behooves me to talk about the rest of us."

Citation: Rubel Shelly; Nashville, Tennessee; source: Abilene Reporter-News *(5-18-00)*

JUDGMENT

SEASON OF GRACE

MATTHEW 24:45-51; MATTHEW 25:1-13; ROMANS 2:4-10; 2 CORINTHIANS 6:1-2; 2 PETER 3:9-12

Day of the Lord; Grace; Judgment; Repentance; Urgency

Unlike other countries that have a pay-as-you-use toll system on major roads, Switzerland expects drivers using its autoroute system to pay an annual fee of 40 Swiss francs. When you pay, you get a windshield sticker you display for the rest of the year.

Traditionally, traffic police give motorists the whole month of January to purchase the sticker. There is no penalty for driving without it during that month—it is a month of grace. But when the first days of February come, expect to see the traffic police on the autoroute exit ramps checking for cars without the sticker. No more excuses are accepted; no more time is given. The grace period has ended.

Citation: Alan Wilson; Switzerland

■

JUSTIFICATION
CLOTHED FOR ENTRANCE TO HEAVEN

GALATIANS 3:26-29

Assurance; Christ our Righteousness; Heaven; Imputation of Righteousness; Jesus Christ; Justification; Righteousness; Salvation and Lostness

I make no claim to being a good golfer, but I love to play golf, watch golf, and on good nights I even dream golf.

So when I was invited to attend the Masters Golf Tournament, I was thrilled. A pass to the Masters is the golfer's Holy Grail. Mine came via pro golfer Scott Simpson.

Off we went to Augusta National Country Club in Georgia where golf heritage hangs like moss from the trees. I was a kid in a candy store. It wasn't enough to see the course and walk the grounds; I wanted to see the locker room where the clubs of Ben Hogan and Paul Azinger are displayed.

But they wouldn't let me in. A guard stopped me at the entrance. I showed him my pass, but he shook his head. I told him I knew Scott, but that didn't matter. "Only caddies and players," he explained.

Well, he knew I wasn't a player or a caddie. Caddies are required to wear white coveralls. My clothing was a dead giveaway. So I left, knowing I had made it all the way to the door but was denied entrance.

God has one requirement for entrance into heaven: that we be clothed in Christ.

When someone prays, "Take away my [sinful] rags and clothe me in your grace," Jesus, in an act visible only to the eyes of heaven, removes the stained robe and replaces it with his robe of righteousness.

What did Jesus do for you and me? He put on our coat of sin and wore it to the cross. As he died, his blood flowed over our sins and they were cleansed. Because of this, we have no fear of being turned away at the door of heaven.

Citation: Max Lucado, "Back Door," Christian Reader (May/June 2000), p. 96

K

KINDNESS

AN UNEXPECTED WINNER

MARK 10:31; 1 CORINTHIANS 1:26-31
Handicaps; Kindness; Weakness; Youth

Andrew Dooyema, a 17-year-old senior at Luverne High School in Minnesota, is no star athlete, high academic achiever, or model of fashion. But that didn't keep 450 classmates from overwhelmingly voting Andrew, a student with Down syndrome, their homecoming king.

Each year, seniors select five boys and five girls as candidates for king and queen of the school. The entire student body then chooses the winners by secret ballot.

"I wasn't expecting it," Andrew said. "I thought I'd be on the bottom."

Now that he is king, Andrew has gently let friends and family know they may call him "King Andrew" and provide shoe-tying services.

Sometimes the last are first even here on earth.

Citation: From Associated Press, Arizona Daily Star (10-7-00), p. A8; submitted by Loren D. McBain; Tucson, Arizona

KNOWING GOD

KNOWING GOD'S ACCEPTANCE

Numbers 14:17-20; Matthew 7:7-11; John 17:13; Ephesians 1:17; Ephesians 3:17-19; Colossians 1:10

Acceptance; Anger; Experiencing God; Family; Fathers; Happiness; Knowing God; Laughter; Parenting

In his book *Connecting*, Larry Crabb writes:

A friend of mine was raised in an angry family. Mealtimes were either silent or sarcastically noisy. Down the street was an old-fashioned house with a big porch where a happy family lived. My friend told me that when he was about ten, he began excusing himself from his dinner table as soon as he could without being yelled at, and walking to the old-fashioned house down the street. If he arrived during dinnertime, he would crawl under the porch and just sit there, listening to the sounds of laughter.

When he told me this story, I asked him to imagine what it would have been like if the father in the house somehow knew he was huddled beneath the porch and sent his son to invite him in. I asked him to envision what it would have meant to him to accept the invitation, to sit at the table, to accidentally spill his glass of water, and hear the father roar with delight, "Get him more water! And a dry shirt! I want him to enjoy the meal!"

Crabb goes on to say, "We need to hear the Father laugh. Change depends on experiencing the character of God."

Citation: Source: Larry Crabb, Connecting *(Word, 1997); submitted by David Slagle; Lawrenceville, Georgia*

L

LEADERSHIP

FOLLOWING THE LEADER'S HEART

ROMANS 12:8; 1 TIMOTHY 4:12-16; TITUS 2:7-8

Desire, spiritual; Goals; Inspiration; Leadership; Motivation; Passion, motivational; Vision

An Olympic equestrian champion was asked, "How does your horse know when it has to leap the hedges and hurdles, and why do some horses turn away or stumble?"

The woman answered, "That's simple. You tear your heart out of your body and throw it over the hedge. The horse knows how desperate you are to catch up to your heart. So it leaps."

Citation: Martin Marty's foreword to Communicating for Life *by Quentin Schultze (Baker, 2000), p. 10; submitted by Jeffrey Arthurs; Portland, Oregon*

LICENSE

MISTAKING GRACE FOR LICENSE

ROMANS 6:1-2; 1 CORINTHIANS 6:9-11; 2 CORINTHIANS 7:1; GALATIANS 6:7-8; HEBREWS 10:26-31; 1 PETER 1:14-17; 1 JOHN 3:3; JUDE 1:4

Forgiveness; Grace; Holiness; Judgment; License; Repentance

D. A. Carson, a professor at Trinity Evangelical Divinity School, used to meet with a young man from French West Africa for the purpose of practicing their German. He writes:

Once a week or so, we had had enough, so we went out for a meal together and retreated to French, a language we both knew well. In the course of those meals we got to know each other. I learned that his wife was in London, training to be a medical doctor. He was an engineer who needed fluency in German in order to pursue doctoral studies in engineering in Germany.

I soon discovered that once or twice a week he disappeared into the red-light district of town. Obviously he went to pay his money and have his woman.

Eventually I got to know him well enough that I asked him what he would do if he discovered that his wife was doing something similar in London.

"Oh," he said, "I'd kill her."

"That's a bit of a double standard, isn't it?" I asked.

"You don't understand. Where I come from in Africa, the husband has the right to sleep with many women, but if a wife is unfaithful to her husband she must be killed."

"But you told me you were raised in a mission school. You know that the God of the Bible does not have double standards like that."

He gave me a bright smile and replied, "*Ah, le bon Dieu, il doit nous pardonner; c'est son metier* [Ah, God is good. He's bound to forgive us; that's his job]."

Citation: D. A. Carson, "God's Love and God's Wrath," Bibliotheca Sacra *(October 1999)*, p. 387; submitted by Aaron Goerner; New Hartford, New York

■

LISTENING
LISTENING WELL LEADS TO SUCCESS

JOSHUA 1:6-9; PROVERBS 18:15; MATTHEW 7:24-25; MARK 4:1-25; LUKE 8:18; LUKE 10:38-42; JAMES 1:22-25

Courage; Direction; Discernment; Discipleship; Following; Guidance; Hearing God; Listening; Obedience; Spiritual Direction; Spiritual Formation; Spiritual Perception

Erik Weihenmayer is blind, yet on May 25, 2001 (Nepal time), he reached the peak of Mt. Everest. Suffering from a degenerative eye disease, he lost his sight when he was 13, but that didn't stop him. On a mountain where 90 percent of climbers never make it to the top—and 165 have died trying since 1953—Erik succeeded, in large measure because he listened well.

He listened to the little bell tied to the back of the climber in front of him, so he would know what direction to go.

He listened to the voice of teammates who would shout back to him, "Death fall two feet to your right!" so he would know what direction not to go.

He listened to the sound of his pick jabbing the ice, so he would know whether the ice was safe to cross.

When we take a perilous journey, listening well can make all the difference.

Citation: Source: Time (6-18-01); Bill White; Paramount, California

LOSS

WILLIAM CAREY: TRUST DESPITE LOSS

PSALM 46:10; ROMANS 8:28

Faith; God, sovereignty of; Loss; Ministry; Sovereignty; Suffering; Trials; Trust

William Carey, often called the father of modern missions, faced a ministry disappointment of overwhelming proportions. Carey began his missionary career to India in 1793. He labored in that country for 40 continuous years, never once returning to his native England. Carey was a prodigious translator, translating portions of Scripture into over a dozen Indian languages.

One afternoon after 20 years of plodding labor in that country, a fire raged through his printing plant and warehouse. All of his printing equipment was destroyed, but most tragically, many of his precious manuscripts were completely consumed by the fire. Of course, Carey had no computer backup files or Xerox masters. Twenty years of nonstop labor were gone within a few hours.

How would he respond to this crushing devastation? Carey wrote to his pastor-friend, Andrew Murray, in England:

The ground must be laboured over again, but we are not discouraged. . . . We have all been supported under the affliction, and preserved from discouragement. To me the consideration of the divine sovereignty and wisdom has been very supporting. . . . I endeavored to improve this our affliction last Lord's Day, from Psalm 46:10, "Be still and know that I am God." I principally dwelt upon two ideas:

God has a sovereign right to dispose of us as he pleases.

We ought to acquiesce in all that God does with us and to us.

Citation: Bill Mills and Craig Parro, Finishing Well in Life and Ministry (Leadership Resources International), pp. 101-102; submitted by Dave Parsons; Santa Rosa, California

■

LOVE, DIVINE
GOD'S LOVE FOR ADULTEROUS HUMANITY

EZEKIEL 16:15-63; HOSEA 1:2; JAMES 4:4

Depravity; God, love of; Idolatry; Love, divine; Sin

Have you ever had to literally turn a lover over to a mortal enemy to allow her to find out for herself what his intentions toward her really were? Have you ever had to lie in bed knowing she was believing his lies and [being intimate] with him every night? Have you ever sat helplessly by in a parking lot, while your enemy and his friends took turns [taking advantage of] your lover even as you sat nearby, unable to win her heart enough so she would trust you to rescue her? Have you ever called this one you had loved for so long . . . and asked her if she was ready to come back to you, only to have her say her heart was still captured by your enemy? Have you ever watched your lover's beauty slowly diminish and fade in a haze of alcohol, drugs, occult practices, and infant sacrifice until she is no longer recognizable in body or soul? Have you ever loved one so much that you even send your only son to talk with her about your love for her, knowing that she will kill him?

All this and more God has endured because of his refusal to stop loving us.

Citation: Brent Curtis and John Eldredge, The Sacred Romance (Thomas Nelson, 1997), p. 106; submitted by Pete Briscoe; Dallas, Texas

LOVE FOR ENEMIES

VULNERABILITY OF GOD

MATTHEW 1:18-22; JOHN 3:16-17; ROMANS 5:8; ROMANS 8:31-32

Brotherly Love; Christ, humanity of; Christ, incarnation of; Deliverance; God; Grace; Humanity; Jesus Christ; Love for Enemies; Reconciliation; Sacrifice; Salvation and Lostness; Salvation, gift of; Savior; Surrender

World War II was drawing to a close. The German army was sending children to man the lines in a futile effort to stop the Allied invasion into their homeland. It was March 1945. Dr. Karl H. Schlesier, a German soldier, remembers this time:

I was . . . in a battalion of teenage grenadiers fresh out of training [and] was sent into the front line east of the Rhine River after American forces had established a foothold on the east bank.

Fresh American units were pushed across, and our battalion was ordered to plug a hole in the front line. We dug in three companies abreast on a slight rise in front of the little town of Kirchhellen. I was with the 1st Company in the center of the position. My company . . . numbered about 80 teenagers.

In bitter fighting American troops pushed through on both sides but got stuck in front of my company. About 17 or 18 of us were left. . . . We huddled in two-man foxholes.

On the morning of March 28, amid smoldering tanks and twisted bodies, there suddenly came an eerie silence.

"I looked over the hole I shared with a buddy and saw no life but a movement in the busted roof of a farmhouse about 200 yards away," Schlesier said. Feeling sudden panic, Schlesier stood up in his foxhole and fired four rapid shots at nothing in particular.

The eerie silence was broken by a single voice. A lone American soldier had walked . . . calmly toward the entrenched Germans, saying in a calm and low voice, "Come on out. Come on out."

[Schlesier remembers:] . . . The American soldier had two machine guns trained on him, and we were sure he knew this, but he just kept on coming. To have shot him would have seemed like murder because he was not a threat. He just wanted us to give up.

[Schlesier's] foxhole happened to be directly in the path of the approaching American soldier, so Schlesier and his buddy were the first to confront him. He was startled to see that the soldier was an American Indian. He had the classic face of an Indian, and it was not threatening to the German soldiers.

The German soldiers did as he said. They dropped their weapons and took off their helmets, tossing them back into the foxhole.

The Indian soldier . . . told them to put their hands over their heads. Then he turned and walked toward the American lines without looking back as the German soldiers followed. Schlesier was overwhelmed.

"He must have been the most reasonable man, the most perceptive, the most understanding, and by far the most brave. We had not expected to live, and he must have seen how idiotic this wall was, and he acted on his own to save us, risking his life in the process."

Later in the prisoner-of-war camp we talked about him. If he had not come to get us, we would have died in our foxholes. His action was a personal one. He was not ordered to do what he did. . . . I owe him my life and have lived it.

Citation: Tim Giago, Spokesman-Review *(8-24-00)*

M

MANIPULATION

PRAYER AND GOD'S SOVEREIGNTY

Isaiah 55:6-9; Luke 2; Hebrews 5:7; 1 John 5:14-15
Children; Christmas; Desire; Gifts; God, sovereignty of; Grace; Humanity;
Manipulation; Prayer; Will, human

A small boy was writing a letter to God about the Christmas presents he
badly wanted. "I've been good for six months now," he wrote.

But after a moment's reflection he crossed out "six months" and wrote
"three." After a pause, that was crossed out, and he put "two weeks."
There was another pause, and that was crossed out too.

He got up from the table and went over to the little nativity scene that
had the figures of Mary and Joseph. He picked up the figure of Mary and
went back to his writing and started again: "Dear God, if ever you want to
see your mother again . . ."

Citation: Mark Ashton, A Voice in the Wilderness *(OM Publishing); submitted by Owen*
Bourgaize; Guernsey, United Kingdom

MARRIAGE

A NEW TYPE OF WEDDING VOW

MATTHEW 19:4-12; 1 CORINTHIANS 7
Commitment; Divorce; Marriage; Vows

A recent study, out in May of 2001, found 43 percent of first marriages end in divorce or separation in the first 15 years. Is there a problem with the marriage vows?

USA Today, in an article titled "Couples Take Their Vows in a New Direction," reported the following:

The Bible is losing ground on the wedding aisle, and *forever* may follow *obey* into oblivion, particularly for those who marry in civil or non-denominational ceremonies.

Editor [of *Bride's* magazine] Millie Martini Bratten says many couples prefer to start their lives together with "guidelines, not a straightjacket of rules." In a recent reader survey, *Bride's* found 72 percent will marry in a house of worship, but 66 percent will edit *obey* out of the vows, and 26 percent will write their own.

The Rev. Ena Drouillard, who has specialized in San Francisco-area, nondenominational ceremonies since 1976, says the Apache Blessing is her most requested vow. Countless versions of the questionably authentic blessing are on the Internet. Still, she says, "A lot of people don't even want readings. They're tired of the Apache Blessing, tired of the Bible. It's 'been there, done that,' " she says.

She says 50 percent of her couples now refuse the word *forever* because they really don't believe in it. Many of her outside-the-church clients don't invite God either: 30 percent refuse any reference to religion. She has a draft of soul-free basic vows in her repertoire.

Citation: Cathy Lynn Grossman, "Couples Take Their Vows in a New Direction," USA Today (5-30-01); submitted by Van Morris; Mount Washington, Kentucky

MARRIAGE

GARRISON KEILLOR ON MARRIAGE

EPHESIANS 5:21-32

Fidelity; Marriage; Perseverance

In *Wobegon Boy*, Garrison Keillor tells the fanciful tale of John Tollefson. John leaves Minnesota, moves to New York, and makes a life for himself far from Lake Wobegon.

Although the story is spun from Keillor's marvelous imagination, it contains gems of insight. For example, John calls home and tells his parents about something his girlfriend had said: "There's no such thing as a successful marriage. There are marriages that give up, and marriages that keep on trying; that's the only difference."

Citation: Garrison Keillor, Wobegon Boy *(Penguin USA, 1998), p. 142; submitted by Rubel Shelly; Nashville, Tennessee*

MARRIAGE

LINEBACKER CHRIS SPIELMAN HELPS WIFE

PSALM 15:4-5; EPHESIANS 5:25-33

Faithfulness; Family; Husbands; Integrity; Loyalty; Marriage; Priorities; Support

When Chris Spielman played for the Buffalo Bills, he was everything a middle linebacker should be: tough, strong, and smart, with passion, total commitment, and loyalty to the game. He played the entire 1995 season with a torn pectoral muscle that he sustained in the season opener.

But the game took a distant second place in his thinking during the 1998 season. He chose to stay home. He cooked, took care of his kids, and cared for his wife—by choice. Stephanie, Chris's wife, was struggling through the stark reality of breast cancer. Surgery, chemotherapy, and nausea were Stephanie's opponents. During her fight, Chris was at her side. His actions supported his "family before job" credo.

Asked by a reporter from the *Rochester Democrat and Chronicle* if he'd consider a return to the Bills late in the season, Spielman said, "I'd play in a heartbeat, but what kind of man would I be if I backed out on my word to her? I wouldn't be a man at all."

Football fans saw Spielman as a man because of his aggressive, leave-it-all-on-the-field style of play. But what really makes him a man? It's his personal sacrifice and unending commitment and loyalty to his wife.

Citation: Rob Bentz, Sports Spectrum *(March 1999); quoted in* Men of Integrity *(January/February 2001)*

MARRIAGE
THE POWER OF PAIRS
GENESIS 1:26-31; GENESIS 2:4-25; ACTS 18:24-26; EPHESIANS 5:22-32
Marriage; Ministry

When the time came for a strategic decision during his ministry, Jesus made an interesting choice. He gathered 70 workers, like regional representatives, and sent them to various towns to prepare people for his visits (see Luke 10:1). He could have sent each disciple separately and reached more towns. Instead, he chose to send 35 teams of two. An efficiency expert might criticize that decision for duplicating effort and cutting productivity in half, but Jesus knew that some ministries are performed best by two, not one. When two people work together, one can protect the other. One can encourage another. Two can split the work, offset each other's weaknesses, and draw on each other's strengths. Companionship makes two more effective, not less, than one.

Today, Jesus sends our Christian couples just like he sent those pairs of disciples, because a pair has power. When we felt God was calling us to write this book, we knew neither of us could do it alone. I needed Kevin's skills in writing; he needed my background in marriage counseling. Together, with God's help, we could minister in a more powerful way.

Most Christians have been trained to think of serving Christ individually—all alone. How often might our ministries—and our marriages—be strengthened if we could find a way to draw on our spouse's strengths? It's not always possible, and it's not always easy. But God has called you to serve him. He also has called you to be married. Those two callings not only CAN go together, they SHOULD go together. When they do, you'll find a stronger Christian life and a stronger Christian marriage.

Citation: Kevin and Karen Miller, More Than You and Me, Touching Others Through the Strength of Your Marriage

MATERIALISM

IMPOSTOR HUSBAND SPENDS THOUSANDS

PROVERBS 11:24-25; ECCLESIASTES 5:8-15; EPHESIANS 5:25

Deception; Family; Generosity; Golden Rule; Marriage; Materialism; Money; Responsibility

Several men in the locker room of a private exercise club were talking when a cell phone lying on the bench rang. One man picked it up without hesitation, and the following conversation ensued:

"Hello?"

"Honey, It's me."

"Sugar!"

"I'm at the mall two blocks from the club. I saw a beautiful mink coat. It is absolutely gorgeous! Can I buy it? It's only $1,500."

"Well, okay, if you like it that much."

"Thanks! Oh, and I also stopped by the Mercedes dealership and saw the new models. I saw one I really liked. I spoke with the salesman, and he gave me a great price."

"How much?"

"Only $60,000!"

"Okay, but for that price I want it with all the options."

"Great! Before we hang up, there's something else. It might seem like a lot, but, well, I stopped by to see the real estate agent this morning, and I saw the house we had looked at last year. It's on sale! Remember? The beachfront property with the pool and the English garden?"

"How much are they asking?"

"Only $450,000, a magnificent price, and we have that much in the bank to cover it."

"Well then, go ahead and buy it, but put in a bid for only $420,000, okay?"

"Okay, sweetie. Thanks! I'll see you later! I love you!"

"I love you, too."

The man hung up, closed the phone's flap, and raised it aloft, asking, "Does anyone know who this cell phone belongs to?"

Citation: John Fehlen; Stanwood, Washington

MEANING OF LIFE

LEO TOLSTOY QUESTIONS MEANING OF LIFE

PSALM 16:11; MATTHEW 6:19-21; 1 TIMOTHY 1:12-17

Conversion; Meaning of Life; Pleasure; Purpose; Questions; Significance; Sin; World; Worldliness

Leo Tolstoy wrote what the *Encyclopedia Britannica* describes as "one of the two or three greatest novels in world literature"—*War and Peace.* But he also wrote a book in 1879 called *A Confession,* which tells the story of his search for meaning and purpose in life.

Rejecting Christianity as a child, Tolstoy left his university seeking pleasure. In Moscow and Saint Petersburg, he drank heavily, lived promiscuously, and gambled frequently.

His ambition was to become wealthy and famous, but nothing satisfied him. In 1862, he married a loving wife and had 13 children; he was surrounded by what appeared to be complete happiness. Yet one question haunted him to the verge of suicide: "Is there any meaning in my life which will not be annihilated by the inevitability of death, which awaits me?"

Nicky Gumbel, in *Questions of Life,* explains what triggered Tolstoy's conversion:

He searched for the answer in every field of science and philosophy. As he looked around at his contemporaries, he saw that people were not facing up to the first-order questions of life ("Where did I come from?" "Where am I going?" "Who am I?" "What is life all about?"). Eventually he found that the peasant people of Russia had been able to answer these questions through their Christian faith, and he came to realize that only in Jesus Christ do we find the answer.

A hundred years later, nothing has changed. Freddie Mercury, the lead singer of the rock group Queen, who died of AIDS at the end of 1991, wrote in one of his last songs on *The Miracle* album: "Does anybody know what we are living for?"

Citation: Source: Nicky Gumbel, Questions of Life *(Kingsway Publications, 1993), pp. 14-15; submitted by David Holdaway; Stonehaven, Kincardinshire, Scotland*

MERCY

WORST ERROR FORGIVEN

Matthew 7:12; Matthew 18:21-35; Ephesians 4:32; I John 1:9

Forgiveness; Forgiveness, human; Grace; Mercy; Mistakes

Professional golfer Ian Woosnam was tied for the lead on the last day of the 2001 British Open. Woosnam, whose career had been sliding for years, knew time was running out for him to win a major tournament. As he stood on the second tee on Sunday, having nearly made a hole-in-one, he turned to his caddie, Miles Byrne, for his club—only to hear Miles say, "You're going to go ballistic."

"Why?" Woosnam responded.

"Because we've got two drivers in the bag," his caddie replied. Woosnam knew immediately what those words implied. Only 14 clubs are allowed, and they obviously had too many: an immediate two-stroke penalty. Woosnam lost the tournament.

It would be easy to assume that a golfer with so much on the line would have immediately fired his caddie. Instead, he responded, "It's the biggest mistake he will make in his life. He won't do it again. He's a good caddie. He will have a severe talking to when I get in, but I'm not going to sack him."

Citation: Gary Sinclair; Mahomet, Illinois; source: newspaper accounts

MESSIAH

AWAITING THE MESSIAH

JOHN 7:25-27; ROMANS 12:17-21

Anger; Christ; Hatred; Messiah; Revenge; Vengeance; War

In March 2001, a little Jewish girl was killed in the tit-for-tat fighting in Hebron on the West Bank while she sat in her stroller. On a wall near where she died, there is a poem in her memory. According to the *Chicago Tribune:*

It is an elegy to her pinchable cheeks, her sweet smile, her kerchiefed cuteness—and to the urgent need of revenge. "We will take revenge; we will scream for revenge in body and spirit and await the coming of the Messiah," the poem says.

That is how people thought of the Messiah in Jesus' day, too. That is why they were so unprepared for a Messiah who preached repentance and faith, who paid scant attention to the Romans, who said he would win freedom by dying for sins.

Citation: Chicago Tribune (4-04-01); submitted by Lee Eclov; Lake Forest, Illinois

MINISTRY

GOD'S GREATNESS THROUGH US

LUKE 10:17; JOHN 14:12

God, works of; Ministry

Donald Grey Barnhouse writes:

Aboard a United States submarine in the waters of the Pacific, a sailor was stricken with acute appendicitis. The nearest surgeon was thousands of miles away. Pharmacist Mate Wheller Lipes watched the seaman's temperature rise to 106 degrees. His only hope was an operation. Said Lipes: "I have watched doctors do it. I think I could. What do you say?" The sailor consented. In the wardroom, about the size of a Pullman drawing room, the patient was stretched out on a table beneath a floodlight. The mate and assisting officers, dressed in reversed pajama tops, masked their faces with gauze. The crew stood by the diving planes to keep the ship steady; the cook boiled water for sterilizing. A tea strainer served as an antiseptic cone. A broken-handled scalpel was the operating instrument. Alcohol drained from the torpedoes was the antiseptic. Bent tablespoons served to keep the muscles open. After cutting though layers of the muscle, the mate took twenty minutes to find the appendix. Two hours and a half later, the last catgut stitch was sewed, just as the last drop of ether gave out. Thirteen days later, the patient was back at work.

Admittedly this was a much more magnificent feat than if trained surgeons in a fully equipped operating room of a modern hospital had performed it. Study this analogy and you will know the real meaning of Christ's words: "Greater works than these shall he do; because I go unto my Father." For Christ, perfect God, to work directly on a lost soul to quicken and bring out of death and into life is great, but for him to do the same thing through us is a greater work.

Citation: Let Me Illustrate: Stories, Anecdotes, Illustrations (Revell, 1967), pp. 358-59; submitted by Kevin Miller; Wheaton, Illinois

■

MIRACLES
GOD INTERVENES

EXODUS 15:26; PSALM 103:3; JEREMIAH 32:17; MATTHEW 8:17; 1 CORINTHIANS 12:7-11
Birth; God, power of; Healing; Hearing God; Miracles; Revelation; Spiritual Gifts; Supernatural Occurrences

On February 23, 1996, three to four months into a pregnancy, Mary Clarke (name changed) of Downers Grove, Illinois, remembers, "I was not feeling very well. I was having a hard time breathing and was very dizzy."

Her doctor said she should come in for an examination. As the nurse started to examine Mary, she said, "We'll be able to hear the baby's heartbeat." The nurse tried to pick up that heartbeat for a while but was unable to locate it.

When the doctor came into the examining room, the nurse asked him to try to locate the baby's heartbeat. The doctor tried for 10 or 15 minutes without success. He then decided to move Mary to an ultrasound room.

In the ultrasound room, the doctor located the baby and tried again to hear the heartbeat. He couldn't, so he asked the nurse to call another doctor. The second doctor tried to locate the heartbeat—for 15 minutes or more—but could not.

At this point, the doctor told Mary and her husband, Ron, "I'm sorry, but the baby has died. I can't tell you why, but these things happen. I'm very sorry, but you will have to be induced."

Mary says, "Ron's heart and my heart were broken. We had lost our precious baby."

The nurse took Mary and Ron to the birth center and explained what would happen when they induced labor. The doctor also requested testing to find out why Mary was having difficulty breathing.

"As I was lying in bed," Mary says, "I prayed that God would watch over our child until we could meet him or her in heaven. My heart was broken, but I was filled with the hope that I would one day see my child."

Meanwhile, Ron called Mary's sister, who called a woman at their church, Pat Bailey, to ask her to pray. When Pat got the call, she said something startling: "That baby's not dead. Tell them to double-check, to get a second opinion."

Ron and Mary talked about it and decided they would talk to the doctor one more time before anything was done, just to confirm the decision. To appease the couple, the doctor ordered another ultrasound.

Back in the ultrasound room, a new nurse, who did not know why this couple was there, started the ultrasound. In a moment she said matter-of-factly, "And there's the heartbeat."

Mary asked her, "Are you sure the baby is okay?"

The nurse told her, "The baby's heartbeat is perfect, no problems."

Mary turned and looked at the nurse from the birth center: "Her jaw dropped, and her eyes were as round as saucers." The nurse called the doctor to come look at the monitor. "I can't believe it," he finally said. "If I had not seen this, I would not have believed it. This is not the same baby I saw on the other ultrasound."

As a precaution, Mary was admitted to Good Samaritan Hospital for observation. The doctor came to her room later. "I would like to give you an explanation for what happened," he managed, "but I have none. A diagnosis like this is always verified by a second doctor. But," he went on, "there are times when medical science cannot explain everything. Sometimes the only explanation is that God intervened."

Mary says, "I did not need an explanation. I knew that God had performed a miracle, and that was all I needed to know."

On August 22, 1996, Jamie Andrew Clarke (name changed) was born—a healthy, beautiful boy. The doctor who delivered him was the same doctor who had seen the lifeless baby on the ultrasound. He said to Mary and Ron, "This baby is special."

Citation: Kevin A. Miller, vice president, Resources, Christianity Today International

■

MIRACLES

GULF WAR MIRACLE

MATTHEW 17:20-21; MATTHEW 19:26; LUKE 1:37; JAMES 5:13-16
Dependence on God; Faith; Miracles; Prayer; Supernatural Occurrences; Trusting God

General Charles Krulak (USMC, retired) had this story to tell about his experience in the Gulf War in 1991:

There is a precious commodity in the Middle East. It's been fought over for hundreds of years. Christians fought for it, Muslims fought for it, nation states swept across the Arabian Peninsula and fought for it. And during the Desert Storm War, this commodity was critical to both the Iraqi army and the United States forces. Oil? No. Water.

Here was the ground scheme of maneuver of the United States Marine Corps during Desert Storm. We were to assault up the Saudi Arabian coast with the Persian Gulf on our right into southern Kuwait, push through the minefields in southern Kuwait, and capture Kuwait City. To effect the movement of eighty thousand Marines up that coast we had to build a logistics support base. We built that base at a location called Kabrit, 30 kilometers south of Kuwait and 30 kilometers in from the Persian Gulf. We picked Kabrit because it was an old airfield that had water wells that provided one hundred thousand gallons of water a day. The United States Marine Corps was going to need that much water on a daily basis to carry its forces into Kuwait.

Fourteen days before the war began, General Norman Schwarzkopf, commander in chief of the central command, decided to make a daring move, called the "great left hook." It was a sweep of forces—instead of right up the gully, so to speak—a flanking of the Iraqi army. That forced the Marine Corps to move 140 kilometers to the northwest and locate a new logistic space at a place called the Gravel Plains.

There was no water at the Gravel Plains. For 14 days we had engineers digging desperately to find water. We went to the Saudi government and asked them if they knew of any water in this area, and their answer was no. We brought the exiled Kuwaiti government down to our command post and pored over maps and asked them, "Do you know if there's any water in this area?" They said no. We went to the Bedouin tribes and the nomads, the people who lived in that area, and said, "Do you know where there's water on the Gravel Plains?" They said, "No, there's no water there." We kept digging wells hundreds of feet deep—to no avail.

In 1976 I had become a Christian, and every morning at 7:15 since that day I've held devotions. During this 14-day period, I obviously asked the Lord to help us with this need for water.

Finally on the Sunday before we were to go into Kuwait I was in a tent where we were holding a chapel service and were praying for water when a colonel came to the tent and asked to see me. I went outside and he said, "General, I need to show you something."

We got in his vehicle and drove down a road we had built through the desert from the Gravel Plains to the border of Kuwait. I had driven down that road at least 70 times. Over sixty thousand Marines had passed down that road. We drove about a mile down that road, and the officer said, "Look over there." About 20 yards off the road was a tower that reached 15 feet into the air. It was a white tower, and at the top of the tower was a cross. Coming off the ends of the cross were canvas sleeves—sleeves used in old train stations to put water into train engines. At the base of that cross was an eight-foot-high pump newly painted red. Beside that pump was a diesel engine. Beside the diesel engine were four batteries still in their plastic. It was a diesel engine. The United States military in Desert Storm did not use diesel fuel. We had no diesel fuel. But beside this engine was a 500-gallon tank filled with diesel fuel.

On the engine was an "on" button and an "off" button, and between those two buttons was a keyhole. I asked the officer, "Has anybody seen the key?" He said, "Sir, there is no key."

I pushed the "on" button, and the engine kicked over immediately. I called one of my engineers and said, "I want you to test the flow coming out of these pipes." In my heart I knew what his answer was going to be. An hour later he said, "Sir, it is putting out one hundred thousand gallons a day."

I went back to the well five days later. The wind and sand had sand-blasted the new paint off. A reporter from the *London Times* wrote an article entitled "The Miracle Well" that made the front page.

Citation: General Charles Krulak, in a message given at the Wheaton, Illinois, Leadership Prayer Breakfast, October 2000; Linda Gehrs; Oak Park, Illinois

MISSIONS
COST OF MISSIONS

MATTHEW 5:14-16; MATTHEW 28:18-20; JOHN 8:12; 2 CORINTHIANS 6:4-10
Evangelism; Light; Missions; Outreach; Witness

As a child I heard a memorable story at a holiness revival meeting in New York. It seems a certain missionary, home on leave, was shopping for a globe of the world to take back to her mission station. The clerk showed her a reasonably priced globe and another one with a lightbulb inside. "This is nicer," the clerk said, pointing to the illuminated globe, "but of course, a lighted world costs more."

Citation: Leonard Sweet, Aqua Church *(Group Publishing, 1999); submitted by Bonne Steffen*

MONEY
FAMILY INCOME IN 2000

DEUTERONOMY 8:17-18; MATTHEW 6:19-33; LUKE 16:10-13
Daily Bread; Family; Finances; Lifestyle; Money; Poverty; Provision; Wealth

The average U.S. family earned $63,410 during the previous 12 months, according to Census 2000. The percentage of the USA's 70.8 million families who in the previous year earned:

$150,000 and up: 5.5
$100,000–$149,999: 9.7
$75,000–$99,999: 12.3

$50,000–$74,999: 22.0

$35,000–$49,999: 16.8

$15,000–$34,999: 23.3

Less than $15,000: 10.4

Citation: Sam Ward, "Average Family Earned $63,410," USA Today Snapshots (8-24-01); source: Census 2000 Supplementary Survey

MONEY

FRANK SINATRA'S INSECURITY

ECCLESIASTES 4:8; ECCLESIASTES 5:10; MATTHEW 6:19-34; LUKE 12:22-34; PHILIPPIANS 4:10-19

Aging; Ambition; Anxiety; Career; Contentment; Fathering; Fear; Greed; Idolatry; Money; Motives; Retirement; Stress; Success; Work

Frank Sinatra's daughter Tina recalls her father's unceasing drive to succeed and make money, even when his health was at risk:

His health was in tatters and his life mired in financial wrangles, but my father refused to stop giving concerts. "I've just got to earn more money," he said.

His performances, sad to say, were becoming more and more uneven. Uncertain of his memory, he became dependent on TelePrompTers. When I saw him at Desert Inn in Las Vegas, he struggled through the show and felt so sick at the end that he needed oxygen from a tank that he kept on hand. At another show he forgot the lyrics to "Second Time Around," a ballad he had sung a thousand times. His adoring audience finished it for him.

I couldn't bear to see Dad struggle. I remembered all the times he repeated the old boxing maxim "You gotta get out before you hit the mat." He wanted to retire at the top of his game, and I always thought he would know when his time came, but pushing 80 he lost track of when to quit. After seeing one too many of these fiascos, I told him, "Pop, you can stop now; you don't have to stay on the road."

With a stricken expression he said, "No, I've got to earn more money. I have to make sure everyone is taken care of."

Since his death there have been constant family wrangles over his fortune.

Citation: Tina Sinatra with Jeff Coplon, My Father's Daughter *(Simon and Schuster, 2000); submitted by David Holdaway; Stonehaven, Kincardinshire, Scotland*

MONEY

MONEY IRRELEVANT TO HAPPINESS

PROVERBS 13:7; ECCLESIASTES 5:8-15

Happiness; Money; Poverty; Wealth

It's pretty hard to tell what does bring happiness. Poverty and wealth have both failed.

Citation: Ken Hubbard, quoted in "Reflections," Christianity Today (6-12-00)

MONEY

MONEY IS MY GOD

EXODUS 20:1-3; MATTHEW 6:24

Greed; Idolatry; Money; Worldliness

What is the chief end of man? To get rich. In what way? Dishonestly if we can; honestly if we must. Who is God, the one and only true? Money is god. Gold and Greenbacks and Stock—father, son, and ghosts of same, three persons in one; these are the true and only god, mighty and supreme.

Citation: Mark Twain, quoted in "Reflections," Christianity Today (6-12-00)

MONEY

MONEY REVEALS CHARACTER

PROVERBS 22:1; MATTHEW 19:23-24

Character; Money

If you were a jerk before, you'll be a bigger jerk with a billion dollars.

Citation: Warren Buffet, quoted in "Reflections," Christianity Today (6-12-00)

■

MONEY

RICHARD PRYOR CALLS ON GOD

MATTHEW 6:19-34; LUKE 16:19-31

Crisis; Dependence on God; God, love of; Health; Illness; Materialism; Money; Needs; Pain; Security in God; Seeking God

Comedian Richard Pryor was critically burned in an accident in 1980. Appearing later on the *Johnny Carson Show,* he insisted that when you are seriously ill, money isn't important: "All that I could think of was to call on God. I didn't call the Bank of America once."

Citation: Peter Graystone, Ready Salted (Scripture Union, 1998), p. 114; submitted by David Holdaway; Stonehaven, Kincardinshire, Scotland

■

MONEY

WORTHLESS MONEY

PROVERBS 11:4; EZEKIEL 7:19; MATTHEW 6:19-21; 1 TIMOTHY 6:17-19

Eternal Life; Heaven; Money; Values

On January 1, 2002, 12 European countries [began] switching from their existing currencies—the lira, franc, mark, and so on—to a new currency, the euro. After a grace period of six or eight weeks, all traditional currency [became] worthless. According to the *Chicago Tribune,* two men in Berlin "plan to fill an empty swimming pool with nearly $45 million worth of deutsche marks, and invite people to dive in. The German government will use about 128 shredding machines to dispose of old banknotes. The state government of Hesse will burn its marks in a heating system, and organizers of the Cologne carnival want to use shredded notes as confetti. . . . The Austrians plan to turn their schillings into 560 tons of compost."

Likewise, there will come a day when all our money will become no more valuable than compost.

Citation: Kevin Miller; Wheaton, Illinois; source: Ray Moseley, "Euro Conversion Spurs a Frenzy: Many Getting Rid of Cash Before It Becomes Worthless," Chicago Tribune (6-04-01)

MORTALITY

LIFE IS SHORT

Job 8:9; Job 14:1-2; Psalm 39:4-6; Psalm 90:12; Isaiah 40:6-8; 1 Peter 1:24-25
Death; Life, short; Mortality

A man went in for his annual checkup and received a phone call from his physician a couple of days later.

The doctor said, "I'm afraid I have some bad news for you."

"What's the news?" the man asked.

"Well, you have only 48 hours to live."

"That is bad news!" said the shocked patient.

"I'm afraid I have even worse news," the doctor continued.

"What could be worse than what you've already told me?" the patient stammered.

"I've been trying to call you since yesterday."

Citation: Rubel Shelly; Nashville, Tennessee

MOTHERHOOD

VALUING MOM

Exodus 20:12; Matthew 6:19-21
Affection; Children; Family; Motherhood; Values

My three young children love to get up early and watch out the window for the garbage truck. They take great delight in watching the waste hauler empty the can, then work the lever that causes the truck to compact the trash.

On the morning of my thirty-fifth birthday, my husband said to the children with a smile, "Kids, do you know what makes today so special?"

It should have been no surprise to us when our 5-year-old rushed past my outstretched arms to the window and replied, "It's garbage day!"

Citation: Sheri B.; Portage, Michigan, "Life in Our House," Christian Parenting Today *(March/April 2000)*

MOTIVATION

MOTIVATIONAL SPEECHES FAIL

1 CORINTHIANS 10:31; COLOSSIANS 3:17; COLOSSIANS 3:22-25
Jobs; Motivation; Purpose; Work

According to *USA Today,* firms are spending billions of dollars to fire up workers—with little results. The article states:

There has been exhaustive academic research trying to find out what motivates workers, and it has turned up almost no evidence that motivational spending makes any difference.

Poll-taker Gallup analyzed its massive database and determined in March [2001] that 55 percent of employees have no enthusiasm for their work—Gallup uses the term "not engaged"—based on several criteria, including loyalty and the desire to improve job performance. One in five (19 percent) are so uninterested or negative about their jobs that they poison the workplace to the point that companies might be better off if they called in sick.

Further into the article, Spencer Johnson, author of *Who Moved My Cheese?* states he "believes research may one day show that the only long-lasting motivation will come from employees who bring it to work in the form of God, spirituality, or something else that causes them to 'rise to a higher purpose.' "

Citation: USA Today (5-10-01); submitted by Van Morris; Mount Washington, Kentucky

MYSTERIES

GOD BEYOND OUR UNDERSTANDING

PSALM 139:6; ISAIAH 55:8-9
God; Mysteries

Since it is God we are speaking of, you do not understand it. If you could understand it, it would not be God.

Citation: Augustine, quoted in "Reflections," Christianity Today (7-31-00)

N

NEEDS

DANGEROUS WATER

Matthew 10:42; Matthew 25:31-46; Titus 3:14

Needs; Provision

More people die each year from unsafe drinking water than from all forms of violence, including war. More than a billion people—one in every five on earth—do not have access to safe drinking water. Percentage of the population with access to safe water:

Ethiopia: 18

Sudan: 45

Pakistan: 56

Mexico: 72

USA: 99

Citation: Lori Joseph and Sam Ward, "Water Unsafe in Much of the World," USA Today Snapshots (5-17-01)

NEW MAN

DON'T RECYCLE OLD LIFE

2 CORINTHIANS 5:1-17; EPHESIANS 4:20-32; EPHESIANS 5:1-17; PHILIPPIANS 3:7-16;
1 JOHN 3:8-10

Change; Christian Life; Conversion; Faith and Works; Growth, spiritual; New Life; New Man; Redemption; Regeneration; Repentance; Sanctification; Spiritual Formation

In the late 1920s my grandparents married and moved into Grandpa's old family home. It was a clapboard house with a hall down the middle. In the '30s they decided to tear down the old house and build another to be their home for the rest of their lives.

Much to my grandmother's dismay, many of the materials of the old house were reused in their new house. They used old facings and doors, and many other pieces of the finishing lumber. Everywhere my grandmother looked, she saw that old house—old doors that wouldn't shut properly, crown molding split and riddled with nail holes, unfinished window trimming. It was a source of grief to her. All her life she longed for a new house.

When God brings us into the kingdom, the old way of living must be dismantled and discarded.

Citation: Len Sullivan; Tupelo, Mississippi

O

OFFERINGS

GIFTS PLEASING TO GOD

PHILIPPIANS 4:18

Fatherhood of God; Gifts; Giving; God, goodness of; God, love of; Ministry; Money; Offerings; Tithing

One of the things my father taught all his sons was how to use a crosscut saw. His daddy and his daddy's daddy had taught their sons, and my father was not going to let this rite of passage for rural Southern manhood end with him. One brisk fall morning, we began sawing on a log that we did not know had a rotten core. When we had just sawed partially through the log, it split and fell off the sawing frame. The timber hit the ground so hard that a large piece was sheared off the rotten log. In my childhood imagination the unusual shape of the sheared piece looked like a horse head. It so captured my interest that I took it home with me after that day of sawing.

For my father's next birthday, I attached a length of two-by-four board to that log head, attached a rope tail, and stuck on some sticks to act as legs. Then I halfway hammered in a dozen or so nails down the two-by-four, put a bow on it, and presented it to my father. When he took off the wrapping, he smiled and said, "Thank you, it's wonderful . . . what is it?"

"It's a tie rack, Dad." I said. "See, you can put ties on those nails going down the side of the horse's body." My father smiled again and thanked me. Then he leaned the horse against his closet wall (because the stick legs could not keep it standing upright) and for years he used it as a tie rack.

Now when I first gave my father that rotten-log-horse tie rack, I really thought it was "good." In my childish mind this creation was a work of art ready for the Metropolitan Museum. But as I matured, I realized that my work was not nearly as good as I had once thought. In fact, I understood ultimately that my father had received and used my gift not because of its goodness but out of *his* goodness. In a similar way our heavenly Father receives our gifts, not so much because they deserve his love, but because he *is* love.

Citation: Bryan Chapell, Holiness By Grace *(Crossway, 2001), pp. 76-77; used by permission of Crossway Books, a division of Good News Publishers; Wheaton, Illinois 60187, www.crosswaybooks.org*

■

OFFERINGS

GIVING BENEFITS YOU, NOT GOD

PSALM 50:8-15; PROVERBS 11:24-25
Giving; Greed; Money; Offerings

I do not think I exaggerate when I say that some of us put our offering in the plate with a kind of triumphant bounce as much as to say, "There—now God will feel better!" . . . I am obliged to tell you that God does not need anything you have. He does not need a dime of your money. It is your own spiritual welfare at stake in such matters as these. . . . You have the right to keep what you have all to yourself—but it will rust and decay, and ultimately ruin you.

Citation: A. W. Tozer, quoted in "Reflections," Christianity Today *(6-12-00)*

■

OFFERINGS

PAID TO PREACH?

MATTHEW 10; 1 CORINTHIANS 9
Christian Life; Giving; Ministry; Offerings; Preaching

Recently, I tried something different in our worship service. Instead of preaching at the end, I did it first, with music, the offering, and Scripture reading afterward.

As I stood behind the pulpit, I could see people getting ready for the offering, until they realized I was starting my message.

Caitlyn, a first grader in the congregation, was perplexed by this change of routine, and whispered frantically to her mom, "Doesn't he know we haven't paid him to talk yet?"

Citation: Gordon Wood; Ellison Bay, Wisconsin, "Kids of the Kingdom," Christian Reader (July/August 2000)

OMNISCIENCE OF GOD

GOD IS WATCHING

JOB 31:4; PSALM 33:13; PSALM 139; MATTHEW 10:28-30; HEBREWS 4:13

Conscience; God, omnipresence of; God, omniscience of; Greed; Honesty; Omnipresence of God; Omniscience of God

Children lined up for lunch in the cafeteria of a religious school. At the head of the table was a large pile of apples. The teacher made a note: "Take only one; God is watching." At the other end of the table was a large pile of chocolate-chip cookies. A boy wrote a note: "Take all you want; God is watching the apples."

Citation: Pastor Tim's Clean Laugh List; submitted by Mark Moring

---

OUTREACH

INDIFFERENCE FOR THE LOST

MATTHEW 28:19; LUKE 15

Apathy; Compassion; Emotions; Evangelism; Hell; Lostness; Outreach; Salvation

The following is a dialogue from the once-popular sitcom *Seinfeld*, between Elaine and her boyfriend.

Elaine asks, "Do you believe in God?"

"Yes," her boyfriend replies.

Elaine asks, "Is it a problem that I'm not religious?"

"Not for me," her boyfriend answers.

"How's that?" she asks.

Her boyfriend says, "I'm not the one going to hell."

Citation: John Fehlen; Stanwood, Washington

■

OVERCOMING

PLAYING BAD HANDS

ECCLESIASTES 8:14; PHILIPPIANS 2:14

Advice; Complaining; Counsel; Mothers; Overcoming; Self-pity

President Dwight Eisenhower described his mother as a smart and saintly lady. "Often in this job I've wished I could consult her. But she is in heaven. However, many times I have felt I knew what she would say."

One night in their farm home, Mrs. Eisenhower was playing a card game with her boys. "Now, don't get me wrong," said the former president, "it was not with those cards that have kings, queens, jacks, and spades on them. Mother was too straitlaced for that." President Eisenhower said the game they were playing was called Flinch.

"Anyway, Mother was the dealer, and she dealt me a very bad hand. I began to complain. Mother said, 'Boys, put down your cards. I want to say something, particularly to Dwight. You are in a game in your home with your mother and brothers who love you. But out in the world you will be dealt bad hands without love. Here is some advice for you boys. Take those bad hands without complaining and play them out. Ask God to help you, and you will win the important game called life.'" The president added, "I've tried to follow that wise advice always."

Citation: Norman Vincent Peale, This Incredible Century *(Tyndale, 1991)*

P

PARENTING

DAY CARE LINKED TO AGGRESSION

EPHESIANS 6:4; TITUS 2:4-5

Children; Family; Motherhood; Mothers; Parenting; Work

In the United States, 96 percent of fathers and 65 percent of mothers with children under the age of 6 work outside the home. Many of those young ones spend various amounts of time with nannies, in preschools, and in day-care facilities.

The federal government conducted a study of over 1,300 of these children in 10 U.S. cities. The findings? The more hours children spend in non-maternal day care, the more aggressive they are toward classmates and the more defiant they are toward their teachers. Study author and psychologist Jay Belsky summarized the findings as a simple equation: "As time in day care goes up, so do problem behaviors."

Citation: Drew Zahn, assistant editor, Leadership; source: Marilyn Elias, "Day Care Linked to Aggression," USA Today (4-19-01)

■

PARENTING

PARENTAL INVOLVEMENT DETERS DRUG USE

1 SAMUEL 2:12-36; 1 KINGS 1:6; PROVERBS 22:6

Alcohol; Children; Drugs; Education; Family; Parenting; Teenagers

According to a survey conducted by Columbia University's Center on Addiction and Substance Abuse (CASA), "Almost one in five American teens say they live with 'hands-off' adults who fail to consistently set rules and monitor their behavior. These youth are at a four-times greater risk for smoking, drinking, and illegal drug use than their peers with 'hands-on' parents."

In a survey of 1,000 children in the age group of 12- to 17-year-olds, it was found that:

Teens who believe their parents would "not be too upset" if they used marijuana are more than three times as likely to use drugs than those who believe their parents would be "extremely upset."

Likewise, teens with parents who are "very unaware" of their academic performance are almost three times more likely to engage in substance use than their peers whose parents are "very aware" of their school performance.

Joseph A. Califano Jr., president of CASA, remarked that, "Mothers and fathers who are parents rather than pals can greatly reduce the risk of their children smoking, drinking, and using drugs." In addition, he notes that "the family is fundamental to keeping children away from tobacco, alcohol, and drugs."

Citation: Reuters News Service, (2-21-01); submitted by Derek and Jeannie Chinn

PATIENCE

PATIENCE PREACHED BUT NOT GRASPED

PROVERBS 14:29; 1 CORINTHIANS 13:4
Patience; Preaching

Gladys and Rhonda walked along the sidewalk after church. They were on their way home, thinking about meals planned for later that afternoon and casually discussing the morning service.

"That was a great sermon on patience," remarked Rhonda.

Gladys replied, "Yeah, but he went five minutes long."

Citation: Adapted from an original cartoon by Dave Veeman and Larry Thomas, The Best Cartoons from Leadership Journal, *Volume 1 (Broadman & Holman, 1999)*

PEACE

ORDINARY PERSON, UNCOMMON FORGIVENESS

PROVERBS 24:29; MATTHEW 5:43-44; 1 JOHN 4:7-8; 1 JOHN 4:19-21

Forgiveness; Peace; Reconciliation; Unity

In 1987 an IRA bomb went off in a town west of Belfast. Eleven died; 63 were wounded. Gordon Wilson, a cloth merchant and devout Methodist, was buried with his 20-year-old daughter under five feet of concrete and brick. "Daddy, I love you very much," were Marie's last words, grasping her father's hand.

From his hospital bed, Wilson said, "I've lost my daughter, but I bear no grudge. Bitter talk is not going to bring Marie back. I shall pray every night that God will forgive them."

Once recovered, Wilson crusaded for reconciliation. Protestant extremists who had planned to avenge the bombing decided, because of the publicity surrounding Wilson, that such behavior would be politically foolish. Wilson wrote a book about his daughter and spoke out against violence, constantly repeating, "Love is the bottom line."

He met with the IRA, personally forgave them, and asked them to lay down their arms. "You've lost loved ones, just like me," he told them. "Surely, enough blood has been spilled."

When he died in 1995, all Ireland and Britain honored this ordinary citizen for his uncommon forgiveness.

Citation: Philip Yancey, What's So Amazing About Grace? *(Zondervan, 1997)*

PEER PRESSURE

SELFISH BIRD, COMPETITIVE FLOCK

GALATIANS 5:13-15; EPHESIANS 4:31-32; PHILIPPIANS 2:3-4; 1 PETER 2:16-17

Character; Community; Competition; Jealousy; Peer pressure; Selfishness; Sharing; Strife

It's easy to see why people like the seagull. I've sat overlooking a craggy harbor and watched one. He exults in freedom. He thrusts his wings backward with powerful strokes, climbing higher and higher until he's above all the other gulls, then coasts downward in majestic loops and circles. He constantly performs, as if he knows a movie camera is trained on him, recording.

In a flock, though, the seagull is a different bird. His majesty and dignity melt into a sordid slough of in-fighting and cruelty. Watch that same gull as he dive-bombs into a group of gulls, provoking a flurry of scattered feathers and angry squawks to steal a tiny morsel of meat. The concepts of sharing and manners do not exist among gulls. They are so fiercely competitive and jealous that if you tie a red ribbon around the leg of one gull, making him stand out, you sentence him to execution. The others in the flock will furiously attack him with claws and beaks, hammering through feathers and flesh to draw blood. They'll continue until he lies flattened in a bloody heap.

Citation: Philip Yancey, as quoted in The Strong-Willed Child *by James Dobson (Tyndale, 1995); submitted by Greg Asimakoupoulos; Naperville, Illinois*

PERSECUTION
FORCED TO RENOUNCE CHRISTIANITY
Matthew 5:10-12; Matthew 10:16-23; Revelation 2:8-11
Hardship; Oppression; Persecution; Suffering

If you become an evangelical Christian in Laos, the Communist neighbor of Vietnam and Cambodia, you likely will be "asked" to sign a fill-in-the-blank form. And it's not a membership card at your neighborhood church.

The form reads, in part:

I, (name), who live in (location), believe in a foreign religion, which the imperialists have used for their own benefit to divide the united front and to build power for themselves against the local authorities. Now I and my family clearly see the intentions of the enemy and regret the deeds which we have committed. We have clearly seen the goodness of the Party and the Government. Therefore, I and my family voluntarily and unequivocally resign from believing in this foreign religion.

If you sign, you promise not to participate in this "foreign religion"—Christianity in every reported case—under punishment of law. If you don't sign, you can expect humiliation, harassment, and persecution, including probable imprisonment and torture.

The document's widespread use by Laotian officials has been authenticated by the World Evangelical Fellowship's Religious Liberty Commission and other sources. Hundreds of rural Christians reportedly have been forced to sign the form in public, then compelled to participate in animistic sacrifices.

Citation: Baptist Press (10-9-00 article); submitted by Ken Taylor; New Orleans, Louisiana

PERSEVERANCE

PAYTON ENDURES REPEATED BLOWS

PROVERBS 24:16; ROMANS 5:3-5; 1 CORINTHIANS 9:24-27; GALATIANS 6:9-10; HEBREWS 10:36; JAMES 1:2-4

Courage; Endurance; Failure; Perseverance; Persistence; Sports; Strength; Success; Winning and Losing

At just 5-foot-10 and 202 pounds, Walter Payton was not a particularly big running back for the National Football League. But he set one of sport's greatest records: the all-time rushing record of 16,726 yards. During his twelve-year career, Payton carried the football over nine miles!

What is truly impressive, though, is that he was knocked to the ground on average every 4.4 yards of those nine miles by someone bigger than himself. But he kept getting up, and he kept getting up, and he kept getting up. Great victories await those with great endurance.

Citation: Bill White; Paramount, California

PERSEVERANCE

REWARDS OF PERSEVERANCE

1 TIMOTHY 4:13-16; JAMES 1:12

Evangelism; Fruitfulness; Ministry; Outreach; Perseverance; Preaching; Results

A single page from the journal of John Wesley reads:

Sunday A.M., May 5—Preached in St. Ann's; was asked not to come back anymore.

Sunday P.M., May 5—Preached at St. John's; deacons said, "Get out and stay out."

Sunday A.M., May 12—Preached at St. Jude's; can't go back there either.

Sunday P.M., May 12—Preached at St. George's; kicked out again.

Sunday A.M., May 19—Preached at St. Somebody Else's; deacons called special meeting and said I couldn't return.

Sunday P.M., May 19—Preached on the street; kicked off the street.

Sunday A.M., May 26—Preached out in a meadow; chased out of meadow when a bull was turned loose during the service.

Sunday A.M., June 2—Preached out at the edge of town; kicked off the highway.

Sunday P.M., June 2—Afternoon service, preached in pasture; 10,000 people came.

Citation: Bob Hartman, Plugged In *(9-16-97), p. 6; submitted by David Holdaway; Stonehaven, Kincardinshire, Scotland*

■

PERSISTENCE

FACING THE IMPOSSIBLE

LUKE 1:37; LUKE 18:27; HEBREWS 12:7

Challenges; Endurance; Overcoming; Perseverance; Persistence; Preparation; Study

George Danzig was a senior at Stanford University during the Depression. All the seniors knew they'd be joining unemployment lines when the class graduated. There was a slim chance that the top person in the class might get a teaching job. George was not at the head of his class, but he hoped that if he were able to achieve a perfect score on the final exam, he might be given a job.

He studied so hard for the exam that he arrived late to class. When he got to class, the others were already hard at work. He was embarrassed and just picked up his paper and slunk into his desk. He sat down and worked the eight problems on the test paper; then he started on the two written on the board. Try as he might, he couldn't solve either of them. He was devastated. Out of the ten problems, he had missed two for sure. But just as he was about to hand in the paper, he took a chance and asked the professor if he could have a couple of days to work on the two he had missed. He was surprised when his professor agreed.

George rushed home and plunged into those equations with a vengeance. He spent hours and hours, but he could find the solution for only one of them. He never could solve the other. It was impossible. When he turned in the test, he knew he had lost all chance of a job. That was the darkest moment of his life.

The next morning a pounding on the door awakened George. It was his mathematics professor, very excited. "George! George!" he kept shouting, "You've made mathematics history!"

George didn't know what his professor was talking about. The professor explained. Before the exam, he had encouraged the class to keep trying in spite of setback and failure. "Don't be discouraged," he had counseled. "Remember, there are classic problems that no one can solve. Even Einstein was unable to unlock their secrets." He then wrote two of those problems on the blackboard. George had come to class late and missed those opening remarks. He didn't know the problems on the board were impossible to solve. He thought they were part of his exam and was determined that he could work them. And he solved one!

He did the impossible.

That very morning the professor made George Danzig his assistant. He taught at Stanford until his retirement.

Citation: Taken from Defining Moments, *2001 by Rick Ezell. Used by permission of InterVarsity Press, P.O. Box 1400, Downers Grove, IL 60515-1426. www.ivpress.com*

PERSISTENCE

JOHN GRISHAM: REWARDS OF PERSEVERANCE

Romans 5:3-5; James 1:2-4; James 5:11
Perseverance; Persistence; Success

Success seldom comes without pain and perseverance. Take the case of author John Grisham.

Grisham is the world's most commercially successful novelist of the last decade. He has well over 100 million books in print in 31 languages. Yet Grisham was hardly an overnight success in his transition from attorney to writer.

A Time to Kill, Grisham's first novel, was rejected by 28 agents and publishers. When an agent finally did take him as a client, the book's first press run was only 5,000 copies. Grisham himself purchased 1,000 and hawked his work to bookstores from the trunk of his car.

Only after his second novel, *The Firm,* hit the best-seller list did he get his big break. Six of his books have now been made into movies, and the press run of his most recent volume, *A Painted House,* was a phenomenal 2.8 million copies.

Citation: Rubel Shelly; Nashville, Tennessee, from various news stories and reviews of John Grisham, A Painted House *(Doubleday, 2001)*

PERSPECTIVE

HUMOROUS LESSONS FROM NOAH

GENESIS 6; 1 PETER 3:20

Attitudes; Christian Life; Perspective; Preparation; Teachability

There is a well-known book titled *Everything I Need to Know I Learned in Kindergarten.* Let me suggest another: *Everything I Need to Know I Learned from Noah:*

Don't miss the boat.

We are all in the same boat.

Plan ahead. It wasn't raining when Noah built the Ark.

Stay fit. When you're 600 years old, someone may ask you to do something big.

Don't listen to critics; just do the job that needs to be done.

Build your future on high ground.

For safety's sake, travel in pairs.

Speed isn't always an advantage. The snails were on board with the cheetahs.

When you're stressed, float a while.

Remember, the Ark was built by amateurs; the *Titanic* by professionals.

No matter the storm, when you are with God, there's always a rainbow waiting.

Citation: Source unknown; submitted by Jon Mutchler; Ferndale, Washington

PERSPECTIVE

ROSIE: LIFE MORE THAN LIPSTICK

PSALM 90:12; JOHN 6:63

Appearance; Disease; Life and Death; Perspective; Pride; Priorities; Sickness; Values

The July 2001 issue of Rosie O'Donnell's magazine, *Rosie*, features a cover photo of the TV personality herself—dressed in a hospital smock, grimacing, unkempt, and sporting a hefty bandage on her hand. She had gone through a terrifying experience in which she nearly died from a staph infection following surgery on her hand. (See "Staph Stinks.") She strikes a sharply contrasting pose to the typical primped and digitally altered covergirl.

When asked why she appeared without makeup or beauty preening, she responded, "I've just gotten out of the hospital and almost died. Who has time for lipstick?"

Citation: "Quoteworthy," Chicago Tribune *(6-6-01); see* Rosie *(June and July 2001)*

POOR

GIVING A BUM A HUG

ISAIAH 58:6-18; MATTHEW 25:35-45; LUKE 10:25-37; JAMES 2:2-4

Brotherly Love; Care; Love; Poor; Servanthood; Service

I walked down Chestnut Street in Philadelphia. There was a filthy bum, covered with soot from head to toe. He had a huge beard. I'll never forget the beard. It was a gigantic beard with rotted food stuck in it. He held a cup of McDonald's coffee and mumbled as he walked along the street. He spotted me and said, "Hey, Mister. You want some of my coffee?"

I knew I should take some to be nice, and I did. I gave it back to him and said, "You're being pretty generous giving away your coffee this morning. What's gotten into you that you're giving away your coffee all of a sudden?"

He said, "Well, the coffee was especially delicious this morning, and

I figured if God gives you something good you ought to share it with people."

I figured, *This is the perfect setup.* I said, "Is there anything I can give you in return?" *I'm sure he's going to hit me for five dollars.*

He said, "Yeah, you can give me a hug."

I was hoping for the five dollars.

He put his arms around me. I put my arms around him. And I realized something. He wasn't going to let me go. He was holding on to me. Here I am an establishment guy, and this bum is hanging on me. He's hugging me. He's not going to let me go. People are passing on the street. They're staring at me. I'm embarrassed. But little by little my embarrassment turned to awe.

I heard a voice echoing down the corridors of time saying, *I was hungry. Did you feed me? I was naked. Did you clothe me? I was sick. Did you care for me? I was the bum you met on Chestnut Street. Did you hug me? For if you did it unto the least of these, my brothers and sisters, you did it to me. And if you failed to do it unto the least of these, my brothers and sisters, you failed to do it unto me.*

Citation: Tony Campolo, "Year of Jubilee," Preaching Today *(212)*

PORNOGRAPHY

HIDDEN EXTENT OF PORNOGRAPHY USE

Job 31:1; Matthew 5:27-30; Romans 1:21-32

Desire, sinful; Lust; Money; Pornography; Sex; Sin

According to *U.S. News & World Report,* Americans spent no more than $10 million on pornography in 1973. By 1999, however, they were spending $10 billion a year—a thousandfold increase. As *U.S. News* put it, it's an amount much larger than Hollywood's domestic box-office receipts and larger than all the revenues generated by rock and country music recordings.

A recent survey conducted by the National Coalition for the Protection of Children and Families provides us with a clue as to how big the problem of Christians and pornography may be. The Coalition surveyed students at five Christian colleges. Sixty-eight percent of the male students said they had intentionally looked for pornography on the Internet. Ten percent of those surveyed admitted to frequent use of pornography, and five percent acknowledged having a problem with pornography.

Another Christian college, Seattle Pacific University, examined all the Web sites accessed by its students during a three-week period. Officials were dismayed to learn that nearly 7 percent of all sites visited were pornographic. And, one in five of all campus computers had been used to view pornography.

Citation: "BreakPoint with Charles Colson" (2-19-01); submitted by Aaron Goerner; New Hartford, New York

■

POVERTY

REAL WORLD NEEDS

LUKE 6:20
Poor People; Poverty; Riches; Wealth

On a hot spring day in 1968, Bobby Kennedy, fighting for the Democratic nomination for the presidency, crisscrossed streets in some of the poorest neighborhoods in Spanish Harlem. Lester and Irene David write in *Bobby Kennedy: The Making of a Folk Hero,* that after five hours, Kennedy was caked with dirt and soaked in perspiration. His guide that day was former boxing champion Jose Torres.

"Torres wondered why the rich man's son came to the ghettoes and worked so hard and long, often 16 hours a day. At the car, Torres asked, 'Why are you doing this? Why are you running?'

"Bobby replied in a very low voice, 'Because I found out that my world wasn't the real world.' "

Citation: Gordon MacDonald, Forging a Real-World Faith *(Nelson, 1989); quoted in* Men of Integrity *(March/April 2001)*

■

POVERTY

WELFARE ROLLS DWINDLE

MATTHEW 26:11; 2 THESSALONIANS 3:6-15

Economics; Government; Money; Poor People; Poverty; Work

The 5.8 million welfare recipients in the USA in 2000 was the lowest number since the 1960s. Recipients by year:
    1965: 4.3 million
    1971: approximately 10 million
    1981: approximately 11.5 million
    1989: approximately 11 million
    1994: 14.2 million
    2000: 5.8 million

Citation: Adrienne Lewis reporting U.S. Health and Human Services Department statistics in USA Today Snapshots, (5-15-01)

■

POWER

POWERLESS CHRISTIANITY

1 CORINTHIANS 1:24; 1 CORINTHIANS 4:20; 2 TIMOTHY 3:5

Holy Spirit; Power; Power, divine; Prayer

While visiting Grand Coulee Dam, my family and I were surprised to see that the visitors' center was dark. It was a sunny day, so we thought the center might have tinted windows, but as we got closer we realized there were no lights on. We went in and saw that none of the displays were working. Suddenly it became clear: there was no power to the center. Due to a technical difficulty of some kind, the visitors' center that sat only hundreds of feet from a hydroelectric dam had no power.

How could something be so close to the power source, yet not be "plugged in"?

Citation: Paul Dawson; Pendleton, Oregon

PRAYER

FIRST, CALL DAD

PSALM 46:1; MATTHEW 6:9; 1 PETER 5:7

Communication; Crisis; Dependence on God; Desperation; Faith; Family; Fatherhood; Fatherhood of God; Fathers; Help from God; Needs; Prayer; Trouble; Trust

While kayaking in southern England off the Isle of Wight, Mark Ashton-Smith, a 33-year-old lecturer at Cambridge University, capsized in treacherous waters. Clinging to his craft and reaching for his cell phone, Ashton-Smith's first inclination was to call his father. It didn't matter to the desperate son that his dad, Alan Pimm-Smith, was at work training British troops in Dubai 3,500 miles away. Without delay, the father relayed his son's mayday to the Coast Guard installation nearest to his son's location. Ironically, it was less than a mile away. Within 12 minutes, a helicopter retrieved the grateful Ashton-Smith.

Like this kayaker, when we are in peril, our first impulse should be to call our Father—the one we trust to help us.

Citation: Greg Asimakoupoulos; Naperville, Illinois; source: Reuters News Agency

PRAYER

HEALED FROM ANGER

LUKE 8:35-36; JAMES 1:20; JAMES 5:13-16

Anger; Anger, human; Attitudes; Death; Healing; Illness; Mind; Miracles; Prayer; Prayer, answered; Prayer, unanswered; Renewing the Mind; Thoughts

In *Preaching Today,* author and speaker Tony Campolo tells this story:

I was in a church in Oregon not too long ago, and I prayed for a man who had cancer. In the middle of the week, I got a telephone call from his wife. She said, "You prayed for my husband. He had cancer."

I said, "Had?" *Whoa,* I thought, *it's happened.*

She said, "He died." I felt terrible.

She continued, "Don't feel bad. When he came into that church last

Sunday he was filled with anger. He knew he was going to be dead in a short period of time, and he hated God. He was 58 years old, and he wanted to see his children and grandchildren grow up. He was angry that this all-powerful God didn't take away his sickness and heal him. He would lie in bed and curse God. The more his anger towards God grew, the more miserable he was to everybody around him. It was an awful thing to be in his presence. After you prayed for him, a peace had come over him and a joy had come into him. Tony, the last three days have been the best days of our lives. We've sung. We've laughed. We've read Scripture. We prayed. Oh, they've been wonderful days. And I called to thank you for laying your hands on him and praying for healing."

And then she said something incredibly profound. She said, "He wasn't cured, but he was healed."

Citation: Tony Campolo, "Year of Jubilee," Preaching Today #212

PRAYER

PRAYER BETTER THAN SELFISHNESS

Romans 1:21-32; Romans 6:16; 2 Corinthians 3:17-18; Colossians 3:1-3; Colossians 4:2-4
Attitudes and Emotions; Ego; Freedom; Prayer; Self-centeredness; Selfishness

Those people who pray know what most around them either don't know or choose to ignore: centering life in the insatiable demands of the ego is the sure path to doom. . . . They know that life confined to the self is a prison, a joy-killing, neurosis-producing, disease-fomenting prison.

Citation: Eugene Peterson, quoted in "Reflections," Christianity Today (7-31-00)

PRAYER, ANSWERS TO

AUGUSTINE'S MOTHER'S PRAYER ANSWERED

Luke 11:11-13; Philippians 4:6-7; 2 Thessalonians 1:11-12
Faith and Prayer; Prayer; Prayer, answers to; Prayer, persistence in; Prayer, power of; Seeking God

In his book *Legacy of Sovereign Joy*, John Piper writes:

At the age of 16 in the year 371, Augustine sneaked away from his mother in Carthage. During the night he sailed away to Rome, leaving her alone to her tears and her prayers.

How were these prayers answered? Not the way Monica [Augustine's mother] hoped at the time. Only later could she see that praying is the deepest path to joy.

Augustine himself wrote, "And what did she beg of you, my God, with all those tears, if not that you would prevent me from sailing? But you did not do as she asked you. Instead, in the depth of your wisdom, you granted the wish that was closest to her heart.

"For she saw that you had granted her far more than she used to ask in her tearful prayers. You converted me to yourself, so that I no longer placed any hope in this world, but stood firmly upon the rule of faith. And you turned her sadness into rejoicing, into joy far fuller than her dearest wish, far sweeter and more chaste than any she had hoped to find."

Citation: John Piper, The Legacy of Sovereign Joy *(Crossway, 2000); submitted by Van Morris; Mount Washington, Kentucky*

PRAYER, UNANSWERED

STUDENT'S IMPOSSIBLE PRAYER UNANSWERED

MATTHEW 21:22; ROMANS 8:26-27
Christian Life; Prayer; Prayer, unanswered; Truth

However much he may want to, I do not believe God will answer the prayer of the student who turned in his test and prayed, "O God, please let Paris be the capital of England!"

Citation: Nicky Gumbel, "How and Why Should I Pray," Alpha Evangelism Series (HTB Publications, 1994); submitted by Bill White; Paramount, California

PRESENCE OF GOD

MOTHER BRINGS PEACE DURING CRISIS

Psalm 139; Proverbs 31:10-31; Matthew 28:20; Hebrews 13:5-6

Afterlife; Children; Child-rearing; Crisis; Death; God, omnipresence of; Heaven; Hope; Motherhood; Mothers; Omnipresence of God; Parenting; Peace; Presence of God

Cindy Holmes is a writer and pediatric nurse in Houston, Texas. She wrote an article about a mother and child she got to know at the hospital who were both suffering from full-blown AIDS. The child, Tyler, was born infected with HIV. From the outset he had been dependent upon all kinds of medical treatment. . . . Sometimes he needed supplemental oxygen.

But Cindy said it didn't slow him down. He was all boy—a little dynamo. He frequently raced through his Houston neighborhood with a little backpack on that held medications he had to take. . . . Sometimes he would pull an oxygen canister in the little red Radio Flyer wagon, but that didn't slow him down. Off he would go through the neighborhood playing like children play.

Cindy Holmes got to know them best when they were confined to the hospital in the last stages of their illnesses, when they both were dying. When it became obvious to Tyler's mother that he was probably going to die first, she decided she'd better talk with him about what was going to come next.

She pulled him up into her bed, and they talked about life, love, and fun. Then she brought up the topic of heaven. She said, "You know, Tyler, I was kind of hoping that you'd do your growing up here, but the doctors say your body is telling them that you might want to move on and grow up in heaven." She continued, "You know, I made a decision."

Tyler asked, "What's that, Mommy?"

She said, "I've decided that if you're going to go live in heaven, I'm going to do that, too, because wherever you are, that's where I want to be."

A few days later, Cindy Holmes was in Tyler's room. She said he looked up at her and said, "Miss Holmes, will you do me a favor?"

Cindy said, "Sure, Tyler. What do you need?"

He asked, "When I die, would you put a red shirt on me?"

Cindy answered, "Tyler, why do you want me to do that?"

Tyler explained, "Well, I'm going to grow up in heaven, and I've been told it's fun over there. I'm going to have friends, and I'm going to play. But my mommy is going to come over there, too, and she's going to be looking for me. And if I'm real busy and don't see her coming, I want her to see me. So it's really important I have on something she can see. So would you give me a red shirt?" Tyler looked up from his bed and continued, "You know, heaven wouldn't be heaven without Mommy."

Cindy Holmes said, "I was overwhelmed by this inexpressible sense of peace that was on his face even at a time of inexpressible crisis. And suddenly I understood where it was coming from. His peace was the result of his mother's presence with him through his life, throughout his illness, and her promise that no matter where he went and no matter what happened, she would still be there."

Citation: Michael Brown, pastor of the United Methodist Church in Winston-Salem, North Carolina, from sermon "Acquainted with the Night" (8-13-00)

PRIDE

300 MEN CONFESS PRIDE

PSALM 32:1-7; PSALM 51:1-19; JAMES 5:16; 1 JOHN 1:9

Confession; Intercession, prayer; Prayer; Prayer, need for; Pride; Sin; Sin, confession of

During the Great Awakening, when the Spirit of God revived much of our nation's early faith, Jonathan Edwards was presiding over a massive prayer meeting. Eight hundred men prayed with him.

Into that meeting a woman sent a message asking the men to pray for her husband. The note described a man who had become unloving, prideful, and difficult.

Edwards read the message in private and then, thinking that perhaps the man described was present, made a bold request. Edwards read the note to the 800 men. Then he asked if the man who had been described would raise his hand, so that the whole assembly could pray for him. Three hundred men raised their hands.

Citation: Bryan Chapell, Holiness By Grace *(Crossway, 2001), p. 80. Used by permission of Crossway Books, a division of Good News Publishers, Wheaton, Illinois*

■

PRIDE

CHUCK YEAGER FINDS THE PROBLEM

Joshua 7; Galatians 6:1-5; James 5:19-20

Accountability; Cause and Effect; Change; Community; Consequences; Cooperation; Disobedience; Folly; Pride; Responsibility; Self-confidence; Self-will; Stubbornness; Teamwork; Work

Chuck Yeager, the famed test pilot, was flying an F-86 Sabre over a lake in the Sierras when he decided to buzz a friend's house near the edge of the lake. During a slow roll, he suddenly felt his aileron lock. Says Yeager, "It was a hairy moment, flying about 150 feet off the ground and upside down."

A lesser pilot might have panicked, with fatal results, but Yeager let off on the G's, pushed up the nose, and sure enough, the aileron unlocked. Climbing to 15,000 feet, where it was safer, Yeager tried the maneuver again. Every time that he rolled, the problem reoccurred.

Yeager knew three or four pilots had died under similar circumstances, but to date, investigators were puzzled as to the source of the Sabre's fatal flaw. Yeager went to his superior with a report, and the inspectors went to work. They found that a bolt on the aileron cylinder was installed upside down.

Eventually, the culprit was found in a North American plant. He was an older man on the assembly line who ignored instructions about how to insert that bolt, because, by golly, he knew that bolts were supposed to be placed head up, not head down. In a sad commentary, Yeager says that nobody ever told the man how many pilots he had killed.

Citation: Matt Friedeman, The Accountability Connection *(Victor Books, 1992), story from Chuck Yeager,* Yeager *(Bantam, 1985)*

PRIORITIES

FIRST BASE FIRST

Proverbs 3:9-10; Matthew 6:33

Discipleship; Honoring God; Priorities; Sports; Values; Worship

Tennessee Titans center Kevin Long, who played under Coach Bobby Bowden at Florida State University, said his college coach inspired the team with parables. Long recounted a favorite story:

[Bowden] was playing college baseball, and he had never hit a home run. Finally he hit one down the right-field line, into the corner. He rounds first and looks to the third-base coach. He turned at second, was halfway to third and the coach was still waving him on. He got to home; he hit the plate. He had his first home run. He was so excited and everybody was slapping him five. Then the pitcher took the ball, threw to the first baseman, and the umpire called him out.

[Coach Bowden] said, "If you don't take care of first base, it doesn't matter what you do. If you don't honor the Lord first, it doesn't matter what else you do."

Citation: The Tennessean (9-29-00); submitted by Rubel Shelly; Nashville, Tennessee

PRIORITIES

ON CHRISTMAS: FOOTBALL OR JESUS?

Luke 2:7

Christmas; Power; Priorities; Values

Saint John the Evangelist Catholic Church in Indianapolis sits directly across the street from the main gate of the RCA Dome, home of the NFL's Indianapolis Colts in downtown Indianapolis. The church petitioned the National Football League to change the starting time of the Colts Christmas Eve game against the Minnesota Vikings. The 4:15 game would interfere with the church's 5:30 Christmas Eve mass. The church becomes virtually inaccessible during games due to traffic and parking problems. The team refused to cooperate, and NFL spokesman Greg Aiello says the league would not change the time of kickoff. As a result the church was forced to cancel its traditional Christmas Eve service. The controversy has sparked little if any heat in Indianapolis.

Citation: Sports Illustrated (11-27-00), p. 32

■

PROMISES

KEEPING PROMISES

Deuteronomy 23:21; Psalm 15:1-4; Ecclesiastes 5:4; Malachi 2:10-16; Ephesians 4:25
Commitment; Covenant; Devotion; Faithfulness; Family; Freedom; Future; Marriage; Promises; Relationships; Speaking; Speech; Uncertainties; Vows; Words

Writer and speaker Lewis Smedes says:

Yes, somewhere people still make and keep promises. They choose not to quit when the going gets rough because they promised once to see it through. They stick to lost causes. They hold on to a love grown cold. They stay with people who have become pains in the neck. They still dare to make promises and care enough to keep the promises they make. I want to say to you that if you have a ship you will not desert, if you have people you will not forsake, if you have causes you will not abandon, then you are like God.

What a marvelous thing a promise is! When a person makes a promise, she reaches out into an unpredictable future and makes one thing predictable: she will be there even when being there costs her more than she wants to pay. When a person makes a promise, he stretches himself out into circumstances that no one can control and controls at least one thing: he will be there no matter what the circumstances turn out to be. With one simple word of promise, a person creates an island of certainty in a sea of uncertainty.

When a person makes a promise, she stakes a claim on her personal freedom and power.

When you make a promise, you take a hand in creating your own future.

Citation: Lewis Smedes, "The Power of Promises," A Chorus of Witnesses, edited by Long and Plantinga (Eerdmans, 1994)

PROSPERITY

MILLION-DOLLAR HOME SALES SOAR

Psalm 49:1-20; Luke 12:13-21

Luxury; Money; Prosperity; Values

Buyers in 2000 smashed records for homes sold for more than $1 million. The analysis is based on sales of residential real estate recorded with local governments across the USA:

1995: 2,520 (estimate)
1996: 3,380 (estimate)
1997: 4,895 (estimate)
1998: 7,155 (estimate)
1999: 10,300 (estimate)
2000: 15,595 (estimate)

Citation: Bob Laird, "Million-dollar Home Sales Soar," USA Today (12-06-00); source: DataQuick Information Systems

PROSPERITY

PROGRESS DOESN'T GUARANTEE CIVILITY

Matthew 6:33; 2 Timothy 3:1-5

Comfort; Community; Conflict; Convenience; Humanity; Lawlessness; Life; Morality; Murder; Prosperity; Violence

Here are some of the measurements of improved living made over the past 100 years in the United States:

Percentage of homes with a flush toilet in 1900: 10; in 1999: 98.

Percentage of homes with electricity in 1900: 2; in 1999: 99.

Average hourly pay in manufacturing (adjusted for inflation) in 1900: $3.80; in 1999: $13.90.

Enormous prosperity in material terms, however, doesn't necessarily translate into greater civility. In spite of the progress as measured by most material indicators, Harvard political scientist Robert Putnam says his research shows that most people believe social and moral values are getting worse, the average American is less trustworthy, and the break-down of community is a serious problem.

As evidence, the number of murders in the U.S. in 1900: 140; in 1999: 16,000.

Citation: Rubel Shelly; Nashville, Tennessee; source: Andrew Curry, "Pursuing Happiness by the Numbers," U.S. News & World Report (12-18-00), p. 56

■

PROTECTION

DADDY'S PROTECTIVE CARE

GENESIS 28:20-21; JOHN 10:27-30; JOHN 11:25-26; 1 CORINTHIANS 15; 1 THESSALONIANS 4:13-18; HEBREWS 2:15

Children; Death; Family; Fatherhood; Fatherhood of God; Fathers; Fear; Human Condition; Human Limitations; Protection; Savior

About a month ago I bought my two-year-old daughter, Sarah, an aquarium. We went together to the pet store to pick out four fish to put in the tank. One of the fish died two weeks ago when Sara was at her grandparents' house. My wife flushed it down the toilet and didn't tell my daughter about it.

This morning Sarah found one of the other fish dead. She found it caught up in one of the fake plastic bushes. My wife called me at the office and said that Sarah had something to tell me. In her two-year-old way, she explained to me the fish had died, she found it in the bushes, and she and Mommy were going to have a funeral for it in the backyard.

I realized that this was the first of many losses she would experience in life. I broke into tears, however, when the last thing she said to me before she hung up the phone was, "Daddy, keep me from getting caught in the bushes."

Citation: Steve Nickles

Q

QUESTIONS

LARRY KING RESPECTS BELIEVERS

GENESIS 22:1-19; JOHN 6:29; JOHN 20:1-30; 2 TIMOTHY 3:16; 2 TIMOTHY 4:1; 2 TIMOTHY 4:8; HEBREWS 9:27; HEBREWS 12:23; JAMES 4:12

Agnosticism; Authority of Scripture; Belief; Bible; Faith; God, will of; Judgment, divine; Questions; Scripture; Seekers; Seeking God; Testing; Tests

In *World* magazine, interviewer Larry King said:

I can't make that leap that a lot of people around me have made into belief that there's some judge somewhere. I have a lot of respect for true people of faith. . . . I've done so many interviews on it. I've always searched. But as someone said, "Did you ever sit down and read the Bible cover to cover?" The answer's no, because I don't know who wrote it. I'm too in my head to be into faith. Faith is a wonderful thing. I envy people who have it. I just can't make the leap.

I remember as a kid, my father died when I was young, and that was unexplainable to me. The God of the Old Testament, I didn't like things he did. "Abraham, sacrifice your son." That always bothered me as a kid. I remember thinking, *Why would he do that to Abraham? As a test?* So I said to myself, *I don't know. I just don't know.* That's still true to this day.

Citation: Bob Jones, "It's Good to Be King," World (7-28-01), p. 22

R

REASON

WITNESS GREATER THAN REASON

ACTS 1:8

Apologetics; Conversion; Ideologies and Belief Systems; Reason; Salvation and Lostness; Witness

God has given enough reason in this world to make faith a most reasonable thing. But he has left out enough to make it impossible to live by reason alone.

Blaise Pascal is considered one of history's greatest scientists. But Pascal's conversion was not through his scientific queries.

When his carriage was once suspended on a bridge, hanging between life and death, the only thing Pascal could think of was the Christian conviction of his sister and the witness of Christ she had in his life.

He was the inventor of the barometer. He was tremendously brilliant as a philosophical scientist. But the one thing that kept piercing his heart was not the scientific laws; it was the Christian witness of his sister.

Citation: Ravi Zacharias, author, "Absolute Truth in Relative Terms" Part I; submitted by Aaron Goerner; New Hartford, New York

RECONCILIATION

INHERITING HATRED

MATTHEW 5:21-24; EPHESIANS 4:26-27

Bigotry; Conflict; Forgiveness; Hatred; Prejudice; Reconciliation

Two decades after the Civil War, North and South still had not achieved reconciliation. Such a reconciliation would not succeed unless it was achieved by the generation that fought the war. Should that generation die unreconciled, its hatreds would become the next generation's legacy, and would be perpetuated. It is a historical truism that inheriting hatreds is a near inevitability, eradicating them a near impossibility.

Citation: Alyn Brodsky, Grover Cleveland: A Study in Character *(St. Martin's Press, 2000); submitted by Van Morris; Mount Washington, Kentucky*

RECONCILIATION

RECONCILIATION REQUIRES SACRIFICE

ROMANS 5:9-11; 2 CORINTHIANS 5:14-21

Christ, love of; Forgiveness; Reconciliation; Sacrifice

On January 26, 2001, Seiko Sakamoto, a plasterer working in a Tokyo subway station, fell into the path of an oncoming train. Lee Su Hyun, a Korean student in Japan for language studies, leaped down on the tracks to save Sakamoto. Both Hyun and Sakamoto were unable to exit the path of the oncoming train and were killed.

This selfless act by the Korean student on behalf of the Japanese laborer has caused many people in Japan to reconsider their long-held prejudices directed toward Koreans. Strong feelings of distrust between the two countries go back to World War II atrocities inflicted upon Koreans by the Japanese. Many Japanese people, including the prime minister of Japan, have openly expressed sorrow over their previously held stereotypes of Koreans and have begun to talk about reconciliation. Nobuaki Fujioka, a 62-year-old Japanese, said, "I felt a kind of shame. A young foreigner sacrificed his life for a Japanese. This is not an easy thing to do."

Reconciliation rarely occurs without sacrifice. By giving his one and only Son, God took the initiative in healing our broken relationship with him. He made the supreme sacrifice for us that we might be reconciled to him.

Citation: David A. Slagle, Lawrenceville, Georgia; source: an article in the Washington Post *by Shigehiko Togo and Doug Struck with Joohee Cho*

RECONCILIATION

RICH MULLINS SHOWS REPENTANCE

Matthew 18:15-20; 2 Corinthians 7:9-11; Colossians 3:12-15

Apology; Conflict; Healing; Reconciliation; Relationships; Repentance

The late musician Rich [Mullins] taught me an invaluable lesson about the true meaning of repentance. One rainy day he got into a blistering argument with his road manager, Gay Quisenberry.

Angry words were hurled back and forth, and Rich stormed out the door. Early the following morning, Gay was awakened from a sound sleep by the loud buzz of a motor outside her house.

Groggily, she looked out the window and saw Rich mowing her lawn!

Citation: Brennan Manning in forward to Rich Mullins: His Life and Legacy *by James Bryan Smith (Broadman & Holman, 2000), p. xi; submitted by Clark Cothern; Tecumseh, Michigan*

REDEMPTION

PEARL HARBOR VILLAIN BECOMES EVANGELIST

Matthew 5:9; 1 Timothy 1:12-17; 2 Peter 3:9

Bible; Conversions; Evangelism; Fasting; Forgiveness; Gospel; Grace; Missions; Peacemakers; Reconciliation; Redemption; Regret; Salvation and Lostness; War

In the *Christian History* Online Newsletter, editor Elesha Coffman writes:

America's latest blockbuster, *Pearl Harbor*, has already been blamed for dwelling on a shallow love triangle, ignoring the sacrifices of Japanese Americans, downplaying the Japanese empire's aggression, and generally Disney-fying the "date which will live in infamy." No surprises there; as director Michael Bay told Reuters, "It's not a history lesson." But it's far too easy to shoot holes in Hollywood history. Instead, I'm going to fault the movie for missing a poignant and inspiring Christian story: the saga of Mitsuo Fuchida.

Fuchida grew up loving his native Japan and hating the United States, which treated Asian immigrants harshly in the first half of the twentieth century. Fuchida attended a military academy, joined Japan's Naval Air Force, and by 1941, with 10,000 flying hours behind him, had established himself as the nation's top pilot. When Japanese military leaders needed someone to command a surprise attack on Pearl Harbor, they chose Fuchida.

Fuchida's was the voice that sent his aircraft carrier the message "Tora! Tora! Tora!" (Tiger! Tiger! Tiger!) indicating the success of the surprise mission. Later, he too was surprised when he learned that, of the 70 officers who participated in the raid, he was the only one who returned alive. He had another close call when he was shot down during the battle of Midway in 1942, but despite serious injuries, he survived again.

By 1945 he had attained the position of the Imperial Navy's Air Operations Officer. On August 6 he was eating breakfast in Nara, Japan, where a new military headquarters was under construction, when he heard about a bomb dropped on Hiroshima. He flew to investigate, then sent a grim report to the Imperial Command.

On the same day, an American POW named Jacob DeShazer felt moved by the Holy Spirit to pray for peace. DeShazer had been in captivity since 1942, when, as a member of Doolittle's Raiders, he had dropped bombs near Tokyo and then was forced to parachute into China. While imprisoned, first in Nanjing and later in Beijing, DeShazer had become a Christian. He found his heart softened toward his Japanese captors. After being liberated, DeShazer wrote a widely distributed essay, "I Was a Prisoner of the Japanese," detailing his experiences of capture, conversion, and forgiveness.

Fuchida and DeShazer met in 1950. DeShazer had returned to Japan in 1948 as a missionary. Fuchida had read DeShazer's testimony, bought a Bible, and converted from Buddhism to Christianity. DeShazer had recently finished a 40-day fast for revival in Japan when Fuchida came to his home and introduced himself. DeShazer welcomed the new convert and encouraged him to be baptized. While DeShazer continued to plant churches throughout Japan, Fuchida became an evangelist, spreading a message of peace and forgiveness in his native country and throughout Asian-American communities.

Fuchida died on May 30, 1976. Like dynamite inventor Alfred Nobel, who wished his legacy to be one of peace rather than destruction, Fuchida wanted the message of his changed heart to supersede the memory of his infamous attack. He wrote, "That morning [December 7] . . . I lifted the curtain of warfare by dispatching that cursed order, and I put my whole effort into the war that followed. . . . [But] after buying and reading the Bible, my mind was strongly impressed and captivated. I think I can say today without hesitation that God's grace has been set upon me."

Citation: Elesha Coffman, "Beyond Pearl Harbor," Christian History Online Newsletter (6-01-01); submitted by Kevin Miller; Wheaton, Illinois

REDEMPTION

TEAM PRESIDENT REDEEMS ATHLETE

JOB 19:25; ROMANS 3:24; ROMANS 8:3-4; 1 CORINTHIANS 1:30; 2 CORINTHIANS 5:16-21; EPHESIANS 1:7; COLOSSIANS 1:14

Grace; New Life; New Man; Redeemer; Redemption; Salvation

Lou Johnson, a 1965 World Series hero for the Los Angeles Dodgers, tried for 30 years to recover the championship ring he lost to drug dealers in 1971. Drug and alcohol abuse cost him everything from that magical season, including his uniform, glove, and the bat he used to hit the winning home run in the deciding game.

When Dodger president, Bob Graziano, learned that Johnson's World Series ring was about to be auctioned on the Internet, he immediately wrote a check for $3,457 and bought the ring before any bids were posted. He did for Johnson what the former Dodger outfielder had been unable to do for himself.

Johnson, 66, who has been drug-free for years and a Dodger community relations employee, wept when given the gold ring. He said, "It felt like a piece of me had been reborn."

Countless Christians can testify to a spiritual rebirth as a result of the price that Jesus paid on the cross in their place. He did for them what they could not do for themselves.

Citation: Bill Plaschke, Los Angeles Times (2-10-01); submitted by Rick Kauffman

■

REGRET

TORMENTED OVER SACRIFICIAL DEATH

Romans 5:8; 1 Peter 3:18

Christ, substitute for humanity; Jesus Christ; Regret

Former college football coach and Promise Keepers founder Bill McCartney tells about a man named Ivan who is a Vietnam veteran. Ivan lives in Denver, and his life is in ruins because of something that happened three decades ago.

While in Vietnam, Ivan's squad befriended some Vietnamese village children who would visit the men daily to peddle candy. Ivan became friendly—no, paternal—with a little seven-year-old girl named Kim. He picked her up and whirled her around. He held her on his lap. He told her he loved her.

Then one day Kim was used by the Vietcong as a *kamikaze*. She showed up alone at the soldiers' camp, wired with explosives. But before she got too close, she unbuttoned her blouse to show the soldiers the bomb. It was her way of telling the Americans she would kill them if they allowed her to come any closer. Ivan was one of the men who shot her.

As McCartney puts it, "This guy is in pure torment over what he did that day. He can't receive what Kim offered. His life! She gave her life so he could live."

Citation: Bruce Weber, "Bill McCartney, Away From the Sideline, Brings His Inspirational Message to the Bowery," New York Times (6-20-97); submitted by Rubel Shelly

RELATIONSHIPS

WIFE TAKEN FOR GRANTED TOO LONG

PROVERBS 31:28-31; EPHESIANS 5:25-33

Gratitude; Husbands; Love; Marriage; Relationships; Thankfulness; Wives

A man accompanied his friend home for dinner and was impressed by the way he entered his house, asked his wife how her day went, and told her she looked pretty. Then, after they embraced, she served dinner. After they ate, the husband complimented his wife on the meal and thanked her for it. When the two fellows were alone, the visitor asked, "Why do you treat your wife so well?"

"Because she deserves it, and it makes our marriage happier," replied the host.

Impressed, the visitor decided to adopt the idea. Arriving home, he embraced his wife and said, "You look wonderful!" For good measure he added, "Sweetheart, I'm the luckiest guy in the world."

His wife burst into tears. Bewildered, he asked her, "What in the world's the matter?"

She wept. "What a day! Billy fought at school. The refrigerator quit and spoiled the groceries. And now you've come home drunk!"

Citation: Robert Leslie Holmes, God's Man *(Kregel, 1998)*

RELIGION

STATS ON WORLD RELIGIONS

MATTHEW 13:31-33; MATTHEW 28:19; ACTS 1:8; COLOSSIANS 1:6

Ideologies and Belief Systems; Missions; Religion; Religion, non-Christian

The second edition of the *World Christian Encyclopedia* (Oxford University Press, 2001) reports the following statistical estimates:

Christianity has become the most universal religion in history with believers today composing a majority of the population in two-thirds of the world's 238 countries.

Christianity began and ended the century as the world's biggest religion with 555 million believers or 32.2 percent of world population in 1900 and 1.9 billion or 31 percent as of last year.

Those counted Christians are divided among 33,820 denominations or similar distinct organizations. Some 386 million believers are in independent churches. Apart from the historic Catholic, Orthodox, Anglican, and Protestant branches, Christians counted as belonging to "other" groups have quadrupled since 1970, with huge increases noted among Pentecostal and Charismatic movements.

Islam ranks second worldwide, and during the last century grew from 200 million, or 12.3 percent of the population, to 1.2 billion, or 19.6 percent.

Other current totals: Hinduism, 811 million; Buddhism, 360 million; Sikhism, 23 million; and Judaism, 14 million.

In the United States, while there is considerable disagreement over numbers for non-Christian religions, there are 5.6 million Jews, 4.1 million Muslims (a more than fourfold increase in 30 years), 2.4 million Buddhists, and 1 million Hindus. There are 192 million people in U.S. Christian groups.

Citation: "New Book Tallies Religions," Associated Press (1-17-01); source: World Christian Encyclopedia; submitted by Kevin Miller

■

REPENTANCE

MANY REPENT FOR STEALING

Exodus 20:15; Acts 26:20; Romans 13:9

Bible; Preaching; Repentance; Scripture; Sin, conviction of; Stealing; Ten Commandments; Word of God

In May 2001, English evangelist J. John spoke in Liverpool, England, on one of the Ten Commandments: You shall not steal. The results of the preaching were dramatic. Cedric Pulford writes:

Conscience-stricken people have handed in large quantities of stolen goods, including hotel towels, a bathrobe, and cash, after attending a church rally at which a preacher urged them to repent.

The inventory of pilfered items included hospital crutches, library

236

books, CDs, videotapes—and about $560 [U.S.]. There were also several letters of confession.

The items were left in large special containers at the Anglican cathedral in Liverpool, northern England, after May 15 when a congregation of 3,000 heard renowned preacher J. John speak at the cathedral on the Eighth Commandment: "Thou shalt not steal."

John, 43, has been preaching on the Ten Commandments in a series of meetings in Liverpool. . . .

John said goods are commonly handed in after his meetings, with stolen items ranging from computers to shovels.

"Stealing any item, however small, is wrong. The commandment doesn't say, 'Don't steal over one pound [sterling] at a time,' " John said.

"A man who is now a vicar took towels from the Wimbledon tennis championships years ago when he was working there. He kept them all these years and has now returned them."

Citation: Cedric Pulford, "Repentant Pilferers Return Hotel Towels and Cash after Sermon on Theft," ENI (6-12-01); submitted by Kevin Miller, vice president, Christianity Today International

■

RESENTMENT

RESENTFUL HUSBAND RETREATS

Matthew 18:15-35; Ephesians 5:22-33; Colossians 3:18-19

Anger; Bitterness; Forgiveness; Gratitude; Husbands; Ingratitude; Marriage; Relationships; Resentment; Wives

I collect old newspapers. I was humored by a story in a 1930s edition of the *Chicago Herald Examiner* about a husband and a wife. The article, "Man Spites His Wife by Staying Blindfolded in Bed Seven Years," reads:

The strange story of Harry Havens of Indiana, who went to bed—and stayed there—for seven years with a blindfold over his eyes because he was peeved at his wife, was revealed here today when he decided to get out of bed. Havens was the kind of husband who liked to help around the house—hang pictures, wipe the dishes, and such. His wife scolded him for the way he was performing one of these tasks, and he resented it. He is reported to have said: "All right. If that's the way you feel, I'm going to bed. I'm going to stay there the rest of my life. And I don't want to see you or anyone else again." His last remark explains the blindfold. He got up, he explained, when the bed started to feel uncomfortable after seven years.

Citation: Van Morris; Mount Washington, Kentucky; source: Chicago Herald Examiner (11-17-1930)

■

RESOURCEFULNESS
RESOURCEFUL STEWARDSHIP
MATTHEW 10:16; MATTHEW 25:14-30
Money; Resourcefulness; Stewardship; Wisdom

Before going to Europe on business, a certain man drove his Rolls-Royce to a downtown New York City bank and went in to ask for an immediate loan of $5,000. The loan officer, taken aback, requested collateral. The man replied, "Well then, here are the keys to my Rolls-Royce."

The loan officer promptly had the car driven into the bank's underground parking for safekeeping and gave him $5,000.

Two weeks later, the man walked through the bank's doors and asked to settle up his loan and get his car back. "That will be $5,000 in principal, and $15.40 in interest," the loan officer said. The man wrote out a check, got up, and started to walk away.

"Wait sir," the loan officer said. "While you were gone, I found out you're a millionaire. Why in the world would you need to borrow $5,000?"

The man smiled. "Where else could I safely park my Rolls-Royce in Manhattan for two weeks for only $15.40?"

Citation: Adapted from a commercial; submitted by Michael Herman; Glen Ellyn, Illinois

RESPONSIBILITY

I DON'T WANT FAMILY

EPHESIANS 5:22-33

Family; Marriage; Responsibility

When my youngest sister Dorothy and her boyfriend, Sonny, both 19 years old, decided they wanted to get married, they approached my no-nonsense father with the news.

"You're mighty young to be taking on a family," he said to my future brother-in-law.

"But I don't want the whole family," protested Sonny. "I just want to marry Dorothy."

Citation: Ruth A. Walton; Barron, Wisconsin; "Lite Fare," Christian Reader
(May/June 2000)

REST

REST IS PRODUCTIVE, TOO

EXODUS 20:8-11; PSALM 127:1-2

Energy; Preparation; Rest; Sabbath; Success; Work

The story is told of two men who had the tiring job of clearing a field of trees. The contract called for them to be paid per tree.

Bill wanted the day to be profitable, so he grunted and sweated, swinging the axe relentlessly. Ed, on the other hand, seemed to be working about half as fast. He even took a rest and sat off to the side for a few minutes. Bill kept chopping away until every muscle and tendon in his body was screaming.

At the end of the day, Bill was terribly sore, but Ed was smiling and telling jokes. Amazingly, Ed had cut down more trees! Bill said, "I noticed you sitting while I worked without a break. How'd you outwork me?"

Ed smiled. "Did you notice I was sharpening my axe while I was sitting?"

Citation: Stand Firm *(June 2000), p.13; submitted by Bonne Steffen; Wheaton, Illinois*

RESTITUTION

SHOPLIFTER COMES CLEAN ... ALMOST

Exodus 20:15; Matthew 6:24; Ephesians 4:28

Confession; Conscience; Guilt; Honesty; Integrity; Repentance; Restitution; Sleep; Stealing

The story is told of a shoplifter who writes to a department store and says, "I've just become a Christian, and I can't sleep at night because I feel guilty. So here's $100 that I owe you."

Then he signs his name, and in a little postscript at the bottom he adds, "If I still can't sleep, I'll send you the rest."

Citation: Bill White; Paramount, California

RESURRECTION OF CHRIST

PROOF OF THE RESURRECTION

Acts 1:3; 1 Corinthians 15

Christ, resurrection of; Easter; Jesus Christ; Resurrection; Resurrection of Christ

Science says if there is any such thing as infallible proof, it is the repetition of the same experiment.

Jesus rose from the dead, and Mary Magdalene encountered him—experiment one. The women encountered him—experiment two. The disciples encountered him—experiment three. The apostles encountered him—experiment four. Five hundred people saw him after the Resurrection—experiment five.

Each one of these is the repetition of the same experiment. They all encountered the same phenomenon. What was it? He was alive! That's what changed the history of the world.

Citation: Walter Martin and Jill Martin Rische, Through the Windows of Heaven *(Broadman & Holman, 1999)*

REVENGE

NEIGHBORLY FEUDS

Romans 12:17-21; Romans 13:10; James 2:8
Anger; Bitterness; Conflict; Hate; Neighbors; Revenge

It all started in 1998 when Michael Zwick of Glenview, Illinois, complained about his neighbor's new fence. It left a dark area behind the garage where gang members might hang out, he felt. In response to his complaint, the neighbor, Jean Craft, according to the *Chicago Tribune*, told Zwick not to put his recycling bins on the public parkway in front of her house because they were killing the grass.

In retaliation, Zwick "blew leaves back onto her property, let his weeds grow 12 inches high, and aimed a fake security camera at her yard." Then she "moved his recycling bins, complained to police about snow plowed onto her land and bought new shades and draperies to cover her windows."

The village of Glenview finally wrote an ordinance that prohibited Zwick from putting his recycling bins close to his neighbor's house. Zwick defies the ordinance and has been given 10 citations and charged $1,000 in fines. The case has now gone to Cook County court.

Says Zwick, "We're digging in."

Citation: Kevin Miller; Wheaton, Illinois; source: Lisa Black, "Glenview Neighbors Recycle Feud from Fence to Weeds to Bins on Parkway," Chicago Tribune *(6-04-01)*

REWARDS

WORLD'S EMPTY PROMISES

Matthew 6:18; Philippians 3:7-14; Hebrews 6:10; Hebrews 11:26; James 1:12
Disappointments; Glory; God, faithfulness of; Hope; Promises; Rewards; Success

When I was a senior in high school, I was voted co-captain and most improved player on the basketball team. At the annual sports assembly I was called forward in front of the entire student body and presented with two trophies, one for each award. It was a day of great pride for me, and I have kept those two tiny trophies for over 30 years. Last year I drove back to my hometown for a 30-year reunion of our school's first football team. I arrived early, so I walked through the old high school to see what it looked like after three decades. I found the lobby where the sports awards are displayed and looked for the two plaques where my name would be inscribed in honor of my awards.

I found both plaques. And I found that in both cases, the name of one of my teammates had been substituted where my name belonged. Now, I'm certain that I won the awards. I remember receiving the awards. I still have the two trophies at home. But my name was not on the plaques where it belonged. My promised "glory" had been stolen from me.

In this sinful world we are often promised rewards that are not delivered to us. We are foolish to place our ultimate hope on any worldly promise of reward. Only our Father in heaven can be trusted to deliver on his promises.

Citation: David Gibson; Idaho Falls, Idaho

■

RICHES

RICHES OBSCURE NEED OF HEAVEN

Luke 23:39-43; 1 Corinthians 15:19; 2 Corinthians 4:16-18; 2 Corinthians 5:1-5; Revelation 21:1-27

Eternal Life; Heaven; Money; Riches; Wealth

For his first sermon in an elementary preaching class, Lawrence, an African student, chose a text describing the joys we'll share when Christ returns and ushers us to our heavenly home.

"I've been in the United States for several months now," he began. "I've seen the great wealth that is here—the fine homes and cars and clothes. I've listened to many sermons in churches here, too. But I've yet to hear one sermon about heaven. Because everyone has so much in this country, no one preaches about heaven. People here don't seem to need it. In my country most people have very little, so we preach on heaven all the time. We know how much we need it."

Citation: Bryan Chapell, The Wonder of It All *(Crossway, 1999); quoted in* Men of Integrity *(January/February 2001)*

RICHES

WEALTH DOESN'T BRING CONTENTMENT

PSALM 49; ECCLESIASTES 5:10-12; 2 CORINTHIANS 6:10; PHILIPPIANS 4:11-13

Contentment; Joy; Materialism; Meaning of Life; Money; Riches

In his autobiography *Just As I Am,* Billy Graham recalls a story demonstrating that true greatness is not defined by wealth or fame, but by character:

Some years ago Ruth and I had a vivid illustration of this on an island in the Caribbean. One of the wealthiest men in the world had asked us to come to his lavish home for lunch. He was 75 years old, and throughout the entire meal he seemed close to tears. "I am the most miserable man in the world," he said. "Out there is my yacht. I can go anywhere I want to. I have my private plane, my helicopters. I have everything I want to make my life happy, yet I am as miserable as hell." We talked to him and prayed with him, trying to point him to Christ, who alone gives lasting meaning to life.

Then we went down the hill to a small cottage where we were staying. That afternoon the pastor of the local Baptist church came to call. He was an Englishman, and he, too, was 75—a widower who spent most of his time taking care of his two invalid sisters. He was full of enthusiasm and love for Christ and others. "I don't have two pounds to my name," he said with a smile, "but I am the happiest man on this island."

Billy Graham relates how he asked his wife Ruth after they left, "Who do you think is the richer man?" She didn't have to reply because they both already knew the answer.

Citation: Billy Graham, Just As I Am (HarperCollins, 1999); submitted by David Holdaway; Stonehaven, Kincardinshire, Scotland

S

SACRIFICE

SACRIFICE WITHOUT REGRET

JOHN 15:13; PHILIPPIANS 2:6-8; PHILIPPIANS 3:7-8
Commitment; Humility; Regret; Sacrifice; Service

When Pearl Harbor was bombed, one of the Americans who volunteered to serve his country was Bob Feller. Bob was a 23-year-old pitcher for the Cleveland Indians, a phenomenon who had already pitched a no-hitter and won 107 games in the Major Leagues.

Bob was reaching his peak years as an athlete, but he gave up those years to shoot down planes in the Pacific. When he returned to baseball after serving his country, Bob went on to throw three no-hitters, 12 one-hitters, and win 266 games.

But his years of military service—during which he could have won another 80–100 games—cost Bob much of the fame he deserved. When baseball fans elected the All-Century Team in 1999, Bob and his 266 victories were ignored in favor of two other pitchers. Some suggest Feller may be the most underrated baseball player of all time.

Feller was once asked if he regretted his wartime service. "No," he said, "I've made many mistakes in my life. That wasn't one of them."

Citation: Based on "Overrated, Underrated," American Heritage (September 2001) and the Bob Feller Museum Web site; submitted by Kevin A. Miller, vice president, Christianity Today International

SALT

FUNCTION OF SALT

MATTHEW 5:13; MARK 9:50; PHILIPPIANS 2:3-4; PHILIPPIANS 2:20-21

Hypocrisy; Pride; Religion; Salt; Self-centeredness; Selfishness

In *The Journal of Biblical Counseling,* Timothy Keller makes the following observation about salt:

The . . . job of salt was to make something taste good. I don't know about you, but I can't stand corn on the cob without salt on it. When I have eaten a piece of corn on the cob that I really like, I put it down, and what do I say? "That was great salt." No, I say, "That was great corn on the cob." Why? Because the job of the salt is not to make you think how great the salt is, but how great the thing is with which it's involved.

What if you are salt in your small group Bible study? If you're salt, people won't go away saying, "That person really knows the Bible and had all the answers. Showed me up!" No. What happens is when you go away from a small group in which you have been the salt, people don't say how great you were. They say, "What a great group." "What fascinating truth."

This is pretty simple. Salt makes you feel better about life. Christians make you feel better. But religious people always make you feel condemned. They make you feel worse.

Citation: Van Morris; Mount Washington, Kentucky; source: Timothy Keller, The Journal of Biblical Counseling *(Volume 19, Winter 2001)*

SALVATION

RESCUE AT GREAT COST

2 KINGS 6:13-18; PSALM 18:1-19; GALATIANS 2:20; EPHESIANS 1:3-14; 1 PETER 1:18-20

Christ, blood of; Evangelism; God, love of; Great Commission; Redeemer; Redemption; Sacrifice; Salvation; Salvation and Lostness

One of the magnificent 19th-century military expeditions conquered no new lands for Queen Victoria. You won't find it mentioned in history books, but because of the monumental logistics, military historians compare the landing in Ethiopia in 1868 to the Allies' invasion of France in 1944.

For four years Emperor Theodore III of Ethiopia had held a group of 53 European captives (30 adults and 23 children), including some missionaries and a British consul, in a remote 9,000-foot-high bastion deep in the interior. By letter, Queen Victoria pleaded in vain with Theodore to release the captives. Finally, the government ordered a full-scale military expedition from India to march into Ethiopia—not to conquer the country and make it a British colony, but simply to rescue a tiny band of civilians.

The invasion force included 32,000 men, heavy artillery, and 44 elephants to carry the guns. Provisions included 50,000 tons of beef and pork and 30,000 gallons of rum. Engineers built landing piers, water treatment plants, a railroad, and telegraph line to the interior, plus many bridges. All of this to fight one decisive battle, after which the prisoners were released, and everyone packed up and went home. The British expended millions of pounds to rescue a handful of captives.

Citation: Jim Reapsome, Current Thoughts and Trends (May 1999); submitted by Darren Wride; Hinton, Alberta, Canada

SALVATION AND LOSTNESS
SAVE THE LAMB TO SAVE THE RAM
LUKE 15:4-7; 1 TIMOTHY 2:3-4

Conversion; Lostness; Salvation and Lostness; Savior, Christ only; Sheep; Shepherd

Several years ago we were kneeling on cushions around a long, low dining table in a private hotel suite in Japan. The air was seasoned with celery and leeks and unknown things.

Through a missionary interpreter, an important Japanese industrialist was addressing my husband: "I have come to this city and invited you to join our family at dinner so that I might ask you a question. During the past year my son has become a Christian. I admit that he was rebellious and hard to handle, and now he is a respectful, good boy. But as you know, Christians in Japan are a very small minority and are looked down upon as being low-class, disloyal to family and to country.

"There are so many sons in Japan. Why would this have to happen to *my* son—to *me?*"

God suddenly gave the translating missionary a parable. He said, "Suppose a shepherd wanted to take his flock to better pastures. But the way was across a raging stream, and one ram was particularly frightened and refused to budge. How would he get that dear sheep to make the trip? Why, he would take his lamb, his precious lamb, and put it on the other side first."

A tear ran down the father's cheek. "Ah, so," he said.

Citation: Anne Ortlund, Up with Worship *(Broadman & Holman, 2001); Drew Zahn; Sandwich, Illinois*

SALVATION AND LOSTNESS

WANDERING FROM GOD'S HOUSE

Psalm 91:14; Luke 15:3-7; Luke 15:11-32

Backsliding; Children; Christ, as shepherd; Coldness; Healing; Motherhood; Parenting; Pursuing Sinners; Redeemer; Redemption; Repentance; Rescue; Restoration; Salvation and Lostness; Sin

On February 24, 2001, a one-year old Canadian girl named Erika somehow wandered out of her mother's bed and house, and spent the entire night in the Edmonton winter.

When her mother, Leyla Nordby, found her, Erika appeared to be totally frozen. Her legs were stiff, her body frozen, and all signs of life appeared to be gone.

Erika was treated at Edmonton's Stollery Children's Health Center, and God helped doctors and rescue workers bring her back to life. To the amazement of all, there appeared to be no sign of brain damage, and doctors gave Erika a clear prognosis—she would soon be able to hop and skip and play like other girls her age.

Some of us have wandered away from our Father's house, and it has brought us near the point of death. Our hearts have hardened, and our spiritual bodies look as lifeless as the little girl in the snow.

But our Father noticed we were missing and is searching for us. He can take our lifeless spirits and restore us to health. Let the Father pick you up and take you back to his house.

Citation: David Duncan; Edmond, Oklahoma; source: Bob McKeown, "A Tiny Survivor," from the television program Dateline, MSNBC (3-20-01)

SANCTIFICATION

HOW GOD'S CHILDREN CHANGE

ROMANS 7:24-25; ROMANS 8:1-5; 2 CORINTHIANS 6:14-18; 2 CORINTHIANS 7:1;
PHILIPPIANS 3:7-15

Adoption; Change; Children of God; Holiness; Sanctification; Spiritual Formation

When I was a child, my minister father brought home a 12-year-old boy named Roger, whose parents had died from a drug overdose. There was no one to care for Roger, so my folks decided they'd just raise him as if he were one of their own sons.

At first it was quite difficult for Roger to adjust to his new home—an environment free of heroine-addicted adults! Every day, several times a day, I heard my parents saying to Roger:

"No, no. That's not how we behave in this family."

"No, no. You don't have to scream or fight or hurt other people to get what you want."

"No, no, Roger, we expect you to show respect in this family."

And in time Roger began to change.

Now, did Roger have to make all those changes in order to become a part of the family? No. He was made a part of the family simply by the grace of my father. But did he then have to do a lot of hard work because he was in the family? You bet he did. It was tough for him to change, and he had to work at it. But he was motivated by gratitude for the incredible love he had received.

Do you have a lot of hard work to do now that the Spirit has adopted you into God's family? Certainly. But not in order to become a son or a daughter of the heavenly Father. No, you make those changes because you are a son or daughter. And every time you start to revert back to the old addictions to sin, the Holy Spirit will say to you, "No, no. That's not how we act in this family."

Citation: Craig Barnes, author and pastor of National Presbyterian Church; Washington, D.C.; from sermon "The Blessed Trinity" (5-30-99)

SANCTIFICATION

PERFECTION IS POSSIBLE

MATTHEW 5:48; PHILIPPIANS 1:6

Christian Life; Holiness; Perfection; Sanctification

The command "be ye perfect" is not idealistic gas. Nor is it a command to do the impossible. He is going to make us into creatures that can obey that command.

Citation: C. S. Lewis, quoted in "Reflections," Christianity Today (8-21-00)

SATAN

SATAN: APPEARANCES ARE DECEIVING

GENESIS 3:1-7; JOHN 8:44; 2 CORINTHIANS 2:11; 2 CORINTHIANS 11:14-15; EPHESIANS 6:10-18; 1 PETER 5:8

Deception; Devil; Evil; Satan; Truth

In a classic *Twilight Zone* episode from 1960, an American on a walking trip through central Europe gets caught in a raging storm. Staggering through the blinding rain, he chances upon an imposing medieval castle. It is a hermitage for a brotherhood of monks. The reclusive monks reluctantly take him in.

Later that night, the American discovers a cell with a man locked inside. An ancient wooden staff bolts the door. The prisoner claims he's being held captive by the "insane" head monk, Brother Jerome. He pleads for the American to release him.

The prisoner's kindly face and gentle voice win him over. The American confronts Brother Jerome, who declares that the prisoner is actually none other than Satan, "the father of lies," held captive by the Staff of Truth, the one barrier he cannot pass.

This incredible claim convinces the American that Jerome is indeed mad. As soon as he gets the chance, he releases the prisoner—who immediately transforms into a hideous, horned demon and vanishes in a puff of smoke!

The stunned American is horrified at the realization of what he has done. Jerome responds sympathetically. "I'm sorry for you, my son. All your life you will remember this night and whom you have turned loose upon the world."

"I didn't believe you," the American replies. "I saw him and didn't recognize him"—to which Jerome solemnly observes, "That is man's weakness . . . and Satan's strength."

Citation: Kevin Stump, "Is the Devil Dead?" The Plain Truth (March/April 2001)

SECOND COMING

ADVENT: A FORESHADOW OF GOOD

LUKE 2

Advent; Birth of Christ; Christmas; Jesus Christ; Last Things; Second Coming of Christ

Theologian Dale Bruner writes:

David Peterson, former pastor at the First Presbyterian Church in Spokane, Washington, told about a time when he was preparing his sermon. His little daughter came in and said, "Daddy, can we play?"

He answered, "I'm awfully sorry, sweetheart, but I'm right in the middle of preparing this sermon. In about an hour I can play."

She said, "Okay, when you're finished, Daddy, I am going to give you a great big hug."

He said, "Thank you very much." She went to the door and (these are his words) "then she did a U-turn and came back and gave me a chiropractic, bone-breaking hug." David said to her, "Darling, you said you were *going* to give me a hug *after* I finished."

She answered, "Daddy, I just wanted you to know what you have to look forward to!"

One meaning of Christmas is that God wants us to know, through this First Coming, how much we have to look forward to in the great Second Coming.

Citation: Dale Bruner, "Is Jesus Inclusive or Exclusive?" Theology, News, and Notes (October 1999), p. 3

GOLD DOESN'T SAVE

Psalm 49:1-20; Matthew 13:22-23; Hebrews 5:9

Christ, only Savior; Dependence on God; Luck; Materialism; Money; Salvation; Security; Security in God; Trust; Wealth

Lt. George Dixon was a genteel, well-respected man in the Confederate army. In the early days of the war, his fiancée gave him a $20 gold piece. During the battle of Shiloh, a Union minié ball struck him—actually it struck the gold coin, which saved his life. The coin, soundly dented, was to remain with him wherever he went. It became his good luck piece, and he would often be seen kneading the coin in his hand.

And where did Lt. Dixon take the coin? Onto the CSS *Hunley*, the Confederate submarine he staunchly believed could break the Union blockade. After sinking the USS *Housatonic*, the *Hunley* herself sank, taking Lt. Dixon and his crew to their deaths. Ultimately, his golden good luck piece could not save him. Recently the coin was found when the submarine was raised.

Man seeks out and trusts in many forms of security. Ultimately there is only one source of life and security: Jesus.

Citation: "Scientists Find Gold Coin in Confederate Sub," CNN.com; submitted by Len Sullivan; Tupelo, Mississippi

HANDLING LIFE'S PRESSURES

Psalm 16:8; Psalm 62:2-6; Proverbs 10:25; Isaiah 28:16-17; Matthew 7:24-27

Commitment; Faith; Pressure; Security; Trials; Trouble; Trust

I got a ticket for speeding and had to go to traffic school. In the defensive-driving part, they created a scenario: "You're stopped at a stop sign. You look in your rearview mirror and see a car careening toward you that you realize is going to rear-end you. What should you do?"

Almost everybody in the class said you should keep your feet off the brake, so that when that car hits you, you would go forward, absorbing some of the shock.

That was the wrong answer!

We were told: Put your brake on as tight as you can and brace yourself for that collision. If your car is rigid and braced—if it's on its foundation, in other words—then when that horizontal pressure hits, there will be less damage to your car and to the occupants. If your car is not braked, you get the whiplash effect.

I thought to myself, *What our Lord has said is that when our lives are anchored into the rock—when we have found his faithfulness and his love, and we have made that the foundation of our life—then we're better able to handle the horizontal pressures of life.*

Citation: *Earl Palmer,* Preaching Today #26

SELF-IMAGE

ONE HOT PAPA

PSALM 127:3-5; PROVERBS 15:33

Aging; Appearance; Body, human; Family; Fatherhood; Fathers; Maturity; Men; Self-image; Significance

Pastor Ben Patterson writes on the satisfaction of being a father:

Blythe is a desert town on the Arizona-California border. My family and I were on our way back home from vacation when we stopped at a McDonald's in Blythe. Lauretta, my wife, asked me to hold Mary, our eighteen-month-old, while she went to the rest room and our three sons romped in the play area.

Picture me holding my daughter, a few feet from the rest-room doors, as "The Babe from Blythe" emerged from behind those doors. She was gorgeous—tanned and dressed as, well, as young women are wont to dress in warm desert climates.

And she was looking right at me, smiling warmly! I straightened up and smiled back, flush with the adolescent conceit that even though I was much older than she was, I must still be a very attractive man. Babes still take notice!

Our smiles and eyes met for longer than a mere random encounter as she walked past. Then I noticed my reflection in the mirror along the wall and saw who she was smiling at. It was me, all right, but it wasn't Ben Patterson the Mature Hunk. It was Ben Patterson, Mary's Daddy. He was middle-aged, a little lumpy, and holding a precious child. That's what delighted The Babe.

My first reaction was embarrassment. *Silly fool, you aren't what you thought you were!*

But as I continued to look in the mirror, I decided I liked what I saw there more than I liked what I first thought The Babe saw. I like being Mary's Daddy. I like it a lot. Ditto for Dan and Joel and Andy. It's better to be a daddy than a stud. My deflation turned into elation.

Citation: Ben Patterson, "Heart and Soul," Leadership (Spring, 2001)

SELF-SACRIFICE

GIVING HOPE AND LIFE AWAY

Isaiah 50:6-7; Luke 23:44-47; Philippians 2:5-11

Christ, death of; Cross; Jesus Christ; Love; Salvation and Lostness; Self-sacrifice; Unselfishness

If you travel up I-395 through Washington, D.C., and cross over the Potomac, you will likely cross the Arland D. Williams Jr. Memorial Bridge. Who was Arland D. Williams Jr.?

On January 13, 1982, he gave hope to five individuals at the cost of his own life. On that cold January day, Air Florida Flight 90 crashed into the icy Potomac. Ice on the wings prevented the plane from a successful takeoff. Almost all of the passengers perished.

Five different times, a helicopter dropped a rope to save Williams. Five times, Williams passed the rope to other passengers in worse shape than he was. When the rope was extended to Williams the sixth time, he could not take hold and succumbed to the frigid waters.

His heroism was not rash. Aware that his own strength was fading, he deliberately handed hope to someone else over the space of several minutes.

Jesus did not make a rash decision to give his life for ours. That Jesus would be an atoning sacrifice for us was his destiny from eternity past. We need only take the lifeline handed to us by his sacrificial death on the cross.

Citation: David A. Slagle; Lawrenceville, Georgia; source: "A Hero-Passenger Aids Others, Then Dies," Washington Post (1-14-82)

■

SELF-SACRIFICE

POW DIES FOR FRIENDS

JOHN 13:34-35; JOHN 15:13
Bible; Church; Community; Courage; Love; Relationships; Self-sacrifice

In his moving book, *Miracle on the River Kwai,* Ernest Gordon tells his story of life as a Japanese prisoner of war among the men building the infamous Burma Railway. They endured horrific conditions with what seemed to be no hope or purpose to life.

A few Christians, however, formed Bible study groups, which began to bring about amazing transformations within the camps. POWs who had stolen and cheated from one another became men who cared for and gave their lives for their friends. Those death camps became places of hope and life because God's Word was at work.

Gordon recounts:

During one work detail a shovel went missing, and the Japanese guard shouted, insisting someone had stolen it. Striding up and down before the men, he ranted and denounced them for their wickedness, working himself up into a paranoid fury. Screaming in broken English, he demanded that the guilty one step forward to take his punishment. No one moved; the guard's rage reached new heights of violence. "All die! All die!" he shrieked. To show that he meant what he said, he cocked his rifle, put it to his shoulder, and looked down the gun sights, ready to fire at the first man at the end of the line.

At that moment one of the men stepped forward, stood stiffly to attention, and said calmly, "I did it."

The guard unleashed all his whipped-up hatred—he kicked the helpless prisoner and beat him with his fists. Seizing the rifle by the barrel, he lifted it high over his head and, with a final howl, brought it down on the prisoner's skull, who sank limply to the ground and did not move. The men of the work detail picked up their comrade's body, shouldered their tools, and marched back to the camp. When the tools were counted again at the guardhouse, no shovel was missing.

Gordon later completed theological training and became Dean of the Chapel of Princeton University.

Citation: Ernest Gordon, Miracle on the River Kwai *(Collins, 1963), p. 88; submitted by David Holdaway; Stonehaven, Kincardinshire, Scotland*

■

SERVANTHOOD
SERVANTHOOD BEGINS WHEN GRATITUDE ENDS

PROVERBS 16:2; MATTHEW 20:20-28; MATTHEW 25:14-46; JOHN 13:1-17; 1 CORINTHIANS 4:5; PHILIPPIANS 2:6-8; 1 THESSALONIANS 2:3

Church; Ingratitude; Ministry; Motives; Servanthood; Service; Service, motivation for; Service, reward for

Timothy Keller, pastor of Redeemer Presbyterian Church in New York, writes:

Pastors often hear, "I work my fingers to the bone in this church, and what thanks do I get?" Is that the way it is? Your service was for thanks? Are you in your right mind? Servanthood begins where gratitude and applause end.

Citation: Timothy Keller, Ministries of Mercy *(Presbyterian & Reformed Publishing, 1997), p. 139; submitted by Aaron Goerner; New Hartford, New York*

■

SERVICE
GOD VALUES ALL SERVICE

MATTHEW 6:1-4; MATTHEW 20:25-28; 1 CORINTHIANS 15:58; COLOSSIANS 3:23-24

Christian Life; Ministry; Servanthood; Service; Work

There are no such things as prominent service and obscure service; it is all the same with God.

Citation: Oswald Chambers, So Send I You *(Discovery House, 1993); submitted by Kevin Miller, vice president, Resources, Christianity Today International*

SERVICE, FAITHFUL

FINISHING WORK ON EARTH

John 9:4; John 17:4; Colossians 4:17; 2 Timothy 4:7-8

Duty; Heaven; Ministry; Perseverance; Responsibility; Servanthood; Service, faithful; Work

Recently I glimpsed the glory of finishing a task well. At Arlington National Cemetery, I saw the changing of the guard at the Tomb of the Unknowns. I had watched that ceremony several times before, always moved by its solemnity and precision.

This time, however, I witnessed something new. When the changing of the guard was completed, the commanding officer asked us to remain standing in silence. Sergeant Jennings had completed 27 months of this special duty and wanted now to pay his respect to the unknown soldiers. A guard escorted Jennings' family to a place of honor.

The commanding officer handed Jennings four roses. Jennings approached the great Tomb of the Unknown Soldier from the First World War, knelt, and placed a rose before it. Then he moved with solemn dignity to the tombs honoring unknown soldiers from the Second World War, and the wars in Korea and Vietnam, kneeling to place one red rose upon each. He returned to his commanding officer and stood before him. At attention, with their eyes locked, they shook hands. Then Sergeant Jennings carefully removed his white gloves and returned them, his work finished. He saluted his officer, greeted his family, and left.

With tears running down my face I thought of standing before my Lord Jesus someday, taking off my gloves and handing them to him.

Citation: Harry J. Heintz; Troy, New York

SEX

MARRIEDS HAVE BETTER SEX

1 Corinthians 6:15-20; 1 Corinthians 7:3-5

Commitment; Family; Marriage; Pleasure, good; Sex

Married people have better sex lives than single people. Indeed, married people are far more likely to have sex lives in the first place. Married people are about twice as likely as unmarried people to make love at least two or three times a week.

And that's not all: Married sex is more fun. Certainly, at least, for men: Forty-eight percent of husbands say sex with their partners is extremely satisfying, compared to just 37 percent of cohabiting men.

When it comes to creating a lasting sexual union, marriage implies at least a promise of permanence, which may be why cohabiting men are four times more likely to cheat, and cohabiting women eight times more likely, than husbands and wives.

Citation: Linda J. Waite and Maggie Gallagher, Talk *(October 2000), p. 155; submitted by Dave Goetz*

SEXUAL IMMORALITY
BILL MAHER ON SEX

Matthew 5:28-30; Romans 1:24-25
Desire, sinful; Lust; Men; Pornography; Selfishness; Sex; Sexual Immorality; Women

On a recent episode of the ABC television talk show *Politically Incorrect,* host Bill Maher was discussing some rules for relationships from the male perspective. With regards to sex he said, "Don't [gripe] about porn."

When the panel (three of whom were women) asked what he meant, he responded, "Unless you [women] are willing to give us sex whenever we want, you don't have the right to gripe if we use pornography."

Surprisingly, all three women agreed that the rule made sense. This rule and response demonstrate the distorted attitude towards sexuality prevalent in our society. Sex is seen as primarily for one's personal physical pleasure. The other person is merely a tool to be used to that end.

Citation: Politically Incorrect, ABC Television (2-15-01); submitted by Rod Reed; Fresno, California

SIN

HEALING FROM SIN

Exodus 20:1-17; Psalm 19:7-11; Ephesians 6:1-3

Commandments; Freedom; God, goodness of; God, love of; Love; Obedience;
Physicians; Sin; Ten Commandments

Last summer I had an encounter with masked men bearing scalpels. A surgeon operated on my foot, and my life was never in danger. Yet the horizontal recovery time did give me a chance to reflect on pain that we choose voluntarily, sometimes for our own good and sometimes to our peril.

While rehabilitating, I often did exercises that hurt because I knew that working through the soreness would allow my foot to regain its usefulness. On the other hand, the surgeon warned against bicycling, mountain climbing, running, and other activities that might endanger the healing process. Basically, anything that sounded fun, he vetoed.

On one visit I tried to talk him into granting me a premature golf match. "Some friends get together once a year. It's important to me. I've been practicing my swing, and if I use only my upper body and keep my legs and hips very still, could I join them?"

Without a flicker of hesitation, my doctor replied, "It would make me very unhappy if you played golf within the next two months."

"I thought you were a golfer," I said, appealing to his sympathies.

"I am. That's how I know you can't swing without rolling that foot inward and putting weight on the parts that are trying to heal."

The point was obvious. My doctor has nothing against my playing golf; as a fellow golfer, he sympathizes with me. But he has my best interests at heart. It will indeed make him unhappy if I do something prematurely that might damage my long-term recovery. He wants me to play golf next year, and the next, and the rest of my life, and for that reason he could not sanction a match too soon after my surgery.

As we talked, I began to appreciate my doctor's odd choice of words. If he had issued an edict—"No golf!"—I might have stubbornly rebelled. He left me the free choice and expressed the consequences in a most personal way: Disobedience would grieve him, for his job was to restore my health.

The role of a doctor may be the most revealing image in thinking about God and sin. What a doctor does for me physically—guides me toward health—God does for me spiritually. I am learning to view sins not as an arbitrary list of rules drawn up by a cranky Judge, but rather as a list of dangers that must be avoided at all costs—for our own sakes.

Citation: Philip Yancey, "Doctor's Orders," Christianity Today (12-6-99)

■

SIN

HOPEFULNESS OF SIN

Psalm 51; Romans 3; James 5:16

Human Condition; Humanity; Reconciliation; Repentance; Sin

Sin is the best news there is . . . because with sin, there's a way out. . . . You can't repent of confusion or psychological flaws inflicted by your parents—you're stuck with them. But you can repent of sin. Sin and repentance are the only grounds for hope and joy, the grounds for reconciled, joyful relationships.

Citation: John Alexander, quoted in Leadership (Summer 2000)

■

SIN

WHY SIN TASTES GOOD

Romans 7:5

Desire; Human Condition; Law; Sin; Sinful Nature; Temptation

Leann Birch, a developmental psychologist at Penn State University, ran an experiment in which she took a large group of kids and fed them a big lunch. Then she turned them loose in a room with lots of junk food.

"What we see is that some kids eat almost nothing," she said. "But other kids really chow down, and one of the things that predicts how much they eat is the extent to which parents have restricted their access to high-fat, high-sugar food in the past: the more the kids have been restricted, the more they eat."

Birch's study also discovered one reason this happened: the children on restricted diets believed the junk food tasted good primarily because they had been told that junk food was bad for them!

This illustrates Paul's insight that the law arouses in us sinful desires (Romans 7:5). It's not only that we break the law because it's trying to control our sinful natures; we convince ourselves that it's really a lot of fun, that it really tastes good—even when it's making us more spiritually unhealthy, and may even be killing us.

Citation: Mark Galli, managing editor of Christianity Today; *source: Malcolm Gladwell, "The Trouble with Fries: Fast Food Is Killing Us. Can It Be Fixed?"* The New Yorker *(3-5-01)*

SINNER

SIN ISN'T POLITICALLY CORRECT

LUKE 12:2-13; ROMANS 3:23; 1 JOHN 5:17
Sin; Sin, avoidance of; Sinful Nature; Sinner

Four congregation members with concerned faces met in their pastor's office. With earnest and imploring eyes, they presented him with a clip-board filled with sheets of signatures.

"This petition," said the spokesperson of the group, "requests changing the term 'sinner' to 'person who is morally challenged.' "

Citation: From an original cartoon by Dan Pegoda, The Best Cartoons from Leadership Journal, *Volume 1 (Broadman & Holman, 1999)*

SMALL THINGS

SMALL CHANGES NET BIG REWARDS

MATTHEW 10:42; MATTHEW 12:36-37; MATTHEW 25:21; 2 CORINTHIANS 7:1
Christian Life; Lent; Money; Small Things; Spiritual Disciplines; Spiritual Formation; Stewardship

Just by making a few small changes in your life, you can really make a big difference in your savings and retirement," says Bryan Olson of the Schwab Center for Investment Research.

As 2000 was drawing to a close, the center released results of a recent study that showed giving up potato chips with lunch could save $176.80 a year and generate retirement savings of $10,483.62 in 20 years, assuming a 10 percent return. The same principle was illustrated with a number of other common indulgences.

Giving up two doughnuts a week could boost your nest egg by $6,552.26 in two decades. Switch from double latte with whipped cream to regular coffee, and you could save $429 per year—a whopping $27,028.07 at 10 percent over 20 years.

Dropping the potato chips would also eliminate close to 10,000 calories per year. Suppose you eat a bagel with cream cheese three times a week. Just by skipping the cream cheese, you would toss 54,000 calories a year from your diet and save $117—or $7,371.29—over a 20-year investment period.

Olson released these facts to underscore one of the oldest investment maxims in his industry: Regular investments, even in small amounts, will make a big difference in savings and retirement.

All the positive steps you take, even the smallest ones, make a significant difference over time.

Citation: Reuters News Service and CNN; submitted by Rubel Shelly; Nashville, Tennessee

SOWING AND REAPING

SUCCESS AFTER DISCOURAGEMENT

1 Chronicles 28:20; Psalm 31:9-24; 1 Corinthians 15:58; Galatians 6:9-10

Circumstances and Faith; Despair; Discouragement; Endurance; Evangelism; Fruitfulness; Harvest; Ministry; Missions; Outreach; Perseverance; Soul Winners; Sowing and Reaping

My heart is sunk. . . . It seemed to me I should never have any success among the Indians. My soul was weary of my life; I longed for death, beyond measure."

So wrote David Brainerd, describing his early weeks as a missionary to Native Americans at the beginning of the 1700s. Things didn't improve much for the first two years, in fact. He felt his prospects of winning converts "as dark as midnight."

Three years into the work, though, he finally witnessed a revival among the Indians of Crossweesung in New England, and after another year and a half, the number of converts numbered 150—not much by today's mass evangelistic standards, but profoundly significant in his day. Unfortunately, Brainerd died after only five years on the mission field, at age 29.

After Brainerd's death, Jonathan Edwards—whom some consider America's greatest theologian—published Brainerd's journals. These were read widely in America and Europe. In fact, William Carey, the "father of modern missions," the man who ignited the modern Protestant missionary movement, which has been responsible for millions upon millions of conversions worldwide, pointed to Brainerd's journals as a key source of his inspiration to take up the missionary life.

Who, then, can judge whether our work is worthwhile? Certainly we cannot when we're in the midst of discouragement.

Citation: Ruth Tucker, From Jerusalem to Irian Jaya: A Biographical History of Christian Missions *(Zondervan, 1983), pp. 90-93; submitted by Mark Galli, managing editor of* Christianity Today

---

SPIRITUAL DISCIPLINES
NEGLECTING PRAYER

LUKE 18:1; COLOSSIANS 4:2; 1 THESSALONIANS 5:17
Accountability; Community; Devotional Life; Meditation; Prayer; Seeking God; Spiritual Disciplines

In one area of Africa where Christianity began to spread, converts were zealous about daily devotions. They would find their own spot within the wild thickets and pour their hearts out to God. After some time the spots became well-worn, and paths were created. Soon, one's prayer life was made public. If someone began to neglect his or her devotional life, it would soon be noticed by others. Believers would then gently and lovingly remind those in neglect, "The grass grows on your path."

Citation: Submitted by David DeWitt; source: Today in the Word *(June 1992)*

USING A SHEPHERD BOY

PROVERBS 20:24; ROMANS 9:20-21; PHILIPPIANS 2:12-13

Ability; God, sovereignty of; Ministry; Practice; Preparation; Providence; Service; Shepherd; Spiritual Formation

While traveling in Jordan, *Leadership* journal editor Marshall Shelley noted:

While driving through the countryside and small towns, you're impressed by how many Jordanians spontaneously wave at the bus.

Some of those who waved were shepherd boys. Usually alone, a boy perhaps 12 or 14 years old would be standing near a flock of goats or sheep, often in utterly desolate terrain. I wondered how the animals could find enough vegetation to eat among the rocks.

Toward evening, we'd see a boy leading the flock back to the tent where his Bedouin family lives. What does such a boy do all day? There's not much to do in a rocky wilderness, except look for shade and keep the sheep in view. How does a boy keep himself occupied?

The Bible does provide a clue. One such shepherd boy who grew up not far away, named David, must have spent his time singing songs and throwing rocks. Day after day with the sheep, there would have been lots of time to make up songs. And there certainly was an endless supply of rocks.

Did he ever wonder if he was wasting his time by singing songs and slinging rocks?

Interestingly those two skills, honed by hours of solitary practice while watching sheep, proved crucial in God's plans for him. His musical abilities were put to the service of a king, the tormented King Saul, and calmed him at least briefly. Later, his musical abilities had a more lasting effect as David penned the Psalms that we still sing and recite.

And the rock throwing? That skill, of course, led to David's stunning victory over Goliath. The stone slinger emerged as a national hero. As I traveled the rocky landscape of the Holy Land, I pondered the rocks. They're everywhere! Easy to complain about or overlook. Yet for David, they were the raw material that God used mightily.

Citation: Marshall Shelley, editor, Leadership; *submitted by Kevin Miller, Christianity Today International*

SPIRITUAL GIFTS

CHOSEN TO CLAP AND CHEER

Romans 12:3-8; 1 Corinthians 12:1-31; Ephesians 4:11-16
Encouragement; Ministry; Purpose; Service; Spiritual Gifts; Support

Jamie Scott tried out for the play at his elementary school. He had his heart set on being one of the main characters, but his mother feared he would not be chosen. On the day the parts were awarded to the children, Jamie's mother and a friend went to pick him up, just in case he was terribly disappointed.

When Jamie saw his mother, he rushed up to her, his eyes shining with pride and excitement, and said, "Guess what, Mom. I've been chosen to clap and cheer."

Citation: Anonymous from the Internet; submitted by Brad Estep; St. Petersburg, Florida

SPIRITUALITY

NATURE OF SPIRITUALITY

Acts 17:16-32; Ephesians 2:1-10; Ephesians 6:10-17
Religion; Spiritual Growth; Spirituality

Spirituality is not something on the fringes, an option for those with a particular bent. None of us has a choice. Everyone has to have a spirituality, and everyone does have one, either a life-giving one or a destructive one.

Citation: Ronald Rolheiser, The Holy Longing: The Search for a Christian Spirituality *(Doubleday, 1999); submitted by Ginger McFarland*

SPIRITUAL PERCEPTION

UNKNOWN PERIL IN CULTURE

JOHN 1:4-5

Culture; Humanity; Ignorance; Light; Lostness; Postmodernism; Spiritual Perception; Truth

In *Into Thin Air,* Jon Krakauer tells of his harrowing experience climbing Mt. Everest. On May 10, 1996, Krakauer made it to the top. He paused only for a few minutes before heading down, his muscles exhausted, his limbs frozen, and his brain oxygen-deprived. As he descended, some clouds drifted up and enveloped him. Soon, thunder, lightning, and a snowstorm threatened to disorient him, but he was close enough to base camp number 4 to get to the sheltering tents before the full force of the storm hit.

Four climbers arrived at the summit shortly before Jon and did not have time to get to the camp before darkness. The storm caused them to lose their way. Exhausted and lost, they simply lay down to wait out the night. When they awoke in the morning, they found they had lain down just one step from the 4,000-foot precipice of the South Wall. They had slept the night on the edge of a cliff in the middle of a snowstorm.

Our culture can disorient us with the winds of relativism and the dark-ness of unbelief. Many people are unaware that they sleep on the edge of disaster. The light of the gospel reveals our position and points the way to safety.

Citation: Jeffrey Arthurs; Portland, Oregon

SPIRITUAL PERCEPTION

WHY DOES IT HURT?

MATTHEW 7:1-5; LUKE 12:57; JOHN 7:24; 1 CORINTHIANS 2:12-16

Cause and Effect; Consequences; Discernment; Disease; Judgment; Pain; Self-examination; Sickness; Spiritual Perception

A man went to see his doctor in an acute state of anxiety. "Doctor," he said, "you have to help me. I'm dying. Everywhere I touch it hurts. I touch my head and it hurts. I touch my leg and it hurts. I touch my stomach and it hurts. I touch my chest and it hurts. You have to help me, Doc, everything hurts."

The doctor gave him a complete examination. "Mr. Smith," he said, "I have good news and bad news for you. The good news is you are not dying. The bad news is you have a broken finger."

Citation: David Holdaway; Stonehaven, Kincardinshire, Scotland

SPIRITUAL WARFARE
WE KNOW THE ENEMY'S PLANS

2 CORINTHIANS 2:11; EPHESIANS 6:10-18; 1 TIMOTHY 3:7; 1 PETER 5:8-9

Bible; Deception; Satan; Spiritual Warfare; Temptation

The Battle of Antietam in 1862 lasted for 12 hours and ranks as the bloodiest day of the Civil War, with 10,000 Confederate casualties and even more on the Union side. "At last the sun went down and the battle ended," wrote one historian, "smoke heavy in the air, the twilight quivering with the anguished cries of thousands of wounded men."

Though militarily a draw, the mediocre Union General George McClellan was able to end the brilliant Robert E. Lee's thrust into Maryland, forcing him to retire across the Potomac. How was this possible? Two Union soldiers had found a copy of Lee's battle plans and had delivered them to McClellan before the engagement.

In some respects, we are no match for our adversary, Satan, whose wiles we are told to be wary of. But as with General McClellan, our enemy's plans have fallen into our hands. We know his usual strategies—to entice us with lies, lust, greed, and the like. With such knowledge, given us by God's Word and God's Spirit within, we too can resist the enemy's advances.

Citation: Mark Galli, managing editor of Christianity Today; *source: Thomas Bailey and David Kennedy,* The American Pageant, *ninth edition (D.C. Heath, 1991), pp. 456-457*

MONEY CAN COMPLICATE FAITH

MATTHEW 6:24; 1 TIMOTHY 6:10, 17-19

Generosity; Giving; Greed; Money; Stewardship

Warren Bailey died July 14, 2000, at age 88. He had no family. And he wasn't much of a churchgoing man. To the best of anybody's recollection in the town of St. Mary's, Georgia, Mr. Bailey hadn't been to church in at least 20 years. He did, however, make annual donations of around $100,000 to St. Mary's United Methodist Church—a 350-member congregation with an annual budget of less than $300,000.

It probably wasn't a great shock to the members at St. Mary's that the church was remembered in Mr. Bailey's will. But the amount of the bequest was indeed a shock. There was stunned silence among the assembled parishioners when Rev. Derek McAleer broke the news that the man who owned 49 percent of the region's Camden Telephone Company had left the church $60 million.

"It's all unreal to me," said the pastor. "This is a number that doesn't have any reality." Mr. Bailey's will included no instructions on how the money was to be used, so the church has set up an advisory board to decide how to handle its newfound and unexpected wealth as good stewards.

Rev. McAleer reports that he has been besieged by calls asking for money. And he admits to a worry that greed could consume the congregation. This was his lament: "How do we remain a Christian church?"

Citation: Associated Press (10-30-00); submitted by Rubel Shelly; Nashville, Tennessee

STRESS

OVERWORKED AMERICANS

EXODUS 23:12; MATTHEW 11:28-30; HEBREWS 4:1-11

Busyness; Leisure; Rest; Sabbath; Stress; Success; Time; Work

Percentage of Americans who say they:
  Need more fun: 68

Need a long vacation: 67
Often feel stressed: 66
Feel time is crunched: 60
Want less work, more play: 51
Feel pressured to succeed: 49
Feel overwhelmed: 48

Citation: Lori Joseph and Bob Laird, "Americans Working Too Hard," USA Today Snapshots; source: Hilton Generational Time Survey of 1,220 adults in January 2001

STRESS

PARALYZED BY THINGS TO DO

MATTHEW 22:35-40; LUKE 10:41-42; PHILIPPIANS 3:7-8
Burnout; Priorities; Stress; Work

In a day when so many things and people vie for our attention, we can experience a paralysis of personal energy. John Maxwell explains this "frozen feeling" that can easily overwhelm us:

William H. Hinson tells us why animal trainers carry a stool when they go into a cage of lions. They have their whips, of course, and their pistols are at their sides. But invariably they also carry a stool. Hinson says it is the most important tool of the trainer. He holds the stool by the back and thrusts the legs toward the face of the wild animal. Those who know maintain that the animal tries to focus on all four legs at once. In the attempt to focus on all four, a kind of paralysis overwhelms the animal, and it becomes tame, weak, and disabled because its attention is fragmented.

Citation: John Maxwell; Developing the Leader within You (Thomas Nelson, 1993), p. 31; submitted by Eugene A. Maddox; Interlachen, Florida

SUCCESS
RETIREES' NEEDS

PSALM 71:9; MATTHEW 6:19-21; 1 TIMOTHY 6:6-19

Aging; Family; Finances; Money; Purpose; Relationships; Retirement; Success; Work

Ralph Warner, author of *Get a Life: You Don't Need a Million to Retire Well,* urges that people looking toward retirement think about more than financial matters.

In his interviews of more than fifty contented retirees, Warner "couldn't find a major correlation between retirement success and money. By working a little less you're really investing in yourself, in your family. Money is not the most important factor."

The five factors rated most important to satisfaction in the retirement years are these:

1. Health
2. Interest/engagement with life and new things
3. Friends
4. Family relationships
5. Money

Citation: "A Million Is Nice, but a Life Counts More," U.S. News & World Report (6-04-01), p. 74; submitted by Rubel Shelly; Nashville, Tennessee

SUNDAY SCHOOL
ASSUMING THE WORST

JOSHUA 6:1-20

Blame; Children; Communication; Confusion; Conscience; Guilt; Leadership; Leadership of the Church; Sunday school

A new pastor decided to visit the children's Sunday school. The teacher introduced him and said, "Pastor, this morning we're studying Joshua."

"That's wonderful," said the new pastor, "Let's see what you're learning. Who tore down the walls of Jericho?"

Little Johnny shyly raised hand and offered, "Pastor, I didn't do it."

Taken aback the pastor asked, "Come on, now, who tore down the walls of Jericho?"

The teacher, interrupting, said, "Pastor, little Johnny's a good boy. If he says he didn't do it, I believe he didn't do it."

Flustered, the pastor went to the Sunday school director and related the story to him. The director, looking worried, explained, "Well, sir, we've had some problems with Johnny before. Let me talk to him and see what we can do."

Really bothered now by the answers of the teacher and the director, the new pastor approached the deacons and related the whole story, including the responses of the teacher and the director. A white-haired gentleman thoughtfully stroked his chin and said, "Well, Pastor, I move we just take the money from the general fund to pay for the walls and leave it at that."

Citation: Cregg Puckett; Florence, Mississippi

SURRENDER
CONTINUING UNNECESSARY BATTLE

JOHN 19:30; ROMANS 5:1; 2 CORINTHIANS 5:16-21

Conflict; Mission; Peace; Reconciliation; Salvation and Lostness; Stubbornness; Surrender; Works

On March 10, 1974, Lt. Hiroo Onada was the last World War II Japanese soldier to surrender.

Onada had been left on the island Lubang in the Philippines on December 25, 1944, with the command to "carry on the mission even if Japan surrenders." Four other Japanese soldiers were left on the island as Japan evacuated Lubang. One soldier surrendered in 1950. Another was killed in a skirmish with local police in 1954. Another was killed in 1972. Onada continued his war alone.

All efforts to convince him to surrender or to capture him failed. He ignored messages from loudspeakers announcing Japan's surrender and that Japan was now an ally of the United States. Leaflets were dropped over the jungle begging him to surrender so he could return to Japan. He refused to believe or surrender.

Over the years he lived off the land and raided the fields and gardens of local citizens. He was responsible for killing at least 30 nationals during his 29-year personal war. Almost a half million dollars was spent trying to locate and convince him to surrender. Thirteen thousand men were used to try to locate him.

Finally, on March 10, 1974, almost 30 years after World War II ended, Onada surrendered his rusty sword after receiving a personal command from his former superior officer, who read the terms of the cease-fire order. Onada handed his sword to President Marcos, who pardoned him. The war was over.

Onada was 22 years old when left on the island. He returned a prematurely aged man of 52. Onada stated, "Nothing pleasant happened in the 29 years in the jungle."

Like Onada, many people are fighting a lonely battle against the God who is offering reconciliation and peace.

Citation: Summarized from a 1974 story in Newsweek; *submitted by Syd Brestel; Bend, Oregon*

T

T

TAXES

CHEATING ON TAXES

ROMANS 13:6-7

Deceit; Duty; Honesty; Lying; Responsibility; Taxes

More than 40 percent of Americans approve of cheating on income taxes. Percentage of taxpayers who believe it is okay to:

Claim personal automobile use for business: 21.3

Neglect to report a cash income: 14.5

Write off a vacation as a business expense: 10.7

Report a higher donation to charity than was actually given: 6.2

Citation: Darryl Haralson and Sam Ward, USA Today Snapshots *(4-9-01); source: International Communications Research,* Money *magazine*

■

TEACHERS

JOHN WOODEN'S EXAMPLE

HEBREWS 13:7

Example; Integrity; Leadership; Priorities; Success; Teachers; Teaching; Values; Winning and Losing

[John Wooden's] UCLA teams won ten NCAA championships in 12 years. . . . No one speaks more eloquently about Wooden than Bill Walton, who played for UCLA at a troubled time in America, a time of Vietnam and Watergate, a time when young people were asking hard questions, when dissent was in style.

For Wooden, the answers never changed. "We thought he was nuts,"

Walton said. "But in all his preachings and teachings, everything he told us turned out to be true. . . .

"His interest and goal were to make you the best basketball player but first to make you the best person," Walton said. "He would never talk wins and losses but what we needed to succeed in life. Once you were a good human being, you had a chance to be a good player. He never deviated from that.

"He never tried to be your friend. He was your teacher, your coach. He handled us with extreme patience."

Today, Walton talks with the 90-year-old Wooden frequently. "He has thousands of maxims. He is more John Wooden today than ever. He is a man who truly has principles and ideas. . . . He didn't teach basketball. He taught life.

"When you're touched by someone that special, it changes your life," he said. "You spend your life chasing it down, trying to recreate it.

"He stopped coaching UCLA 25 years ago. Now he just coaches the world."

Citation: Hal Bock, Associated Press, "A Coach for All Seasons," The Spokane-Review (12-4-00), p. C8; submitted by Bob Luhn; Othello, Washington

■

TEAMWORK

ASSISTING BETTER THAN SCORING

Romans 12:5; Ephesians 4:2-3; Ephesians 4:11-16; Philippians 2:4

Church; Community; Help; Humility; Ministry; Servanthood; Teamwork; Unselfishness; Winning and Losing

One evening some friends of ours, Paul and Brenda, were watching their grandson, Scott, play basketball. Scott plays center. He is tall and handles the ball well. That night, every time Scott got the ball, he looked around for someone to pass to instead of shooting.

Later, Paul asked his grandson, "Scott, why don't you shoot when you have a good shot?" Scott thought for a moment and replied, "When you throw the ball out to one of the other guys and he makes two points, then you run down the court giving high fives—that's the real thrill. That's the name of the game."

Citation: Samuel M. Miller; Oconee County, South Carolina

TEAMWORK

YOU NEED THE TEAM

1 Corinthians 3:5-10; 1 Corinthians 12; Ephesians 4:11-16; Philippians 2:3-4

Church, body of Christ; Community; Competition; Ego; Pride; Selfishness; Sports; Teamwork; Unity; Unselfishness

NBA player A. C. Green writes:

Men often talk about their "glory years" in high school. At Benson High School, in Portland, Oregon, I was a sports-minded, egotistical maniac. I was the tallest guy on the team and could have broken scoring records, but Coach Gray wouldn't let me. Even with the brakes on, twice that year I scored 39 points, and in the season finale against Wilson I scored 40. I averaged 27 points per game. As a team we scored more than 100 points in seven games and averaged over 90. I was voted the Oregonian's 1981 All-Metro area player of the year, and joined Dean Derrah on the All-Metro team.

Coach Gray wouldn't allow me to be a hotshot scorer because he was more interested in the final stat—number one. He knew the only way we could reach that championship level was for us to become team players.

In basketball and in life, everyone starts out with a what's-in-it-for-me attitude. Children are selfish. That natural selfishness has to be broken to be a winner. You have to realize you can't do it all by yourself. You need the team. Coach Gray made me pass the ball and play unselfishly. Regardless of individual stats, we, the team, reached the top. We went all the way.

Citation: A. C. Green, Victory *(Creation, 1994), reprinted in* Men of Integrity *(May/June 2000), p. 60*

TELEVISION
EX-MTV VJS AGAINST MTV

PSALM 119:9; 2 CORINTHIANS 7:1; PHILIPPIANS 4:8; 1 TIMOTHY 5:22; 1 JOHN 2:15-17; 1 JOHN 3:2-3

Children; Entertainment; Hypocrisy; Music; Parenting; Popular Culture; Purity; Rock 'n' Roll; Rules; Television; Youth

Good Morning America interviewed former MTV video jockeys about their willingness to let their kids watch MTV:

Mark Goodman said, "My kids are not allowed to watch MTV.... Have you seen what they put on that channel?"

Martha Quinn agreed with Goodman's no-MTV household rule: "Yeah, my kid doesn't watch it."

Citation: World (8-11-01), p. 12; source: interview on ABC's Good Morning America *on the 20th anniversary of the cable music channel*

TEMPTATION
DEVOTION GREATER THAN TEMPTATION

GALATIANS 2:20; GALATIANS 5:15-26; EPHESIANS 6:10-20

Christian Life; Desire, evil; God, love of; Obedience; Sin; Temptation

Henri Nouwen once said in a *Leadership* journal interview:

I cannot continuously say no to this or no to that, unless there is something ten times more attractive to choose. Saying no to my lust, my greed, my needs, and the world's powers takes an enormous amount of energy. The only hope is to find something so obviously real and attractive that I can devote all my energies to saying yes.... One such thing I can say yes to is when I come in touch with the fact that I am loved. Once I have found that in my total brokenness I am still loved, I become free from the compulsion of doing successful things.

Citation: Terry Muck, "Hearing God's Voice and Obeying His Word," Leadership Journal (Winter 1982), p. 16

TEMPTATION

EMPTY PROMISES

Appearances; Fulfillment; Materialism; Meaning of Life; Pleasure, sinful; Promises; Satisfaction; Sin; Temptation; Worldliness

A "Bonehead of the Day" e-mail reported on a newfangled toy recently released for distribution:

A U.S. company has an action figure called Invisible Jim that is selling briskly in Britain for about $2.80 apiece. Why is it called Invisible Jim? Because all you get is the packaging. There is no Jim.

"Lack of darting eyes" and "realistic fake hair," "as not seen on TV," and "camouflage suit sold separately" are some of the boasts made on the package. The company says they have received no complaints about the empty boxes.

A spokeswoman for the distributor says that when the first shipment arrived they thought there was some mistake at the factory—that they sent the packaging without the product.

Good marketing, good packaging, empty box. Sounds a lot like temptation and sin.

Citation: From "Bonehead of the Day" e-mail; submitted by Eric Hulstrand; Portland, North Dakota

TEMPTATION

SAVED FROM DANGER BY LOVE

Christ, love of; Love; Savior, Christ our; Temptation

Several years ago my wife, Kathy, and a friend gathered up their kids and made a trip to the St. Louis Zoo. A new attraction had just opened called "Big Cat Country," which took the lions and tigers out of their cages and allowed them to roam in large enclosures. Visitors observe the cats by walking on elevated skyways above the habitats. As my wife and her friend took the children up one of the skyway ramps, a blanket became entangled in the wheel of the friend's stroller. Kathy knelt to help untangle the wheel while our boys—roughly ages three and five—went ahead. When next she looked up, Kathy discovered that the boys had innocently walked right through a child-sized gap in the fencing and had climbed up on the rocks some 20 or 25 feet above the lion pen. They had been told that they would be able to look down on the lions, and they were doing just that from their hazardous vantage point. Pointing to the lions below, they called back to their mother, "Hey, Mom, we can see them!"

They had no concept of how much danger they were in. Kathy saw immediately. But now what could she do? If she screamed, she might startle the boys perched precariously above the lions. The gap in the fence was too small for her to get through. So she knelt down, spread out her arms, and said, "Boys, come get a hug." They came running for the love that saved them from danger greater than they could perceive.

With similar love, our Savior beckons us from temptation that would devour us.

Citation: Bryan Chapell, Holiness by Grace *(Crossway, 2001), pp. 107; used by permission of Crossway Books, a division of Good News Publishers, Wheaton, Illinois 60187, www.crosswaybooks.org*

■

TEMPTATION

TOXIC SIN

GENESIS 3:1-5; 2 CORINTHIANS 11:3
Devil; Sin; Temptation

A recent news article reported on a dangerous practical joke played by a nursery employee:

A British Columbia-based nursery is trying to track down people who bought poisonous plants that were incorrectly labeled "tasty in soup."

Valleybrook Gardens, which distributed the plants, has worked with government officials to locate the buyers of 17 improperly labeled perennials sold at stores in British Columbia and Ontario from April 18 to 25. Only eight of the plants had been accounted for by Sunday.

The label should have read, "All parts of this plant are toxic," but an employee changed it to, "All parts of this plant are tasty in soup," said

Michel Benoit, the nursery's general manager. "The employee was making a practical joke and thought it would be caught by a horticulturist," said Benoit.

The devil has done the same to us. God put a warning label on sin that declared, "Do not eat from this for you shall surely die." But our enemy switched labels. The label he attached to sin reads, "Looks good. Tastes great. Is desirable to make one wise."

Citation: The Appeal-Democrat (4-30-01); submitted by Tom Tripp; Colusa, California

■

TESTIMONY

A MARINE'S ASTONISHING THANKFULNESS

1 Thessalonians 5:18

Courage; Gratitude; Testimony; Thankfulness; Thanksgiving; Witness

Retired U.S. Marine Corps General Charles Krulak tells of the time when he as a nonbeliever was first confronted with the testimony of a person committed to Christ:

Thirty-five years ago I was a young second lieutenant just graduated from the Naval Academy, married 14 days after I graduated. My wife and I went down to Quantico, Virginia, home of the basic school where officers learn about honor, courage, and commitment. At that time in my life I thought I was a cross between John Wayne and Tom Cruise. Because I was married, I shared a room with another married officer named John Listerman. John was a wonderful human. He exuded goodness. If I asked him for his arm, he would have said, "Where do you want me to cut it off? At the wrist? The elbow?" John was a Christian. That meant nothing to me other than *Gee, what a nice guy. I guess this Christian stuff must be pretty good.*

Upon graduating from basic school, John and I went to Camp Pendleton, California, where we joined the same battalion preparing to go to Vietnam. And I saw another side of John Listerman: he was a tremendous leader—aggressive and technically proficient. People loved him. He was committed to his troops; his troops were committed to him. He was a Marine's Marine.

On a December morning in 1965 John and I went to war. John Listerman's war lasted one day.

We were on patrol moving down a trail through the jungle. We came around a corner in that trail, and we ran into an ambush. John took the first round, a 50-caliber round right in his kneecap. As his kneecap burst, the crack was so loud it sounded like a mortar exploding. It threw him up in the air. As he was dropping, the second round hit him right below the heart and exited out his side. I was wounded also but nowhere near as badly. I saw John about 30 meters away on his back, his leg blown off.

I crawled up to him, and I wanted to say, "Are you okay? Can I do anything?" but before I could do that, his head turned to me and he said, "How are you doing, Chucker? Are you okay?"

I said, "Yes, John. I'm okay." He said, "Are my men safe?" I said, "John, your people are okay." At that point he turned his head and looked to the sky and repeated over and over, "Thank you, Lord. Thank you, Lord. Thank you for caring for my people. Thank you for caring for me."

I was dumbfounded.

(John Listerman and Charles Krulak were evacuated. Krulak later became a Christian.)

Citation: Linda M. Gehrs; Oak Park, Illinois; source: General Charles Krulak, from a message given at the Wheaton, Illinois, Leadership Prayer Breakfast (October 2000)

TESTIMONY

CONSIDERATE WITNESSES

Matthew 10:7-8; Colossians 4:3-6
Consideration; Evangelism; Gospel; Testimony; Witness

While in seminary in Chicago's suburbs, I discovered that a Promise Keepers' convention was coming to Soldier Field. A group of us took a commuter train downtown, then caught a cab to the stadium.

We were running late, but still hoped to get a good seat. I'm sure our driver, a man who spoke little English, felt intimidated as the six of us piled into his taxi, jabbering loudly. Traffic was heavy and got worse near the stadium. We slowed to a crawl. We weren't going to get that good seat after all.

A couple of us started talking about hopping from the cab and running the rest of the way to the stadium. It sounded good to most of us, but

Michael spoke against the plan. He was more concerned about the cabby. If we got out at that point, the driver would be stuck in traffic without being able to refill his taxi. He'd be losing money.

After Michael spoke with us, he turned his attention to our foreign driver. Michael shared about the conference we were going to, and then he shared the good news of Jesus Christ.

I don't know if the man was affected by the message, but I do know Michael's concern provided a base of credibility for sharing the gospel that the rest of us overlooked.

Citation: Greg Huffer, Lebanon, Indiana

TESTIMONY

EXAMPLE IS THE BEST ARGUMENT

2 Timothy 1:13; 1 Peter 5:1-4
Arguments; Example

One example is worth a thousand arguments.

Citation: Thomas Carlyle, quoted in Men of Integrity *(July/August 2000)*

TESTIMONY

GOD TRANSFORMS DAD'S LIFE

Psalm 40:1-4; John 10:10; 2 Corinthians 5:17; Galatians 1:13-24
Anger; Children; Christlikeness; Conversion; Example; Family; Fathers; Men; Salvation and Lostness; Spiritual Formation; Testimony; Transformation

Author, pastor, and onetime atheist Lee Strobel says in one sermon:

How can I tell you the difference God has made in my life? My daughter Allison was 5 years old when I became a follower of Jesus, and all she had known in those 5 years was a dad who was profane and angry. I remember I came home one night and kicked a hole in the living-room wall just out of anger with life. I am ashamed to think of the times Allison hid in her room to get away from me.

Five months after I gave my life to Jesus Christ, that little girl went to my wife and said, "Mommy, I want God to do for me what he's done for Daddy." At age 5! What was she saying? She'd never studied the archaeological evidence [regarding the truth of the Bible]. All she knew was her dad used to be this way: hard to live with. But more and more her dad is becoming different. And if that is what God does to people, then sign her up. At age 5 she gave her life to Jesus.

God changed my family. He changed my world. He changed my eternity.

Citation: Lee Strobel, author and teaching pastor at Saddleback Church; Lake Forest, California, from sermon "The Case for Christ"

■

THANKFULNESS

VERY SHORT GRIPE SESSION

Psalm 66:8-12; Psalm 66:9; Psalm 107:1-9

Attitudes and Emotions; Encouragement; God, goodness of; Thankfulness

A party of pioneers on the Oregon Trail suffered for weeks from a scarcity of water and grass for their animals. Most of the wagons had broken down, causing endless delays in the stifling heat. A feeling of fretfulness and futility prevailed. Optimism and cheer were gone. Courage was in limited supply.

One night the leaders called a meeting to air complaints. When they gathered around the campfire, one man stood up and said, "Before we commence our grief session, don't you think we should at least first thank God that he has brought us this far with no loss of life, with no serious trouble from the Indians, and that we have enough strength left to finish our journey?"

The other settlers agreed. After the brief prayer, all that could be heard were the cries of a distant pack of wolves. There was otherwise stone silence around the campfire, because no one had any grievances they felt were important enough to voice.

They suddenly realized if they couldn't be satisfied with what they'd received, they could at least be thankful for what they'd escaped. Thankfulness enabled them to see the mercies of God they had been overlooking.

Citation: Gregory L. Jantz, Becoming Strong Again (Baker, 1998)

THIRST

WHAT QUENCHES SPIRITUAL THIRST

PSALM 42:1; JOHN 4:6-29

Desire; Discontent; Satisfaction; Thirst

In his book *Sahara Unveiled,* William Langewiesche tells the story of an Algerian named Lag Lag and a companion whose truck broke down while crossing the desert:

They nearly died of thirst during the three weeks they waited before being rescued. As their bodies dehydrated, they became willing to drink anything in hopes of quenching their terrible thirst. The sun forced them into the shade under the truck, where they dug a shallow trench. Day after day they lay there. They had food, but did not eat, fearing it would magnify their thirst. Dehydration, not starvation, kills wanderers in the desert, and thirst is the most terrible of all human sufferings.

Physiologists . . . use Greek-based words to describe stages of human thirst. For example, the Sahara Desert is *dipsogenic,* meaning "thirst provoking."

In Lag Lag's case, they might say he progressed from *eudipsia,* "ordinary thirst," through bouts of *hyperdipsia,* meaning "temporary intense thirst," to *polydipsia,* "sustained excessive thirst." Polydipsia means the kind of thirst that drives one to drink anything.

For word enthusiasts, this is heady stuff. Nevertheless, the lexicon has not kept up with technology. I have tried, and cannot coin a suitable word for the drinking of rusty radiator water. Radiator water is what Lag Lag and his assistant started into when good drinking water was gone. In order to survive, they were willing to drink, in effect, poison.

Many people do something similar in the spiritual realm. They depend on things like money, sex, and power to quench spiritual thirst. Unfortunately, such "thirst quenchers" are in reality spiritual poison, a dangerous substitute for the "living water" Jesus promised.

Citation: William Langewiesche, Sahara Unveiled *(Vintage, 1997); submitted by Jeff Ingram*

TIME

WHAT TIME I HAVE LEFT

MATTHEW 10:39; PHILIPPIANS 3:7-14; 2 TIMOTHY 2:15

Consecration; Entertainment; Life and Death; Preparation; Prisons; Service, faithful; Stewardship; Study; Television; Time

Chuck Colson tells the following story of visiting Mississippi's Parchman Prison:

Most of the death-row inmates were in their bunks wrapped in blankets, staring blankly at little black-and-white TV screens, killing time. But in one cell a man was sitting on his bunk, reading. As I approached, he looked up and showed me his book—an instruction manual on Episcopal liturgy.

John Irving, on death row for more than 15 years, was studying for the priesthood. John told me he was allowed out of his cell one hour each day. The rest of the time, he studies.

Seeing that John had nothing in his cell but a few books, I thought, *God's blessed me so much, the least I can do is provide something for this brother.* "Would you like a TV if I could arrange it?" I asked.

John smiled gratefully. "Thanks," he said, "but no thanks. You can waste an awful lot of time with those things." For the 15 years since a judge placed a number on his days, John has determined not to waste the one commodity he had to give to the Lord—his time.

Citation: Charles Colson, A Dangerous Grace *(Word, 1994)*

TITHING

TITHE TIED UP IN BROOMS

MATTHEW 6:21; LUKE 21:1-4; 2 CORINTHIANS 8:12

Generosity; Giving; Money; Stinginess; Tithing; Treasure

A church member stopped the pastor and angrily complained that the church had purchased five new brooms—an expenditure that he thought was completely unnecessary.

The pastor was surprised at the man's reaction and mentioned it to the church treasurer, who said, "It's understandable. How would *you* feel if you saw everything you gave in the past year tied up in five brooms?"

Citation: Preaching (March/April 1995); submitted by Brad Estep; St. Petersburg, Florida

■

TONGUE

SABBATH FOR THE TONGUE

PROVERBS 12:18; JAMES 1:26; JAMES 3:3-12

Criticism; Family; Sabbath; Speech; Spiritual Formation; Teenagers; Tongue; Words

In his book *Sabbath Time,* Tilden Edwards tells about a family with teenage children who decided, as part of their Sabbath commitments, that they would not criticize each other on Sundays. As the months went on and they kept this commitment, they realized more and more of their children's friends were coming over on Sundays just to hang around. No one in the family had talked about this commitment, but somehow other teenagers knew this home was a good place to be.

Citation: Tilden Edwards, Sabbath Time: Understanding and Practice for Contemporary Christians (Upper Room Books, 1992); submitted by Bonne Steffen; Wheaton, Illinois

■

TRANSFORMATION

TRANSFORMED BY AN ELEVATOR

1 CORINTHIANS 15:50-52; 2 CORINTHIANS 5:17

Aging; Conversion; Growth, spiritual; Salvation and Lostness; Spiritual Formation; Transformation

A family from a remote area was making their first visit to a big city. They checked in to a grand hotel and stood in amazement at the impressive sight. Leaving the reception desk they came to the elevator entrance. They'd never seen an elevator before, and just stared at it, unable to figure out what it was for.

An old lady hobbled towards the elevator and went inside. The door closed. About a minute later, the door opened and out came a stunningly good-looking young woman.

Dad couldn't stop staring. Without turning his head he patted his son's arm and said, "Go get your mother, son."

Citation: Owen Bourgaize; Guernsey, United Kingdom

TRIALS

GOD TURNS PERSECUTION INTO OPPORTUNITY

GENESIS 50:20; JOHN 15:20; ACTS 8:1-8; ROMANS 8:28

Circumstances and Faith; Opportunity; Persecution; Trials; Trust

John Rucyahana, the Anglican bishop of Shyira, Rwanda, served as a pastor in Uganda during the brutal reign of dictator Idi Amin. Amin targeted 200,000 political opponents, Christian leaders, and members of certain ethnic groups for extermination.

One day the government soldiers came for John. He remembers, "One put the cold barrel of a gun against my ear and held his finger on the trigger. They put me in a vehicle and made me sit on a sack of explosives. As we began moving, I thought, *Even the slightest jolt, and I'm dead.*"

The soldiers finally released John, figuring they had successfully intimidated him and that he would no longer speak out.

What the oppressors meant for evil, though, God used for good. Two days after John's harrowing brush with death was Sunday. That day, John walked into the cathedral to find it packed—people were standing in the aisles. People had heard what happened and had come to find out what he would say. Would he speak out for Christ?

John did speak for Christ, only this time to a larger group than he could ever have gathered on his own.

Citation: Kevin A. Miller, vice president, Resources, Christianity Today International

TRUST

NEEDING TRUST OVER CLARITY

PSALM 37:3-6; PROVERBS 3:5-6

Dependence on God; Direction; Guidance; Prayer; Spiritual Perception; Trust

When the brilliant ethicist John Kavanaugh went to work for three months at "the house of the dying" in Calcutta, he was seeking a clear answer as to how best to spend the rest of his life. On the first morning there he met Mother Teresa. She asked, "And what can I do for you?"

Kavanaugh asked her to pray for him. "What do you want me to pray for?" she asked.

He voiced the request that he had borne thousands of miles from the United States: "Pray that I have clarity."

She said firmly, "No, I will not do that."

When he asked her why, she said, "Clarity is the last thing you are clinging to and must let go of."

When Kavanaugh commented that she always seemed to have the clarity he longed for, she laughed and said, "I have never had clarity; what I have always had is trust. So I will pray that you trust God."

Citation: Brennan Manning, Ruthless Trust *(HarperCollins, 2000); submitted by Dave Goetz; Wheaton, Illinois*

TRUTH
PROOF OF FAITH

MATTHEW 7:13-27; MATTHEW 13:40-43; 2 TIMOTHY 2:19
Faith and Works; Fruit; Hell; Judgment; Repentance; Salvation and Lostness; Truth; Works

In his novel *A Painted House,* John Grisham describes a Sunday school teacher eulogizing a mean character named Jerry Sisco, who had been killed the night before in a back alley fight after he picked on one person too many.

In the words of the little boy who had seen the fight with his friend Dewayne: "She made Jerry sound like a Christian, and an innocent victim. I glanced at Dewayne, who had one eye on me. There was something odd about this. As Baptists, we'd been taught from the cradle that the only way you made it to heaven was by believing in Jesus and trying to follow his example in living a clean and moral Christian life. . . . And anyone who did not accept Jesus and live a Christian life simply went to hell. That's where Jerry Sisco was, and we all knew it."

Citation: John Grisham, A Painted House *(Doubleday, 2001), pp. 85-86; submitted by Bob Rogers; Rincon, Georgia*

U

UNBELIEF

C. S. LEWIS DEPICTS UNBELIEF

PSALM 104:24-34; MARK 4:11-12; JOHN 8:47; JOHN 9:35-41; ROMANS 1:18-22;
COLOSSIANS 1:16

Creation; Denial; God, creator; Hardness of Heart; Holy Spirit; Science; Spiritual Perception; Unbelief

In his book *The Magician's Nephew*, C. S. Lewis writes of the creation of fictitious Narnia through the song of Aslan (the lion who represents Jesus in the book). The Creation Song is clearly intended to reveal the majesty and glory of Aslan. As in Genesis 1, it is a grand call to worship.

But there was one (Uncle Andrew) who would not hear it. The consequences were staggering:

When the great moment came and the Beasts spoke, he missed the whole point, for a rather interesting reason. When the Lion had first begun singing, long ago when it was still quite dark, he had realized that the noise was a song. And he had disliked the song very much. It made him think and feel things he did not want to think and feel.

Then, when the sun rose and he saw that the singer was a Lion ("only a lion," as he said to himself) he tried his hardest to make himself believe that it wasn't singing and never had been singing—only roaring as any lion might in a zoo in our own world. *Of course it can't really have been singing,* he thought. *I must have imagined it. I've been letting my nerves get out of order. Who ever heard of a lion singing?*

And the longer and more beautifully the Lion sang, the harder Uncle Andrew tried to make himself believe that he could hear nothing but roaring. Now the trouble about trying to make yourself stupider than you really are is that you very often succeed. Uncle Andrew did. He soon did hear nothing but roaring in Aslan's song. Soon he couldn't have heard anything else even if he had wanted to.

And when at last the Lion spoke and said, "Narnia awake," he didn't hear any words: he heard only a snarl. And when the beasts spoke in answer, he heard only barkings, growlings, bayings, and howlings.

Citation: C. S. Lewis, The Magician's Nephew *(Collier), pp. 125-126; submitted by Eugene A. Maddox; Interlachen, Florida*

UNITY

GENERAL COLIN POWELL ON UNITY

Acts 2:42-47; Romans 13

Church; Conflict; Criticism; Cynicism; Family; Patriotism; Unity

General Colin Powell writes:

On the speech circuit, I tell a story that goes to the heart of America's longing. ABC correspondent Sam Donaldson was interviewing a young African-American soldier in a tank platoon on the eve of the battle in Desert Storm. Donaldson asked, "How do you think the battle will go? Are you afraid?"

"We'll do okay. We're well trained. And I'm not afraid," the GI answered, gesturing toward his buddies around him. "I'm not afraid because I'm with my family."

The other soldiers shouted, "Tell him again. He didn't hear you." The soldier repeated, "This is my family, and we'll take care of each other."

Citation: Colin Powell, My American Journey: An Autobiography *(Random House, 1995); submitted by Rubel Shelly; Nashville, Tennessee*

UNITY

QUESTIONABLE COMMUNITY

1 CORINTHIANS 12:13; EPHESIANS 2:14
Church; Community; Divisions; Unity

Grove Street was lined with lovely mature trees, manicured lawns, and three churches—all right next to each other. The three churches were each built in different styles and shapes, but they each posted a sign out front, proudly displaying the name of the church. The three churches were named First Community Church, Second Community Church, and Third Community Church.

One day the pastors of these three houses of worship all happened to meet on the sidewalk in front of their churches. Said one pastor to the others, "Maybe we need to define what we mean by *community.*"

Citation: Adapted by Drew Zahn from an original cartoon by Ed Koehler, The Best Cartoons from Leadership Journal, *Volume 1 (Broadman & Holman, 1999)*

URGENCY

LIFE-AND-DEATH URGENCY

ISAIAH 55:6-7; ROMANS 13:11-12; 2 CORINTHIANS 6:2
Life and Death; Receiving Christ; Salvation and Lostness; Urgency

Sitting on the hard wooden bleachers at Fort Benning while attending the United States Army Airborne School, we prepared for our first parachute jump. Soon we would soar hundreds of feet above the red Georgia clay and hear the jump-master bark out the orders, "Stand up! Hook up! Check equipment! Stand in the door! Go! Go! Go!" Understandably, the instructors had our undivided attention.

The Airborne sergeant's voice rang out confidently as he explained what to do in case of a parachute malfunction. "If your main parachute should fail to deploy, don't panic—pull the handle of your auxiliary parachute. Should your auxiliary parachute fail to fill with air, don't panic—pull it in toward your body and then vigorously throw it away from yourself. Should your auxiliary chute again fail to deploy, don't panic—vigorously repeat this process."

He paused dramatically, looking intently into our eyes. Then with a slight mischievous grin he slowly stated, "Should this also fail, don't panic. You'll have the rest of your life to get your parachute to deploy."

Citation: Tim Wilson, pastor of Indian Hills Christian Fellowship; Indian Hills, Colorado, from a sermon titled "Urgency"

V

VICTORY

KEEPING DISCOURAGEMENT AT BAY

2 Corinthians 5:7; Hebrews 10:36; Hebrews 11; Hebrews 12:1-2

Attitude; Circumstances and Faith; Confidence; Encouragement; Faith; Overcoming; Perseverance; Persistence; Perspective; Prevailing; Problems; Trust; Victory; Winning and Losing

A man stopped to watch a Little League baseball game. He asked one of the youngsters what the score was. "We're losing 18–0," was the answer.

"Well," said the man. "I must say you don't look discouraged."

"Discouraged?" the boy said, puzzled. "Why should we be discouraged? We haven't come to bat yet."

Citation: Stan Toler, God Has Never Failed Me, but He's Sure Scared Me to Death a Few Times (Honor Books, 1995); submitted by Jerry De Luca; Montreal West, Quebec, Canada

■

VISION

BUILDING GOD'S KINGDOM

Proverbs 29:18; Ecclesiastes 2:24-26; Ecclesiastes 3:22; Ephesians 1:18-19

Ministry; Purpose; Vision; Work

The story is told of the foreman on a building site who asks one of the builders what he is doing. The builder replies, "I'm breaking rocks."

Another worker is asked the same question, and he answers, "I'm earning for my family."

The question is posed to a third worker. With a glint in his eye, he responds, "I'm building a cathedral."

Citation: Submitted by Owen Bourgaize; Guernsey, United Kingdom

W

WAITING ON GOD

THE GIVER'S BIG HANDS

GENESIS 13:9; PSALM 16:5-6; PSALM 23; PSALM 34:8-10; PSALM 81:10; PSALM 84:11; PSALM 100:5; MATTHEW 7:7-11; EPHESIANS 3:20

Ambition; Dependence on God; Faith; Faith and Circumstances; God, goodness of; God, providence of; Grace; Guidance; Patience; Prayer; Selfishness; Striving; Trust; Waiting on God

A young boy went to the local store with his mother. The shop owner, a kindly man, passed him a large jar of suckers and invited him to help himself to a handful. Uncharacteristically, the boy held back. So the shop owner pulled out a handful for him.

When outside, the boy's mother asked why he had suddenly been so shy and wouldn't take a handful of suckers when offered.

The boy replied, "Because his hand is much bigger than mine!"

Citation: Brian Harris; Mt. Roskill, Auckland, New Zealand

WAR

C. S. LEWIS: WAR GIVES IMPORTANT REMINDER

PSALM 90:12; PSALM 103:14-16; COLOSSIANS 3:1-4; 1 PETER 1:13-25

Death; Depravity; Human Condition; Human Limitations; Life and Death; Mortality; Truth; War; Wisdom

War does do something to death. It forces us to remember it. The only reason why the cancer at 60 or the paralysis at 75 does not bother us is that we forget them. War makes death real to us: and that would have been regarded as one of its blessings by most of the Christians of the past. They thought it good for us to be always aware of our mortality. I am inclined to think they were right. All the animal life in us, all schemes of happiness that centered in this world, were always doomed to a final frustration. In ordinary times only a wise man can realize it.

Now the stupidest of us knows. We see unmistakably the sort of universe in which we have all along been living, and must come to terms with it. If we had foolish un-Christian hopes about human culture, they are now shattered. If we thought we were building up a heaven on earth, if we looked for something that would turn the present world from a place of pilgrimage into a permanent city satisfying the soul of man, we are disillusioned, and not a moment too soon.

Citation: C. S. Lewis, "Learning in War-Time," from a sermon preached in the Church of St. Mary the Virgin, Oxford, 1939; submitted by Linda Gehrs; Oak Park, Illinois

---

WEAKNESS

RELY ON FATHER'S STRENGTH

PSALM 46:1; PHILIPPIANS 4:6; PHILIPPIANS 4:13; JAMES 4:2
Dependence on God; Fatherhood of God; Prayer; Strength; Weakness

Minister Bob Russell wrote about a father who watched through the kitchen window as his small son attempted to lift a large stone out of his sandbox. The boy was frustrated as he wrestled with the heavy object because he just couldn't get enough leverage to lift it over the side. Finally the boy gave up and sat down dejectedly on the edge of the sandbox with his head in his hands.

The father went outside and asked, "What's wrong, Son? Can't you lift that rock out?"

"No, sir," the boy said, "I can't do it."

"Have you used all the strength that's available to you?" the father asked.

"Yes, sir," the boy replied.

"No, you haven't," the father said. "You haven't asked me to help you."

Citation: Bob Russell, author and preaching minister, Southeast Christian Church; Louisville, Kentucky; submitted by Van Morris; Washington, Kentucky

WEAKNESS

WEAK PREACHING

ROMANS 1:16; 2 CORINTHIANS 12:8-10
Evangelism; Gospel; Ministry; Preaching; Weakness

Once when he was to preach at the University of Sydney in Australia, John Stott lost his voice. He says:

What can you do with a missionary who has no voice? We had come to the last night of the [evangelistic campaign]. The students had booked the big university hall. A group of students gathered around me, and I asked them to pray as Paul did, that this thorn in the flesh might be taken from me. But we went on to pray that if it pleased God to keep me in weakness, I would rejoice in my infirmities in order that the power of Christ might rest upon me.

As it turned out, I had to get within one inch of the microphone just to croak the gospel. I was unable to use any inflection of voice to express my personality. It was just a croak in a monotone, and all the time we were crying to God that his power would be demonstrated in human weakness. Well, I can honestly say that there was a far greater response that night than any other night. I've been back to Australia ten times now, and on every occasion somebody has come up to me and said, "Do you remember that night when you lost your voice? I was converted that night."

Citation: Student Leadership *(Spring 1993), p. 32*

WITNESSING

EMBARRASSED TO WITNESS

MATTHEW 28:19; 1 CORINTHIANS 9:19-22; 2 CORINTHIANS 5:13; 2 TIMOTHY 1:1-14
Boldness; Evangelism; Shame; Witnessing

As a youth pastor, I'd just entered a convenience store with "Jeff" to pay for the gas I'd put in the church van. It was apparent that the woman behind the counter had been crying. I looked at her and said, "Has anybody let you know today that Jesus really loves you?" Well, Jeff freaked out, took off running, and dived into the van.

As nobody else was in the store, I witnessed for the next few minutes to that woman, who was going through a very difficult time in her life. After she asked Christ to come into her heart, her whole countenance changed.

When I got into the van, Jeff said, "Don't ever do that again!"

"Don't do what again?" I asked.

"Witness to people like that," he replied. "Did you see how embarrassed that lady got?"

I responded, "Jeff, you got more embarrassed than she did. In fact, I prayed with her, and she received Christ."

I took Jeff back into the store to meet the woman, now radiant with the love of God—a complete contradiction of what she had been just a few minutes before.

Citation: Eastman Curtis, Raising Heaven-Bound Kids in a Hell-Bent World *(Nelson, 2000); quoted in* Men of Integrity *(July/August 2001)*

■

WITNESSING

REGRET FOR NOT WITNESSING

MATTHEW 28:19-20; JOHN 14:6-7; COLOSSIANS 4:3-6; 1 PETER 3:15

Depression; Evangelism; Excuses; Outreach; Witnessing

In *Decision* magazine, Peggy DesNoyers writes:

My job as a psychiatric home-health nurse brought me in touch with many people who were hurt or angry and who were searching for answers to problems in their lives. I knew that Jesus was the answer, but I couldn't bring myself to talk to them about him. I was the master of excuses. [Until] one patient changed my life.

Wanda was a 56-year-old widow in chronic depression. All of her family had died, some of them tragically, within a span of 16 years. The loss and her grief overwhelmed her until life for her became a burden she was unable to bear.

One day she quit her job, went home, pulled the curtains, and refused to leave her house. Eventually she stopped eating, and even the smallest of tasks became too difficult for her to do.

An observant neighbor had noticed the chang in Wanda's behavior, and that neighbor made arrangements for her to be taken to a hospital where she was admitted to the psychiatric ward. At the end of her hospital stay, when she went home, I was assigned to be her home-health nurse. I visited her weekly to make sure she was taking her medication and was eating and taking care of herself.

Over the course of six months Wanda continued to recover. Although I knew she needed to meet Jesus as her Savior, I reasoned that she would soon be attending church and would hear about him there.

One day I went to Wanda's house for my regular visit, and I was surprised to find the door ajar. I knocked and when there was no response, I pushed the door open and stepped inside. The living room was vacant, so I went to her bedroom and found her lifeless body on the bed. There were several empty medication bottles beside her, and in her hand she held a note addressed to me.

I sat on the bed beside her and took the note. I read: "Dear Peggy, I'm so sorry. I tried it your way, but I got tired. Please forgive me. I tried. I just couldn't do it. I got tired."

I slid off the bed onto my knees and cried my heart out to my loving, forgiving Father: "Lord Jesus, she tried it my way. I gave her the best that I had. But it was my way. I didn't tell her about you. I didn't tell her about your way."

On my knees beside [Wanda's] lifeless body I promised God that I would never pass by another opportunity to tell someone about him.

Citation: Peggy DesNoyers, "Silent No More," Decision (July/August 2000), p. 36

■

WONDER

HOLINESS IN CREATION

EXODUS 3:5; ROMANS 1:20

Awe; Creation; Holiness; Spiritual Perception; Vision; Wonder; Worship

Earth's crammed with heaven, And every common bush afire with God; But only he who sees takes off his shoes—The rest sit round it and pluck blackberries.

Citation: Elizabeth Barrett Browning, quoted in "Reflections," Christianity Today (7-31-00)

■

WORD OF GOD

LETTERS FROM THE KING

PSALM 119:49; PSALM 119:103; JOHN 1:14

Christ, love of; Christ, the Word; Bible; Kings; Scripture; Word of God

John Kass, a columnist for the *Chicago Tribune*, recently wrote about a waiter named Bouch who works at a tavern in Chicago. Bouch decided to write to the king of his homeland, Morocco. The king, Mohammed VI, is immensely popular because he often interacts with his subjects in public. He has freed political prisoners, and he helps the poor and disabled. When Bouch wrote to him from Chicago, King Mohammed VI, true to nature, wrote back.

"Look at the letters," said Bouch. "These are letters from the king. If I meet him, I'll be so happy."

John Kass, the columnist, muses, "How many guys hauling beer and burgers in a Chicago tavern have a correspondence going with a royal monarch?" The columnist talked to Morocco's deputy counsel general in Chicago and was told that it isn't unusual for the king to write personal letters to his subjects abroad. "It happens a lot," the official said. "He loves his subjects."

You think King Mohammed VI loves his subjects? You ought to meet Jesus, the King of kings, and read his precious letters to you.

Citation: Lee Eclov; Lake Forest, Illinois; source: John Kass, "Waiter's Pen Pal Just a Cool Guy Who Runs a Country," Chicago Tribune (7-23-01)

■

WORK

YOUNG MEN VALUE FAMILY

MALACHI 4:6; EPHESIANS 6:4

Family; Fatherhood; Home; Money; Work

A study from the Radcliffe Public Policy Center revealed that 82 percent of males ages 21 to 29 put family time at the top of their agenda, and 70 percent of the same age group said they'd accept a smaller salary if they could spend more time with their families. In contrast, only 26 percent of males 65 and older would take a pay cut.

"Most of these younger men—70 percent—grew up in families where the mother worked outside the home," says Leslie Cintron, PhD, assistant project manager for the study. "Younger men have seen firsthand how hard it can be to balance family and work."

Citation: Charles Pappas, Working Mother *(September 2000), p. 20; submitted by Dave Goetz*

WORKS

WE CAN'T PAY

ROMANS 3:20-28; EPHESIANS 2:8-9; TITUS 3:5
Atonement; Dependence on God; Grace; Salvation; Self-justification; Works

I took my two daughters, Abby and Flannery, out to get something fun to drink at a coffee stand. Abby got an apple juice, and Flannery got a mango surprise. Despite my insistence that I would pay, my daughters had brought the contents of their piggy banks, a combined total of about 80 cents.

As we were walking up to the counter, one of them said, "I want to pay for mine."

I assured her, "Daddy's gonna get it."

Nonetheless, she insisted, "I'm paying for mine."

As the clerk rang it up, he said, "That'll be $2.06," and she put her change on the counter. "Um, that's . . . that's not enough," the clerk responded.

I felt a little tug at my sweater from my other daughter. I looked down, and she said, "I think I'd like to use your money."

Citation: Tom Allen, pastor of Grace Church Seattle; Seattle, Washington

WORLD

DECEPTIVE APPEAL

JAMES 4:4; 2 PETER 1:4; 1 JOHN 2:15-17

*Appearances; Beauty; Deception; Materialism; New Age; Occult; Spiritual
Perception; Temptation; World; Worldliness*

Joe Gutierrez tells five stories from his 42 years as a steelworker in the
book *The Heat: Steelworkers' Lives and Legends.* In one story, called "Snow
Danced in August," he describes a scene of silvery dust flakes that
frequently floated to the floor in an area of the mill where steel strips
rolled over pads in a tall cooling tower. For years, workers and visitors
alike flocked to the sight, which was especially picturesque at night.

Then they discovered the dust was asbestos. "Everybody breathed it,"
wrote Gutierrez. He now suffers from the slow, choking grip of asbestosis,
as do many plant workers.

"Who am I? I'm everybody. Can't walk too far now. I get tired real fast
and it hurts when I breathe, sometimes. And to think we used to fight
over that job."

How many things in our culture resemble the silver flakes in that steel
mill? Enchanting but deadly.

Citation: *"Steelworkers Break the Mold,"* Chicago Tribune *(6-27-01); submitted by Lee
Eclov; Lake Forest, Illinois*

WORTH

WHEN THE LAST ARE FIRST

MATTHEW 19:30; MARK 10:31

*Career; Humility; Judgment, final; Second Coming of Christ; Self-centeredness;
Self-exaltation; Self-worth; Worth; Servanthood; Work*

The weekend following September 11, 2001, syndicated columnist and
former presidential speechwriter Peggy Noonan drove to Lower
Manhattan to witness the relief effort taking place at Ground Zero. She
found herself focusing on the convoy of trucks filled with rescue workers

coming off their 12-hour shifts. The men in the trucks were construction and electrical workers, police, emergency medical workers, and firemen. It was a procession of the not-so-rich-and-famous.

Nonetheless, these New Yorkers were celebrities in a human drama more significant than any Broadway act. Noonan joined the growing crowd of onlookers cheering the workers with shouts of "God bless you!" and "We love you!" They clapped and blew kisses.

Noonan writes:

I looked around me at all of us who were cheering. And saw who we were. Investment bankers! Orthodontists! Magazine editors! In my group, a lawyer, a columnist, and a writer. We had been the kings and queens of the city, respected professionals in a city that respects its professional class.

And this night we were nobody. We were so useless, all we could do was applaud the somebodies, the workers who, unlike us, had not been applauded much in their lives. . . . I was so moved and, oddly I guess, grateful. Because they'd always been the people who ran the place, who kept it going; they'd just never been given their due.

This reversal Peggy Noonan witnessed is nothing less than a foreshadowing of what Jesus talked about. A day is coming when the first shall be last and the last shall be first.

Citation: Greg Asimakoupoulos; Naperville, Illinois; Source: Peggy Noonan, "Welcome Back, DUKE," Wall Street Journal (10-12-01)

Y

YOUTH

CHILDREN: THE CHURCH'S FUTURE

Matthew 11:25-26; Matthew 18:1-3; Matthew 19:13-15
Children; Church; Church, leadership of; Church, membership; Youth

Forty years ago a Philadelphia congregation watched as three 9-year-old boys were baptized and joined the church. Not long after, unable to continue with its dwindling membership, the church sold the building and disbanded.

One of those boys was Dr. Tony Campolo, author and Christian sociologist at Eastern College, Pennsylvania. Dr. Campolo remembers:

Years later when I was doing research in the archives of our denominations, I decided to look up the church report for the year of my baptism. There was my name, and Dick White's. He's now a missionary. Bert Newman, now a professor of theology at an African seminary, was also there. Then I read the church report for 'my' year: "It has not been a good year for our church. We have lost 27 members. Three joined, and they were only children."

Citation: Marlene LeFever, author

INDEX OF REFERENCES

INDEX OF CATEGORIES

ARE YOUR SERMONS HITTING HOME RUNS?

Your message will score with *PreachingToday.com!*

Need great illustrations that will go straight to the hearts of your congregation? Hit the message home with *PreachingToday.com*.

PreachingToday.com is a premier online resource for preachers—find the perfect illustrations, invaluable sermon skills, and much more:

- Find the right illustrations in a snap with over 7,500 top-quality illustrations, selected by the editors of *Leadership*—all in a powerful searchable database.
- Prepare your sermons and preach confidently with the help of series builders, over 50 full sermon outlines, preaching tips and articles by senior editor Haddon Robinson and many of today's best communicators.
- Preach fresh, timely sermons with 10 NEW illustrations e-mailed to you every week, all indexed by topic and Bible text, including the week's lectionary.
- Broaden your research with links to other great preaching resources from *Leadership* journal, *Christianity Today*, *Christian History*, *Books & Culture*, and more…

90 DAYS FREE!

As a special thank you for purchasing the book "Perfect Illustrations for Every Topic and Occasion," please visit the website below for your FREE 90-DAY TRIAL*!

www.PreachingToday.com/go/Perfect

*Offer subject to cancellation without notice.